Managerial Economics FOR DUMMIES®

by Robert Graham

WILEY

John Wiley & Sons, Inc.

Managerial Economics For Dummies®

Published by
John Wiley & Sons, Inc.
111 River St.
Hoboken, NJ 07030-5774
www.wiley.com

WILEY

About the Author

Robert Graham is a Professor of Economics at Hanover College where he regularly teaches managerial economics, microeconomics, and statistics.

Since earning his doctorate at the University of Illinois, Rob has published articles on a wide range of topics including agricultural mechanization and the usefulness of economic theory. His current research focuses on the institutions associated with a market economy.

Rob's hobbies include bicycle riding and running, which leads to an annual trip to Boston each April.

Dedication

To my parents who provided the encouragement and support that led me to take my first economics course. And to my wife Susan and children Nicholas, Matthew, and Catherine. Their love and support is always there, even when they endure the externalities of having an economist for a husband/father.

Author's Acknowledgments

I am very grateful to my project editor, Kelly Ewing. Her advice and patience made an intimidating project and deadline manageable and enjoyable. More importantly for you, the reader, her editing greatly improves the readability of the book.

I have benefitted from the comments of several reviewers who spotted weak explanations and offered insight on those explanations may be improved. Having their advice and suggestions has led to greater clarity.

Special thanks to Acquisitions Editor David Lutton. His early direction helped me understand the *For Dummies* style and provided a quick start for the book.

I'm indebted to my agent, Grace Freedson, who first introduced me to this project. In addition, Grace handles all the technical aspects associated with publishing letting me use my time in the way I most enjoy — writing.

Finally, thanks to my students. Their suggestions and feedback have strengthened my presentation of difficult concepts.

Publisher's Acknowledgments

We're proud of this book; please send us your comments at http://dummies.custhelp.com. For other comments, please contact our Customer Care Department within the U.S. at 877-762-2974, outside the U.S. at 317-572-3993, or fax 317-572-4002.

Some of the people who helped bring this book to market include the following:

Acquisitions, Editorial, and Vertical Websites

Project Editor: Kelly Ewing

Acquisitions Editor: Stacy Kennedy

Copy Editor: Sarah Faulkner

Assistant Editor: David Lutton

Editorial Program Coordinator: Joe Niesen

General Reviewer: Nicole Bissessar

Senior Editorial Manager: Jennifer Ehrlich

Editorial Supervisor and Reprint Editor: Carmen Krikorian

Editorial Assistants: Rachelle S. Amick, Alexa Koschier

Cover Photos: © sorendls/iStockphoto.com

Cartoons: Rich Tennant (www.the5thwave.com)

Composition Services

Senior Project Coordinator: Kristie Rees

Layout and Graphics: Joyce Haughey, Andrea Hornberger

Proofreaders: Jessica Kramer, Lisa Stiers

Indexer: Maro RioFrancos

Publishing and Editorial for Consumer Dummies

>   **Kathleen Nebenhaus,** Vice President and Executive Publisher

>   **David Palmer,** Associate Publisher

>   **Kristin Ferguson-Wagstaffe,** Product Development Director

Publishing for Technology Dummies

>   **Andy Cummings,** Vice President and Publisher

Composition Services

>   **Debbie Stailey,** Director of Composition Services

Contents at a Glance

Table of Contents

Introduction

*I*f left to my own desires, I would have titled this book *How to Make a Gazillion Dollars*. First, I think you'd be more interested in reading the book if I told you it would help you make a lot of money. Second, the title is a much better descriptor of the book's content than *Managerial Economics*. Can anybody "manage" economics?

I don't mean to say that managerial economics is a bad title; indeed, that's what economists call this subject. But such a term begs the question — what are you managing? The answer is your business, and if you're managing a business, your goal is to make as much profit as possible.

Some people think profit is a bad thing — it's not. Profit serves a crucial signaling function, and trying to make a lot of it means you're paying attention to the signal. If you're making a lot of profit, that means everyone wants the good you're producing. But other business owners see this success and say, "I want to make lots of profit too." So their businesses start making the same or similar products, and all of a sudden the good that consumers really want is supplied in abundance. That's a good thing.

Similarly, if you're losing money, it's because consumers don't want what you're producing — at least not at the price you're charging. So, you go out of business, or you start charging a lower price until consumers are happy. That's also a good thing.

If you're paying attention to profit, you're ultimately interested in helping other people get the things they want. Think about it — your success depends on consumers buying your product. So, in the end, managerial economics is about making consumers happy, and when you do that you'll make a lot of money or profit. If you're interested in doing some good for others while making some money for yourself, *Managerial Economics For Dummies* is the book for you — and it cost a lot less than a gazillion dollars.

About This Book

I wrote this book to make managerial economics easy and fun. I focus on big ideas and avoid the trivial — I was never much good at the game Trivial Pursuit, so I have a strong desire to avoid minutiae.

I especially wrote this book for readers who are interested in discovering how to maximize profit. So, I focus on the methods businesses use to increase their profit. By providing clear explanations of these methods, I hope to give you the ability to apply them to your own unique circumstances.

Admittedly, some readers are discovering how to maximize profit as part of a class in managerial economics. For those readers, I include both graphs and calculus to illustrate how economic concepts are expressed mathematically. My clear, concise explanations eliminate all the minutiae present in the typical textbook, enabling you to focus your efforts on the critical concepts.

But this is also a "how to" book for business owners. You can use the book's concepts to increase your profit. Because the topics stand alone, you can simply go to a specific technique and discover how you use that technique to make more money.

The standalone nature of the book's topics is a critical aspect for any reader. You don't have to read the first 100 pages to understand what's on page 101. I encourage you — both students and business owners — to simply go to the topics of greatest interest to you as you read the book.

Conventions Used in This Book

As an economist, I love the old saying "A picture's worth a thousand words." I love this saying because economists like to use graphs to illustrate ideas, and you'll see lots of graphs, pictures, in this book.

But if a picture is worth 1,000 words, an equation is worth at least 100 pictures. Yes, be warned, I use math in the book. Math makes things easier. This is your mantra, so continue repeating it whenever you're walking somewhere — math makes things easier. Equations and calculus are especially helpful when you have three or more things or variables acting on each other. With a graph, I'm limited to illustrating how two variables relate — one on the horizontal axis and the other on the vertical axis. With math and calculus, I can show how three or more variables relate. Essentially, with math, I can look at unlimited possibilities. And when you're trying to maximize profit, you want to look at as many variables as possible. See, math does make things easier.

That being said, I know not everyone is good at working with graphs and/or equations. So in the book, I explain concepts three ways — verbally, graphically, and mathematically. Choose whichever way works best for you. You can also use one form of explanation to better understand another.

Another convention you should know is that I use *italics* to indicate a term when I define it. The definitions are easy to understand, and they appear when I first introduce the term. Knowing terms helps you better understand the methods I describe in the book. Even more importantly, knowing these terms is magical. By dropping terms at your next business meeting, you're sure to impress everyone.

Finally, the action steps in the examples are **bold.** These steps describe the sequence of actions you must take to get to the right answer. If you need to memorize something for a test, this is it.

When this book was printed, some Web addresses (which all appear in `this font` to make them easy to find) may have needed to break across two lines of text. If that happened, rest assured that I haven't put in any extra characters (such as hyphens) to indicate the break. So, when using one of these Web addresses, just type in exactly what you see in this book, pretending as though the line break doesn't exist.

What You're Not to Read

First, don't read *The Communist Manifesto*. Karl Marx didn't understand the importance of profit in allowing consumers to signal what they do and don't want. Marx wrongly believed that profit came from exploitation, not mutually beneficial exchange. But as long as you're free to choose as a consumer, profit reflects your preferences.

Also, feel free to ignore the technical stuff in this book. I sometimes give you more detailed explanations of the material, marking it with a Technical Stuff icon when I do; you can skip these explanations without losing any critical material.

Finally, I include some stories in sidebars to illustrate the concept I'm explaining at that point. But because they're simply illustrations, you can understand the concept without reading the sidebar.

Foolish Assumptions

One night before bed my wife, Susan, asked what I was reading. I said *Butterfly Economics.* She asked what it was about, and I told her economics and chaos theory. When she asked what class I was reading the book for, I told her I wasn't reading the book for class, I was reading it for fun. Now you understand why Susan thinks I'm weird and why I dedicated this book to her for putting up with me. So, I'll start with the most important assumption I made when writing this book. I assume that unlike me, you're normal. You're like Susan, who wants to know how economics can be useful to her, and that's enough.

I do believe economics is fun, and I hope you'll find it fun too. I didn't write this book for another economist; I wrote it for you. I wrote it for somebody interested in discovering how economics might help them make better business decisions. The ultimate success of this book is in helping you make decisions that improve your business.

I also assume you're a busy person. You have a lot of things you have to do and even more things that you want to do. Thus, I try to make this book as clear and concise as possible. Because you're busy, I want you to learn these concepts as quickly and with as little effort as possible.

Some of you are probably taking a managerial economics course. I wrote this book so you can pick and choose what topics to read without reading a bunch of extra stuff. If you want to learn about game theory in Chapter 12, you can go straight there. You don't have to read the previous 11 chapters.

I also wrote this book knowing that some of you would want to see the math — that's calculus — while others want to avoid math like it's the plague. Either way, you can use this book. I present all theories both with graphs and, where appropriate, with calculus. If you want to skip the calculus, feel free to.

Finally, I assume you want to have fun while learning useful stuff. Although economics is called the dismal science, making lots of money is anything but dismal. So I assume you want to apply these ideas to business decisions. Remember that learning how economics helps your business doesn't have to be boring.

How This Book 1s Organized

I grouped topics together by dividing this book into five parts. I hope that grouping topics together helps you more easily find related ideas. The following section gives you an idea of the concepts I present in each part.

Part 1: The Nature of Managerial Economics

I hope that you associate managerial economics with the famous Broadway play, *How to Succeed in Business Without Really Trying.* The purpose of managerial economics is to give you ideas on how to increase your business's profit. That's success. Part I introduces fundamental aspects of managerial economics. It also introduces the basic theory of price determination — supply and demand. Finally, this part includes a brief calculus review if you're interested in incorporating calculus with business decision-making. But, remember that you can read and understand every economic theory in the book without knowing calculus, so the calculus review is an easy chapter to skip if you want.

Part 11: Considering Which Side You're On in the Decision-Making Process

A common lament goes, "Whose side are you on?" As the lament recognizes, it really matters to note which side you're on. This part separates consumers from producers to look more closely at each side of a market.

I begin by examining in-depth the relationship between price and quantity demanded. I examine why consumers are willing to purchase more at lower prices and that relationship's implication for business decisions, including how business owners can influence that relationship.

On the other side of the market, producers want high prices, so the relationships between inputs and output and production costs and supply are developed. And because innovation affects these relationships, the development of new technology is explored.

Part III: Recognizing Rivals: Market Structures and the Decision-Making Environment

Perhaps nothing is more important in business decision-making than situational awareness. When you're trying to sell your product to consumers, it's critical that you recognize who your rivals are.

The number of rivals you have influences your ability to set price. This part focuses on how you determine price in situations ranging from *perfect competition* (an extremely large number of rivals) to a *monopoly* (no rivals). In addition, I present advanced pricing strategies, such as *price discrimination* (charging different prices for the same commodity) and *bundling* (charging a single price for a bundle of two or more commodities).

Part IV: Anticipating Surprises: Risk and Uncertainty

My son Nicholas introduced me to a great term — flexecute. *Flexecute* means you have to be flexible enough to execute your mission under any circumstance. Your mission as a business owner is to maximize profit. But you need to accomplish this mission in a world that's constantly changing. In this part, I examine risk and uncertainty, and I present methods for making decisions when the outcomes can't be guaranteed.

This part also examines situations where participants have different goals. I introduce techniques that reconcile your goal of maximizing profit with your worker's goal of taking it easy. Finally, I consider government's influence on markets and businesses.

Part V: The Part of Tens

Just like late night show host David Letterman, every *For Dummies* book has its top ten lists. My top ten lists include ten critical concepts — you want to remember these; ten managerial shortcuts — ways to keep things simple; and ten managerial mistakes and how to avoid them — rather than learn from your mistakes, I want you to avoid them all together.

Icons Used in This Book

I couldn't figure out how to include neon lights in the book so instead I include five icons. These symbols call your attention to important ideas and information. If you see one, think of a neon light and pause for a second to check out the idea that follows.

This icon means you're about to read some really exciting shortcut. It's like the GPS on my cellphone that enables me to avoid the big traffic jam — tip: exit here and avoid a 20-minute wait in traffic. I love the GPS function for all the time it saves me, and I include tips in this book so you also save time by avoiding unnecessary "economic" traffic.

This icon identifies a critical concept. This is something to memorize — an idea that helps you make good business decisions. The text explains why the idea is important, but the icon gives you the one little thing that you should remember to key you into all the other good stuff related to that concept. For example, remember managerial economics is fun as you read the rest of the book.

I like to think of this icon as the "Yikes!" symbol. When you see this icon, be careful. Bad things can happen — yikes! This icon is the red stretch of highway on my GPS — avoid at all cost. The purpose of the warning icon is to make sure you don't do any of these bad things. So paying attention to the warning icon is like getting your economics flu shot — it will keep you from feeling sick because you made an economic mistake.

When you see this icon, it means you're about to see some of my favorite stuff. But then, remember, I'm an economist. Text associated with this icon shows some neat twists or extensions or maybe an interesting bell or whistle. I love that kind of stuff. But I also know that bells and whistles can make your ears hurt. So, know that you can skip this material without losing any important ideas, and who knows, maybe your ears won't hurt so much. On the other hand, if you like loud noises or technical stuff, this is the place for you.

Explanations are great, but examples are awesome! After explaining each technique, I include an example of how you can actually apply that technique. The example's purpose is to give you a step-by-step illustration of how you can apply the technique. That way, you can take your own situation or problem and apply the same steps I use in the example to find the answer to your problem.

Where to Go from Here

If this were a mystery book, I would suggest going straight to the end to find out whodunit. But this isn't a mystery. Instead, I suggest that you go to the topic that you think is neatest. If I have a vote, I pick bundling — pricing two goods as one (think Happy Meal). Or maybe price discrimination — charging different prices to different customers for the same good. I'm starting to really love senior citizen discounts. Or, I really enjoy learning how to avoid buying lemons; I've never bought a car in the same decade it was manufactured. But that's the great thing about this book — you pick, not me. So don't think you have to read the chapters in order, or that you need to start with Parts I, II, and III before going to Part IV. Start with the specific topics you're interested in and use the index and table of contents to help you find them.

Or, if you want, you can always start at the beginning.

Finally, if you're wondering what to do after reading this book, I suggest making a gazillion dollars, or at the very least using what you know to impress your coworkers and boss.

Part I
The Nature of Managerial Economics

The 5th Wave
By Rich Tennant

"I've never been good at this part of the job, which is why I've asked 'Buddy' to join us. As you know, the economy has been down lately, and well, Buddy has some bad news for you..."

In this part . . .

Economics studies how people allocate scarce resources to satisfy as many of their wants and desires as possible. By trying to make a profit, businesses turn the scarce resources into the goods that satisfy those wants and desires. Businesses that make lots of profit are providing the goods and services that people value the most. In this part, I establish the foundation for business decision-making that simultaneously satisfies consumer wants and desires while generating maximum profit. I describe how markets work and the determination of a good's price through demand and supply. I examine how the quantity of a good consumers purchase responds to changes in price and other factors such as income. This part also includes a calculus review — an important tool businesses use to minimize costs and maximize profit.

Chapter 1

Managerial Economics: Taking Care of Business

American humorist Frank McKinney Hubbard said, "Lots of folks confuse bad management with destiny." Managerial economics ensures a destiny that includes success for your business. And success has to be earned given that businesses compete for scarce resources.

The basic economic problem — scarcity of resources versus virtually unlimited human wants and desires — requires all societies to determine how to allocate scarce resources among competing uses. However, different methods are used to determine this resource allocation with the most common methods involving markets, government, or some combination of both. In a market economy, the production and distribution of goods is undertaken by firms. And because firms are economic entities, they're best analyzed with economic theory.

Managerial economics is a special subdivision within economics that applies economic theory to business decision-making. In general, economic theory describes how things work. But in managerial economics, economic theory provides tools managers use to make decisions. As a subdivision within economics, managerial economics moves away from mere description. Managerial economics focuses on the decisions managers should make, addressing the question of what action would be best for the firm's owners. For example, economic theory may describe how markets work, whereas managerial economics develops criteria that enable you to determine what price your company should charge in order to reach its objectives. Therefore, while economic theory is descriptive, managerial economics is prescriptive.

In this chapter, I place managerial economics in the broader context of general economic theory. Given this context, I examine business's role in a market economy and your role as a business manager. The concept of opportunity cost provides a fundamental element for business decision-making as does the explicit identification of the business's and manager's goals. I also introduce competition and risk and conclude by examining the time value of money or present value.

Managing Economics

Managerial economics combines economy theory and the decision sciences to develop methods for business and administrative decision-making. It provides a conceptual framework that bridges the gap between economic theory and practice.

Economics consists of two major subdivisions — macroeconomics and microeconomics. *Macroeconomics* is the area of economics that studies the behavior of the national economy, while *microeconomics* is the area that studies the behavior of individual economic agents, such as the firm or a consumer. To a large extent, *managerial economics* applies microeconomic theory to business decision-making. However, business decision-making doesn't take place within a vacuum. National economic conditions, international competition, financial markets, interest rates, and future economic conditions substantially influence individual businesses. Therefore, macroeconomic issues also have substantial impact on the firm and managerial decision-making.

The *decision sciences* provide methods for analyzing the impact of alternative decisions. These sciences include the optimization techniques associated with calculus and statistical techniques. Managerial economics integrates the decision sciences' analytical tools with economics in order to provide a framework for business decision-making.

Resource scarcity requires society to make choices in order to achieve specific goals. In *The Wealth of Nations,* the book published in 1776 that establishes the foundation for modern economics, Adam Smith states that individuals are motivated by self interest. Smith emphasizes that self-interest isn't bad; indeed, the pursuit of self interest generally leads to the best allocation of resources for society. Of course, there are exceptions, but that's the point — there are exceptions, not general problems with pursuing self interest. For business managers this statement means that trying to maximize profit isn't a bad thing. Indeed, by maximizing profit, business owners and managers effectively coordinate markets. That is, their decisions lead to the production of the best or most valuable goods and services.

But it would be a mistake to think that managerial economics applies only to profit-maximizing businesses. The techniques embodied in managerial economics are also of use to nonprofit organizations and governmental agencies. These organizations must also deal with scarce resources, so cost minimization and price determination for specific goals are crucial to their success.

Considering business's role

Firms are the primary instrument used to allocate scarce resources among competing activities in a market economy. Firms direct the transformation of resources into the goods and services that consumers desire. In the course of this transformation, the firm becomes an important agent in answering the three basic economic questions:

- ✔ What commodities should be produced?
- ✔ How should those commodities be produced?
- ✔ For whom are those commodities produced?

Thus, in a market economy, business owners and managers are heroes. As Adam Smith points out, it's through the efforts of business owners — the butcher, the brewer, and the baker — that you and I get our dinner. Their pursuit of profit provides everyone the food they eat. And the same goes for the farmer, the auto industry executive, Bill Gates, and anyone else connected to business. The business owner produces the stuff everyone consumes, employs resources to produce that stuff, and pays for the resources — especially the wages for labor. So, businesses produce the stuff I want and pay me the income that I need to buy that stuff.

Profit then becomes the business scorecard. It's important to use the resources as efficiently as possible — remember, they're scarce. Businesses that use those resources efficiently to produce the stuff that's highly valued get profit. Lots of profit generally means the business is doing a good job with the scarce resources. On the other hand, losses indicate that the business isn't doing well. These businesses are wasting scarce resources either by using them inefficiently or by producing stuff that consumers don't want.

Identifying the manager's role

Business owners and managers make and implement decisions that directly answer two of the major economic questions: "What commodities should be produced?" and "How should those commodities be produced?" They must decide what commodity or combination of commodities their firms should produce. They must decide what combination of inputs should be used in the commodity's production. They must also determine the commodity's price and how much they're willing to pay for various inputs. Profit is their scorecard and is used to evaluate the success or failure of their decisions in these areas.

The manager's tasks are grouped into three major areas:

- ✔ First, managers help develop the firm's goals.
- ✔ After the goals are established, managers must establish strategies for achieving those goals.
- ✔ Finally, managers must acquire and direct the resources necessary for achieving the firm's goals.

While attempting to promote the firm's objectives, managers confront numerous alternative actions. These alternatives are often complex; they may embody contradictions, and they may be subject to a variety of constraints. Because managers have incomplete information upon which to base a decision, uncertainty exists. Therefore, the complexity and uncertainty of the decision-making process require that managers possess a diverse set of skills.

Nothing Is Free: Opportunity Cost

The first thing managers must recognize is that nothing is free. A favorite saying in economics is "There's no such thing as a free lunch." This idea is crucial. If your boss takes you to lunch and offers to pay, it's still not a free lunch to you. You still have a cost. Perhaps the cost is spending time with your boss. Perhaps it's not getting something else done that you wanted to do. Perhaps it's going to a restaurant you don't especially like. No matter what, you made some sacrifice in going to lunch with your boss. You gave up some alternative.

Opportunity cost is the cost of an action or decision as measured by the best alternative you give up. Right now you're incurring an opportunity cost by reading this book. What's the next best alternative you're giving up? Perhaps it's watching television or taking a nap. Maybe you'd rather be bike riding — I would. Whatever the best alternative you're giving up — that's your opportunity cost.

But note that opportunity cost is just the best alternative you give up — it's not every alternative. If my best alternative to reading this book is riding a bike, that's my opportunity cost. Watching television doesn't count because I can't ride a bike and watch television at the same time.

Opportunity cost is the best alternative you give up when making a decision.

Defining Goals

The decision-making process has five major steps:

1. **Establish objectives.**

2. **Identify the problem or problems that prevent the fulfillment of the objectives.**

3. **Specify and evaluate possible solutions to the problem(s).**

4. **Select the best possible solution based upon the information available.**

5. **Implement the solution and subject it to ongoing evaluation.**

The crucial first step in this process is the identification of goals. As English mathematician Lewis Carroll once said, "If you don't know where you are going, any road will get you there." Or American baseball player Yogi Berra has another view, "You've got to be very careful if you don't know where you're going, because you might not get there." The point of both of these quotes is essentially the same — managerial decision-making requires a clear set of objectives.

You can't make a good decision if you don't know what you're trying to accomplish.

The owner's goal in a market economy is generally to maximize profits. Indeed, relative to the rest of the world, U.S. business owners emphasize short-run profits as indicated by publication of firm profits on a quarterly, semiannual, and annual basis.

However, alternative goals to profit maximization can also exist. For example, at times firms might maximize sales revenue or *market share,* where market share is the percentage of an industry's total sales that are held by a single firm. Or a business owner might focus on growth rather than profits as an objective. Other goals may include maximization of value added, or managers pursuing objectives that promote their interests rather than the interests of the firm's owners. In many of these cases, however, the purpose of these goals, which appear to contradict profit maximization, is, rather, a sacrifice of immediate profits in order to increase future profits.

Keeping your job: First things first

As a business manager your goals may differ from the owner's goals. Usually, your first goal is to keep your job. This is important to recognize because this goal may lead to conservative decision-making. Managers often don't pursue high risk–high reward strategies for fear of failure — failure that may lead to the manager being fired. This leads to the principal–agent problem that I discuss in Chapter 17.

Maximizing profit by recognizing all costs

To maximize profit, you must recognize all costs. This recognition takes you back to opportunity cost. But be careful, opportunity cost must consider all aspects of the best alternative.

In the previous section, I mention that managers may not take risks in order to protect their jobs. As a result, new products and new innovations may not be embraced as quickly as they should. But innovation is crucial to business survival. Successful new technologies make existing products and production techniques obsolete. Thus, the manager who avoids taking risks isn't protecting the business; indeed, a manger who avoids risk is probably making the business more vulnerable to its rivals. The business landscape is littered with companies that failed to adopt new technologies. Polaroid and instant developing film were made obsolete by the digital revolution, as were Eastman Kodak and cameras. The development of air transportation and interstate highways all but eliminated passenger rail travel. And many retailers — think of Borders bookstores — are suffering with the development of online marketing.

Staying with the tried and true has its own costs and is likely to threaten a business's survival.

Taking it to the limit with constraints

As a manager, you face numerous constraints when making decisions. These constraints affect your ability to achieve organizational objectives. Broadly defined, constraints fall into the following three categories:

> ✔ **Resource constraints** are often the result of limitations in the availability of certain inputs. These limitations may include shortages of critical raw materials, the inability to obtain labor that possesses the necessary skills, restrictions imposed by existing production facilities, intermediate inputs provided by auxiliary firms, or labor contracts that limit your ability to lay-off workers. In addition, you're constrained by the technical relationship that exists between inputs and the quantity of output produced.

  ✔ **Constraints on output quantity and quality** are typically the result of contractual obligations the firm has. Contracts that the firm has may specify a certain number of units of output. Delivery contracts may specify deadlines for fulfilling the order. Or, contracts may specify minimum standards for quality. These contracts represent obligations the firm must satisfy.

  ✔ **Legal constraints** take a variety of forms. Working conditions, health and safety concerns, child-labor laws, and minimum-wage legislation impose constraints on the firm. Environmental legislation limits your choice of production techniques. Antitrust legislation constrains the firm's relationship with competitors, as well as pricing and marketing strategies.

As a result of constraints, the goal of managerial decision-making is often called constrained optimization.

Taking Sides: Demand and Supply in the Decision-Making Process

Consumers and producers have exactly the opposite view regarding price. Consumers want low prices so they can buy more stuff — this is called *demand.* Producers what high prices so they can earn more profit — this is called *supply.* The great thing about markets is at any given price consumers are free to determine whether or not to buy the good and producers are free to decide whether or not to sell the good. When both consumers and producers simultaneously decide the price is "right," they engage in a mutually beneficial exchange. In other words, the exchange is a win-win situation called *equilibrium.* Consumers purchase the good at a price they're willing to pay, and producers sell the good at a price they're willing to receive. As long as consumers and producers are free to choose, the result of a market transaction benefits all participants.

Looking at Market Structures and the Decision-Making Environment

You don't make decisions in a vacuum. As you try to satisfy customer wants and desires, rival firms are trying to do the same thing. Therefore, it's critical to recognize your competition, including global competition, and what they're doing. Before making any decision, you must carefully note the level of competition you have and thus what market structure you're operating in.

Economists describe the level of competition through the use of market structures. *Market structures* simply reflect differing characteristics related to the number of rival firms and product characteristics. There are four major market structures, ranging from perfect competition, which has the highest degree of competition, to monopoly, which has the lowest degree of competition. Here are the four market structures, starting with the most competitive and moving to the least competitive:

- ✔ **Perfect competition** is the market structure with the highest degree of competition. Perfectly competitive markets have a large number of firms producing identical products. In perfect competition, price is determined by supply and demand in the market, and the individual firm has no influence on that price. The firm's managers must determine what quantity of output to produce given the price. Farmers growing corn, soybeans, and other agricultural commodities generally operate in perfectly competitive markets.

- ✔ **Monopolistic competition** also has a large number of firms but the good produced by the firms isn't identical — there are differences between firms. Because of the differences in the good produced by each firm, customers develop preferences for one firm's product over another firm's product. Differing customer preferences mean that the managers of monopolistically competitive firms can choose both the profit-maximizing quantity and price. Pizza restaurants operate in monopolistically competitive markets.

- ✔ **Oligopoly** is characterized by a small number of large firms. Because there are a small number of firms, you know who your rivals are. The close interaction among rivals leads to mutual interdependence — your actions affect every other firm. Thus, decision-making in oligopoly requires you to take into account how your rivals respond to those decisions.

- ✔ **Monopoly** has a single firm producing a commodity for which there are no close substitutes. Thus, monopolies don't have to consider direct competition. Nevertheless, monopolies are still constrained by consumer demand — if you think the monopoly's price is too high, you won't buy its product.

It should be noted that both perfectly competitive and monopolistically competitive markets are also characterized by easy entry and exit. It's easy for new firms to enter these markets and easy for existing firms to leave. Because of easy entry and exit, over time profit tends toward zero in these markets. Both oligopoly and monopoly have barriers to entry — it's difficult for new firms to enter these markets. Thus, it's easier for oligopolies and monopolies to maintain profit over an extended period of time.

Taking Chances: Recognizing Risk and Uncertainty

There is always risk. Taking chances is part of managerial decision-making. But it's a mistake to rely on blind luck when taking risks. Managerial economics develops criteria for evaluating risk. In addition, the techniques of managerial economics help you to determine the value of additional information. More information reduces risk, but it comes with a cost. Managerial economics provides you techniques to determine whether the information's expected value is worth its cost.

It's also important to recognize that business innovation rewards everyone through economic growth. As businesses produce new products, they enable consumers to satisfy even more wants and desires. Think about what life would be like without computers and cellphones, not to mention electricity and automobiles.

Knowing the Time Value of Money: Present Value

I've read articles that say a dollar today is worth only 25 cents. I want to meet the author of any article that says this, because I can get lots of quarters and trade them one-for-one for any dollars the author has. In fact, because I'm a generous guy, I'll throw in an extra nickel on every trade.

This idea sounds somewhat absurd, and it is. But it's really important to recognize what happens to money over time. A dollar today is worth — surprise — a dollar. However, a dollar today doesn't buy as much stuff as a dollar did 30 years ago because of inflation. Given inflation, I would rather have a dollar right now, rather than a dollar ten years in the future.

Even more important than inflation is the role interest plays in the value of money. If I have a dollar today, I can use it to buy a bond and earn interest. Thus, the dollar I have today will be $1.10 one year from now if the interest rate is 10 percent. Because of interest, you prefer receiving money now instead of in the future.

In making business decisions, it's important that you include the time value of money — the fact that money you hold today can earn interest. Thus, if you spend money today to build a new factory, you're giving up the opportunity to earn interest. In the future, your factory generates profits — at least you believe it will — but you need to know whether or not those profits are large enough to offset the interest you lost by not buying a bond. This is determined by calculating the present value.

The *present value* of money is the value of a future stream of revenue or costs in terms of their current value. Future revenues and costs are adjusted by a *discount rate* that reflects the individual's time and risk preference. Often, the discount rate is some interest rate that represents the individual's best alternative use for money today.

The formula for calculating the present value of a future stream of *net revenue* — future revenues minus future costs — is

$$PV = \sum_{i=1}^{t} \frac{R_t - C_t}{(1+r)^t}$$

where *PV* represents present value, $R_t - C_t$ represents net revenue (revenue minus cost) in year *t*, *r* is the interest rate, and *t* is the year.

Your company accepts a contract that has an anticipated net revenue of $100,000 at the end of each of the next three years. The interest rate is 6 percent. To determine the present value of this future stream of net revenue you take the following steps:

1. **Determine the present value of year one's net revenue.**

   Divide 100,000 by 1.06.

   $$\frac{R_t - C_t}{(1+r)^t} = \frac{100,000}{(1+0.06)^1} = 94,339.62$$

2. **Determine the present value of year two's net revenue.** Divide 100,000 by $(1.06)^2$.

   $$\frac{R_t - C_t}{(1+r)^t} = \frac{100,000}{(1+0.06)^2} = 88,999.64$$

3. **Determine the present value of year three's net revenue.**

   Divide 100,000 by $(1.06)^3$.

   $$\frac{R_t - C_t}{(1+r)^t} = \frac{100,000}{(1+0.06)^3} = 83,961.92$$

4. **Add the present value of net revenue for years one, two, and three.**

   $$PV = \sum_{i=1}^{t} \frac{R_t - C_t}{(1+r)^t} = 94,339.62 + 88,999.64 + 83,961.92 = 267,301.18$$

Thus, the present value of $100,000 net revenue for each of the next three years given an interest rate of 6 percent is $267,301.18.

As an alternative to short-run profit maximization, managerial efforts can maximize the firm's value. Focusing on maximizing the firm's value can resolve the apparent conflict between the goal of immediate profit maximization and other goals, such as sales or growth maximization, that may increase the firm's future profits.

A firm's value is defined as the present value of the firm's expected future profit, π. Therefore,

$$\text{Firm's Value} = PV\left(\text{future profit}\right) = \sum_{i=1}^{n} \frac{\pi_t}{\left(1+r\right)^t}$$

where π_t represents the profit in year t, and r is the interest rate. This is simply a present value calculation that discounts profit earned in the future by the interest rate.

A number of factors influence the firm's value. The firm's marketing department can increase profits through various marketing strategies. Costs are frequently reduced through the firm's engineering or production department. Although research and development expenditures increase current costs and diminish current profits, they may result in higher future profits that more than offset those costs. Thus, maximizing the firm's value encompasses a broad variety of strategies that you may employ as a manager.

Your ultimate goal as manager is to maximize your firm's value. That ensures that your destiny is a good one.

Chapter 2

Supply and Demand: You Have What Consumers Want

· ·

In This Chapter

▶ Buying more with lower prices

▶ Producing more with higher prices

▶ Compromising on price at equilibrium

▶ Moving toward equilibrium when shortages and surpluses occur

▶ Understanding why equilibrium changes

· ·

The Scottish essayist Thomas Carlyle said, "Teach a parrot the terms 'supply and demand' and you've got an economist." Or there's a story about a student standing next to an economist by a bank of elevators. Three elevators passed them on the way to the basement. The student said, "I wonder why everybody in the basement wants to go upstairs." The economist responded, "You're confusing supply with demand." Or finally, there is an old joke, "Talk is cheap. Supply exceeds demand."

The numerous jokes about supply and demand indicate its fundamental importance in economics. Indeed, if the parrot understood what the terms supply and demand meant, it wouldn't be much of an exaggeration to say the parrot qualifies as an economist. The reason this isn't an exaggeration is because understanding supply and demand enables you to understand how prices are determined and what causes prices to change. And in business decision-making, understanding how prices are determined means nearly everything.

How Much Is That Doggie in the Window? Setting Prices through Markets

A popular children's song asks, how much is that doggie in the window? The song's chorus goes:

How much is that doggie in the window?
The one with the waggley tail.
How much is that doggie in the window?
I do hope that doggie's for sale.

The last line of the lyrics — "I do hope that doggie's for sale" — is too vague. To an economist (see, economists can even ruin a children's song), the question is not whether the doggie is for sale. Of course, it's for sale. The question is how much does it cost.

If the price is very low, customers are more likely to buy the dog, but the store does not make much profit; it may even lose money. If the doggie is too expensive, nobody will buy it. So the question is what price will lead to someone buying the doggie while the store owner makes some profit.

This apparent conflict between customers wanting low prices and sellers wanting high prices is resolved in the market — or through supply and demand.

Demanding Lower Prices

The relationship between how much customers must pay for an item and how much customers buy is called *demand*. More precisely, demand shows the relationship between a good's price and the quantity of the good customers purchase, holding everything else constant.

Wow! Holding everything else constant, even the dog's waggley tail? Not quite, but holding things like income, customer preferences, and the price of other goods — say cats — constant. (Are cats a good?)

So quite simply, demand tells you how much customers purchase at each possible price.

Distinguishing between quantity demanded and demand

Quantity demanded and demand sound like the same thing. Indeed, as you read the newspaper, you're likely to see demand all the time and never see quantity demanded. (That's because very few reporters take economics classes.) But to economists, there is a big difference between the terms quantity demanded and demand.

To economists, *quantity demanded* is the amount of the good customers purchase at a given price. Quantity demanded is a specific number.

On the other hand, demand refers to the entire curve. Demand shows how much is purchased at every possible price.

Demand is an equation or line on a graph that indicates how price and quantity demanded are related.

Graphing demand

The graph of the demand curve enables you to focus on the relationship between price and quantity demanded. Figure 2-1 illustrates the demand curve for dog treats. (You want to keep that tail wagging.) The graph shows you that when prices are very high, customers want to buy fewer treats. More specifically, if the price of treats is $5.00, customers want to buy only 50 boxes of treats a week. On the other hand, if the price of treats decreases, say, to $1.00 a box, the quantity demanded of treats increases to 250 boxes a week.

Changing price

Price changes cause movements along the demand curve, or a change in quantity demanded. In Figure 2-1, when the price of dog treats decreased from $5.00 to $1.00, the quantity demanded increased from 50 to 250 boxes per week — a movement from point A to point B on the demand curve in Figure 2-1.

An inverse relationship exists between price and quantity demanded — price and quantity demanded move in opposite directions.

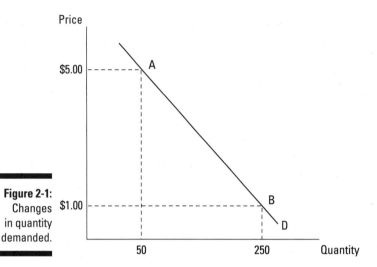

Figure 2-1:
Changes
in quantity
demanded.

Shifting the demand curve

When one of the things being held constant — income, tastes, and the prices of other goods — changes, the entire demand curve shifts. For example, advertisements indicate that treats lead to happy dogs. People want happy dogs, so their preference for treats changes; dog treats become more desirable. So more dog treats are purchased, even though nothing happened to the price of dog treats.

Figure 2-2 illustrates the increase in demand as the curve shifts from D_0 to D_1. Because the desirability of dog treats increases, stores are selling a lot more dog treats. Stores were previously selling 250 boxes of treats per week at a price of $1.00. Now, with the price still $1.00, stores are selling more treats — 350 boxes a week. That point isn't on the original demand shown in Figure 2-1. What happened is the demand curve shifts so that this new point is on the new demand curve, D_1. Because the new demand curve is to the right of the original demand curve, economists say demand has increased.

Any rightward shift in the demand curve is an increase in demand, and any leftward shift in the curve is a decrease in demand.

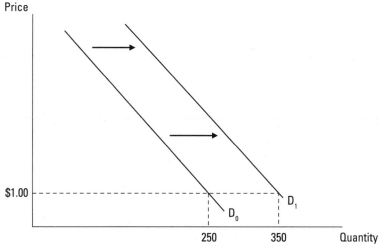

Figure 2-2:
Changes
(shifts) in
demand.

The factors that shift the entire demand curve are

✓ **Consumer tastes or preferences:** A direct relationship exists between desirability (consumer tastes) and demand. Thus, an increase in desirability increases demand.

✓ **Income:** Income's impact on demand is a little more complicated. Economists note two types of goods — normal goods and inferior goods. For *normal goods*, a direct relationship exists between income and demand — an increase in income increases demand. This is the expected, or normal, relationship. For an *inferior good*, an increase in income decreases demand; therefore, an inverse relationship exists between income and demand for an inferior good.

✓ **Prices of other goods:** Changes in the prices of other goods are also a little complicated. If the goods are *consumer substitutes* for one another, they are used interchangeably. Hot dogs and hamburgers at a picnic are an example of consumer substitutes. A direct relationship exists between one good's price and the demand for the second, substitute, good. Thus, when the price of hot dogs increases, the entire demand curve for hamburgers shifts to the right (increases). *Consumer complements* are a second type of goods. Consumer complements are used together, such as coffee and cream. An inverse relationship exists between one good's price and the demand for its consumer complement. As the price of coffee increases, the amount of coffee you drink decreases. This decrease in the quantity demanded of coffee is because you're responding to a change in coffee's price. And because you're drinking less coffee, your demand for cream decreases. The higher price for coffee decreases your demand for cream — an inverse relationship. Even if the price of cream doesn't change, you use less of it.

Supplying Higher Prices

Supply describes the relationship between the good's price and how much businesses are willing to provide. Supply is a schedule that shows the relationship between the good's price and quantity supplied, holding everything else constant.

Holding everything else constant seems a little ambitious, even for economists, but there is a reason for that qualification. By holding everything else constant, supply enables you to focus on the relationship between price and the quantity provided. And that is the critical relationship.

Understanding quantity supplied and supply

You must be able to distinguish between two terms that sound the same, quantity supplied and supply, but mean very different things. It is common for others not to make the distinction and as a result their analysis is confused.

Quantity supplied refers to the amount of the good businesses provide at a specific price. So, quantity supplied is an actual number. Economists use the term *supply* to refer to the entire curve. The supply curve is an equation or line on a graph showing the different quantities provided at every possible price.

Graphing supply

The supply curve's graph shows the relationship between price and quantity supplied. Figure 2-3 illustrates the supply curve for dog treats. The graph indicates that when the price is very high, businesses provide a lot more treats. There's money to be made in dog treats. But if the price of dog treats is very low, there's not much money to be made, and businesses provide fewer dog treats. For example, if the price of treats is $5.00, businesses provide 650 boxes of treats a week. On the other hand, if the price of treats decreases to $1.00 a box, the quantity of treats provided decreases to 50 boxes a week.

Changing price

Figure 2-3 illustrates that price and quantity supplied are directly related. As price goes down, the quantity supplied decreases; as the price goes up, quantity supplied increases.

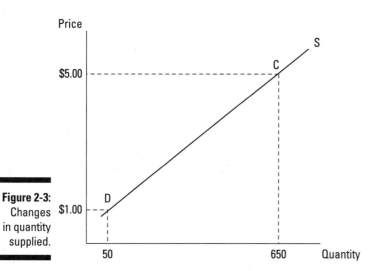

Price changes cause changes in quantity supplied represented by movements along the supply curve. When the price of dog treats decreases from $5.00 to $1.00 in Figure 2-3, the quantity supplied decreases from 650 to 50 boxes per week — a movement from point C to point D on the supply curve. This movement indicates that a direct relationship exists between price and quantity supplied: Price and quantity supplied move in the same direction.

Shifting the supply curve

When economists focus on the relationship between price and quantity supplied, a lot of other things are held constant, such as production costs, technology, and the prices of goods producers consider related. When any one of these things changes, the entire supply curve shifts.

If an increase in supply occurs, the curve shifts to the right, as illustrated in Figure 2-4. In this case, an increase in supply shifted the curve from S_0 to S_1. As a result, more dog treats are provided at every possible price. For example, at a price of $5.00, 750 boxes of dog treats are provided each week instead of 650.

A rightward shift in the supply curve always indicates an increase in supply, while a leftward shift in the curve indicates a decrease in supply.

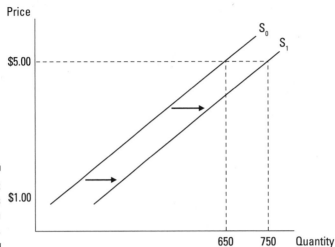

Figure 2-4:
Changes
(shifts) in
supply.

The factors that shift the supply curve include

- ✔ **Production costs:** Input prices and resulting production costs are inversely related to supply. In other words, changes in input prices and production costs cause an opposite change in supply. If input prices and production costs increase, supply decreases; if input prices and production costs decrease, supply increases. For example, if wages or labor costs increase, the supply of the good decreases.

- ✔ **Technology:** Technological improvements in production shift the supply curve. Specifically, improvements in technology increase supply — a rightward shift in the supply curve.

- ✔ **Prices of other goods:** Price changes for other goods are a little complicated. First, in order to affect supply, producers must think the goods are related. What consumers think is irrelevant. For example, ranchers think beef and leather are related; they both come from a steer. However, as a consumer, please don't serve me leather for dinner.

  Beef and leather are an example of *joint products*, products produced together. For joint products, a direct relationship exists between a good's price and the supply of its joint product. If the price of beef increases, ranchers raise more cattle, and the supply of beef's joint product (leather) increases.

  Producer substitutes also exist; using the same resources, a business can produce one good or the other. Corn and soybeans are examples of producer substitutes. If the price of corn increases, farmers grow more corn, and less land is available to grow soybeans. Soybeans' supply decreases. An inverse relationship exists between a good's price (corn) and the supply of its producer substitute (soybeans).

Determining Equilibrium: Minding Your P's and Q's

Business executives face a dilemma: Customers want low prices, and executives want high prices. Markets resolve this dilemma by reaching a compromise price. The compromise price is the one that makes quantity demanded equal to quantity supplied. At that price, every customer who is willing and able to buy the good can do so. And every business executive who wants to sell the good at that price can sell it.

The price that makes quantity demanded equal to quantity supplied is called the *equilibrium price*. It occurs where the demand and supply curves intersect.

Figure 2-5 illustrates the equilibrium price for dog treats — the point where the demand and supply curve intersect corresponds to a price of $2.00. At this price, the quantity demanded (determined off of the demand curve) is 200 boxes of treats per week, and the quantity supplied (determined from the supply curve) is 200 boxes per week. Quantity demanded equals quantity supplied.

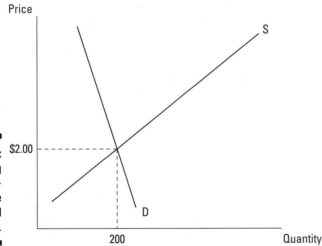

Figure 2-5: Determining the equilibrium price and quantity.

Determining the price mathematically

You can also determine the equilibrium price mathematically. In order to determine equilibrium mathematically, remember that quantity demanded must equal quantity supplied.

The demand for dog treats is represented by the following equation

$$Q_D = 300 - 50P$$

In the equation, Q_D represents the quantity demanded of dog treats, and P represents the price of a box of dog treats in dollars. Because a negative sign is in front of the term 50P, as price increases, quantity demanded decreases.

The supply of dog treats is represented by

$$Q_S = -100 + 150P$$

The quantity supplied of dog treats is represented by Q_S in this equation, and P again represents the price for a box of dog treats in dollars. A positive sign in front of the 150P indicates a direct relationship exist between price and quantity supplied.

To determine the equilibrium price, do the following.

1. **Set quantity demanded equal to quantity supplied:**

   $$Q_D = 300 - 50P = -100 + 150P = Q_S$$

2. **Add 50P to both sides of the equation.**

   You get

   $$300 - 50P + 50P = -100 + 150P + 50P \text{ or } 300 = -100 + 200P$$

3. **Add 100 to both sides of the equation.**

   You get

   $$300 + 100 = -100 + 200P + 100 \text{ or } 400 = 200P$$

4. **Divide both sides of the equation by 200.**

   You get P equals $2.00 per box. This is the equilibrium price.

Producing too much: Stuff lying everywhere

Gas prices keep rising, and customers no longer want to buy large cars with low gas mileage. The car dealer's lot is full of large cars, and more are on the way. The dealership has an excess supply of cars.

REMEMBER

Economists call an excess supply a *surplus*. A surplus means the good's price is too high, and as a result, quantity demanded is less than quantity supplied. Customers want to buy less at the current price than the store wants to sell.

Figure 2-6 illustrates the car surplus. At $35,000 per car, the quantity demanded is only 10 cars per month, while the quantity supplied is 30 cars. Thus, a surplus, or excess supply, of 20 cars exists. The managers don't want these cars sitting on the lot, so they lower the price. At the same time, they cancel future orders, reducing quantity supplied. And because of the lower price, customers buy more cars. In the end, the price per car falls to the equilibrium price of $30,000 in Figure 2-6, the quantity supplied by the dealer decreases from 30 to 15, and the quantity demanded by customers increases from 10 to 15. At the price of $30,000, the market is in equilibrium because quantity demanded equals quantity supplied.

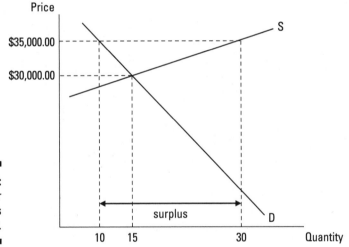

Figure 2-6:
Surplus or
excess
supply.

Producing not enough: The cupboard is bare

It's Christmas, and you know what the "hot" gift is. You know because you have been to six stores and can't find it anywhere. Or it's the biggest basketball game of the year, and you just have to go but the tickets are sold out. In these situations, you're encountering a shortage.

A *shortage* exists when the quantity supplied of a good is less than the quantity demanded; in other words, not enough is being provided, and there is excess demand. Customers want to purchase more than businesses are providing. As a result, some customers who want to purchase the good can't find it. The customers are left with two choices: Do without and be disappointed or offer a higher price to buy the good. At the same time, stores recognize that more customers want the good than they expected, so they raise the price.

Suppose that the hot gift next Christmas is baseball cards of famous economists. (Yes, such things really exist, but bubble gum isn't included.) As illustrated in Figure 2-7, at a price of $5.00 per set, the quantity supplied is 1,500 sets, while the quantity demanded is 5,000 sets. A shortage or excess demand of 3,500 sets exists. As the producer realizes the cards are selling out, the producer raises price to $10.00 per set, and some customers decide the cards are too expensive, so quantity demanded decreases to 3,000 sets. At the same time, the producer also increases production (there is a lot of money to be made in famous economist cards), so the quantity supplied increases to 3,000. The market has reached equilibrium, as illustrated in Figure 2-7, because the quantity demanded of 3,000 equals the quantity supplied. And this occurs at the equilibrium price of $10.00.

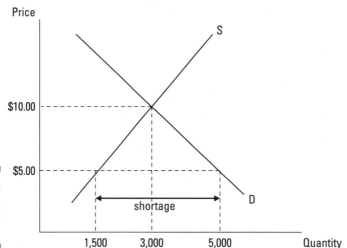

Figure 2-7: Shortage or excess demand.

Changing equilibrium: Shift happens

Markets tend toward equilibrium, the price and quantity that correspond to the point where supply and demand intersect. But equilibrium itself can change.

REMEMBER

Because equilibrium corresponds to the point where the demand and supply curves intersect, anything that shifts the demand or supply curves establishes a new equilibrium. (See the earlier sections "Shifting the demand curve" and "Shifting the supply curve.")

Figure 2-8 illustrates what happens when demand increases. Originally, the market was in equilibrium at price P_0 and quantity Q_0. If demand increases, the demand curve shifts to the right from D_0 to D_1. The quantity demanded associated with the price P_0 is now Q_D. Because this is greater than the quantity producers are providing (still Q_0 as determined off the supply curve), a shortage exists. The market moves from the original equilibrium price P_0 to the new equilibrium price P_1 and from the original equilibrium quantity Q_0 to the new equilibrium quantity, Q_1.

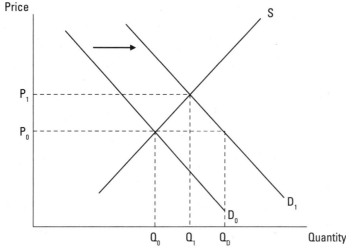

Figure 2-8:
Changing
equilibrium
due to an
increase in
demand.

The impact of an increase in supply is illustrated in Figure 2-9. Originally, the equilibrium price and quantity are P_0 and Q_0, respectively. An increase in supply shifts the supply curve to the right from S_0 to S_1. The supply increase immediately creates a surplus because at P_0, the new quantity supplied Q_S is greater than the quantity demanded, which is still at Q_0. Because there is a surplus, the good's price falls from P_0 to the new equilibrium price P_1, and the quantity demanded and quantity supplied move to the new equilibrium quantity Q_1, which is greater than the original equilibrium quantity Q_0.

There are instances where both demand and supply shift at the same time, and this makes determining the changes in equilibrium price and quantity more difficult.

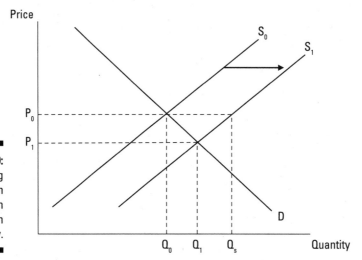

Figure 2-9:
Changing
equilibrium
due to an
increase in
supply.

When both demand and supply shift simultaneously, the change in only one equilibrium characteristic — price or quantity — can be definitely determined.

Figure 2-10 illustrates a simultaneous decrease in both demand and supply — the demand curve shifts left from D_0 to D_1, and the supply curve shifts left from S_0 to S_1. The original equilibrium price and quantity are P_0 and Q_0, corresponding to the intersection of the original demand and supply curves. Given the shifts to D_1 and S_1, the equilibrium quantity decreases from Q_0 to Q_1 while the equilibrium price has not changed — $P_0 = P_1$. But note that in Figure 2-10, the demand and supply curves shift by the same amount.

In Figure 2-11, two decreases in supply are illustrated along with the decrease in demand. The first decrease in supply is a relatively small one, from S_0 to S_A. The new equilibrium quantity decreases from Q_0 to Q_A, and the equilibrium price also decreases from P_0 to P_A. The second decrease in supply is a relatively large one, from S_0 to S_B. In this case, the new equilibrium quantity still decreases, now from Q_0 to Q_B. But note what happens to equilibrium price: It increases from P_0 to P_B. Given the decrease in demand, a small decrease in supply results in a lower equilibrium price, while a large decrease in supply results in a higher equilibrium price.

Figures 2-10 and 2-11 illustrate that when both demand and supply simultaneously decrease, equilibrium quantity always decreases, but equilibrium price can increase, decrease, or remain the same. So, only one equilibrium characteristic — equilibrium quantity — can be definitely determined.

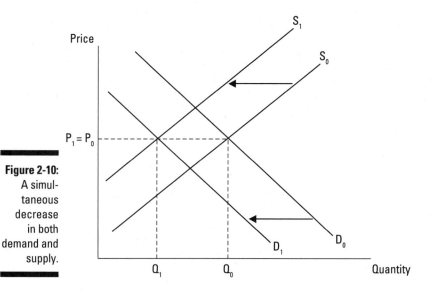

Figure 2-10:
A simul-
taneous
decrease
in both
demand and
supply.

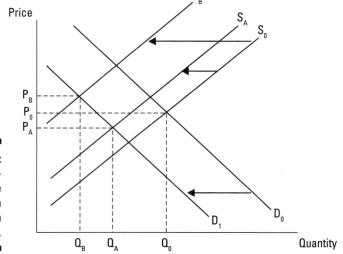

Figure 2-11:
An inde-
terminate
change in
equilibrium
price.

The crucial thing to note is that no matter what happens to supply and demand, the market always adjusts to its equilibrium point.

Chapter 3

Calculus, Optimization, and You

· ·

In This Chapter

▶ Determining the best or optimal decision

▶ Following the rules of calculus

▶ Doing your best given constraints

· ·

I remember once seeing a quote, "Warning: The internet may contain traces of nuts." Well, to be truthful, it's probably a little more than traces. In any case, it is in that spirit that I say, "Warning: This chapter contains traces of calculus."

*E*conomic theories are frequently presented with graphs. But the relationships described on the graphs can also be presented mathematically — especially when problems involve optimization. Consumers maximizing satisfaction, firms minimizing cost, and firms maximizing profit are examples of topics that can be presented both graphically and mathematically. Because you may not be interested in learning how topics are presented mathematically, throughout the book I present them both ways. Remember, however, that the graphs and math are simply tools — they help you determine the best decision. Therefore, you should think of them as a simplification rather than a burden in the decision-making process.

If you want to understand the mathematical approach to optimization in managerial economics, this chapter reviews basic calculus — specifically, derivatives. It assumes you already know calculus but you need a brief refresher on some aspects of it. At the end of the chapter, I present a technique for constrained optimization called the Lagrangian function. This function is a great tool to use in many managerial and business situations.

Describing How Things Are Related with Functions

Graphs easily describe the relationship between two variables; for example, a supply curve describes the relationship between price and quantity supplied. Economic relationships are also expressed as mathematical functions.

A function describes the relationship that exists between two or more variables. For example,

$$q = f(p)$$

is a general statement that indicates the variable q is a function of the variable p. A specific functional form describes the exact relationship that exists between those variables; the function

$$q = 5p$$

indicates that for every one unit increase in p, q's value increases by 5 units, or that q is five times greater than p. By identifying the exact relationship between variables, you've turned a general equation into a specific function.

Two variable functions are easily expressed with either an equation or a graph. However, for functional relationships involving three or more variables, you'll find that equations are not only simpler than graphs, but also often a necessity. A functional relationship among three variables is

$$U = g(x,y)$$

This equation indicates that U is a function "g" of the variables x and y. In such functions, U is called the dependent variable because its value depends upon the values of x and y. The variables x and y are called independent variables because their values are given and determine U's value.

Business decision-making requires knowing the specific relationship among variables. The equation

$U = 2x + 3y$ indicates that a one-unit increase in the variable x causes a two-unit ($2x$) increase in U, while a one-unit increase in variable y causes a three-unit ($3y$) increase in U.

Optimizing Is the Best Decision

You want to make the best possible decision for your business. Doing so is optimization — you're making the optimal decision. You may be trying to maximize sales, minimize costs, and/or maximize profit. In each optimizing situation, you're determining the best possible outcome.

Sometimes, you face constraints when optimizing. As a consumer, you try to maximize your satisfaction given the constraint of your available income. As a manager, you try to minimize the cost of producing a given quantity of output given technological constraints. In these situations, equations and calculus become very helpful tools for you.

You Want Me to Remember Calculus?

Again, you don't have to remember calculus. Managerial economics concepts are presented without calculus. On the other hand, calculus does make things easier, and there's nothing like an equation to dazzle the boss. Let's be honest, if somebody wrote out a big, long equation, you and I would look at it, think "I haven't a clue what it means," but nevertheless be impressed. Well, the calculus you use will impress a lot of people, but more importantly, you'll know what it means and it will help you solve managerial problems.

And as real-world situations become more complicated, calculus may be the only way to develop a solution.

Deriving derivatives

Suppose that the variable y is a function of the variable x, or

$$y = f(x)$$

Thus, a change in x's value causes a change in y's value. The relationship between changes in the values of x and y is described by a derivative.

You may remember from your calculus course that a derivative also represents the function's slope at any given point.

Consider the following quadratic relationship,

$$y = x^2$$

I graph this specific function in Figure 3-1. The derivative of this function is

$$\frac{dy}{dx} = 2x$$

The symbol dy/dx represents the derivative of variable y taken with respect to variable x. In other words, this is the change in y that occurs given a change in x. In Figure 3-1, the derivative is the slope of the function or line. The change in y is often referred to as the *rise*, and the change in x is the *run*. Thus, the derivative is the rise over the run — the function's slope.

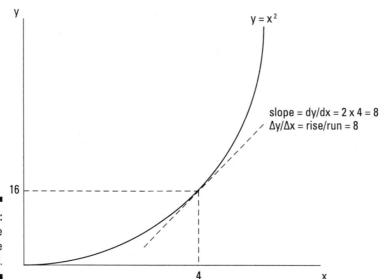

Figure 3-1:
Derivative
and slope
for $y=x^2$.

For any given value of x, the slope of the original function at that point can be determined by substituting x's value into the derivative. For example, at x equals 4, the original function's slope is 8. The tangent illustrating the slope at x equals 4 is illustrated in the figure.

Rules, rules everywhere

Okay, enough general comments on derivatives. This section reviews basic differentiation rules that you use in managerial economics. Again, I assume you already know calculus — this is just a brief refresher for some of the important rules of differentiation. If you need more than a quick refresher, a great place to go is *Calculus For Dummies* (John Wiley & Sons) and its online cheat sheet at www.dummies.com/cheatsheet/calculus.

Constant function rule

If variable y is equal to some constant a, its derivative with respect to x is 0, or if

$$y = a \quad \text{then} \quad \frac{dy}{dx} = 0$$

For example,

$$y = 37 \quad \text{then} \quad \frac{dy}{dx} = 0$$

Power function rule

A power function indicates that the variable x is raised to a constant power k.

The derivative of y with respect to x equals k multiplied by x raised to the k-1 power, or

$$y = ax^k \quad \text{then} \quad \frac{dy}{dx} = kax^{k-1}$$

For example,

$$y = 5x^4 \quad \text{then} \quad \frac{dy}{dx} = 4 \times 5x^{4-1} = 20x^3$$

The power function rule is extremely powerful! You can use it with a variety of exponents. For example,

$$y = \frac{4}{x^3}$$

can be rewritten as

$$y = 4x^{-3} \quad \text{then} \quad \frac{dy}{dx} = (-3) \times 4x^{-3-1} = -12x^{-4} = \frac{-12}{x^4}$$

Be careful with this last derivative. When a variable with an exponent appears in the denominator, such as x^3 in the previous equation, the variable can be moved to the numerator, but the exponent becomes negative. So, $4/x^3$ becomes $4x^{-3}$. Then when you take the derivative, make sure you subtract 1 from -3 to get -4.

As another example, consider

$$y = 3\sqrt{x}$$

can be written as

$$y = 3x^{0.5} \quad \text{then} \quad \frac{dy}{dx} = 0.5 \times 3x^{0.5-1} = 1.5x^{-0.5} = \frac{1.5}{\sqrt{x}}$$

You may remember that square roots are fractional exponents, or the 0.5 (one-half) power.

Finally, note that

$$y = 6x \quad \text{then} \quad \frac{dy}{dx} = 1 \times 6x^{1-1} = 6x^0 = 6$$

Sum-difference rule

Remember, I warned you about the calculus. Again, these sections are intended to refresh your memory about calculus — I assume you've already served your time in a calculus course, or alternatively, you've read *Calculus For Dummies* by Mark Ryan (Wiley). Now, on to the sum-difference rule.

Assume there are two functions, $TR = g(q)$ and $TC = h(q)$. (You may think of the variable *TR* as total revenue, the variable *TC* as total cost, and the variable *q* as the quantity of the product produced. The symbol *g* in the total revenue function and the symbol *h* in the total cost function mean that the relationship between *q* and total revenue is different from the relationship between *q* and total cost.) Further, assume that the variable π (profit) is a function of both *TR* and *TC*, so

$\pi = TR - TC.$

The derivative of π with respect to *q* equals the sum (the functions can be added or subtracted) of the derivatives of *TR* and *TC* with respect to *q*, or,

$$\frac{d\pi}{dq} = \frac{dTR}{dq} \pm \frac{dTC}{dq}$$

For example,

$$TR = 50q - 0.005q^2 \quad \text{and} \quad TC = 12,000 + 20q + 0.0025q^2$$

Then the derivatives of *TR* and *TC* with respect to *q* are

$$\frac{dTR}{dq} = 50 - 0.01q \quad \text{and} \quad \frac{dTC}{dq} = 20 + 0.005q$$

Using the sum-difference rule

$$\frac{d\pi}{dq} = \frac{dTR}{dq} - \frac{dTC}{dq} = 50 - 0.01q - (20 + 0.005q)$$
$$= 50 - 0.01q - 20 - 0.005q = 30 - 0.015q$$

Although in the example the two functions were subtracted, remember that the sum difference rule also works when functions are added.

Product rule

Assume you have two functions, $u = g(x)$ and $v = h(x)$. Further, assume that $y = u \times v$.

The derivative of y with respect to x equals the sum of u multiplied by the derivative of v and v multiplied by the derivative of u, or if

$$y = u \times v \quad \text{then} \quad \frac{dy}{dx} = u\frac{dv}{dx} + v\frac{du}{dx}$$

For example, if

$$y = x^3\left(9 + 4x - 7x^2\right)$$

In this equation, $u = x^3$ and $v = (9 + 4x - 7x^2)$. Thus, the derivative of u with respect to x is

$$\frac{du}{dx} = 3x^2$$

And the derivative of v with respect to x is

$$\frac{dv}{dx} = 4 - 14x$$

Then

$$\frac{dy}{dx} = x^3\left(4 - 14x\right) + \left(9 + 4x - 7x^2\right)3x^2$$
$$= 4x^3 - 14x^4 + 27x^2 + 12x^3 - 21x^4 = 27x^2 + 16x^3 - 35x^4$$

Quotient rule

A quotient refers to the result obtained when one quantity, in the numerator, is divided by another quantity, in the denominator. Assume you have two functions, $u = g(x)$ and $v = h(x)$. So, u is the quantity in the numerator, and it's a function g of x. And v is the quantity in the denominator, and it's a different function of x as represented by h. In addition, assume that $y = u/v$. So y is the quotient of u divided by v.

The derivative of y with respect to x has two components in its numerator. The first component is the original equation for v multiplied by the derivative of u taken with respect to x, du/dx. From that amount, you subtract the numerator's second component, the original equation u multiplied by the derivative of v taken with respect to x, dv/dx. The dominator of this derivative is simply the original equation, v, squared. Thus,

$$y = \frac{u}{v} \quad \text{then} \quad \frac{dy}{dx} = \frac{v\frac{du}{dx} - u\frac{dv}{dx}}{v^2}$$

For example, if the original quotient is

$$y = \frac{x^3}{(5x-2)} \quad \text{then} \quad \frac{dy}{dx} = \frac{(5x-2)3x^2 - x^3(5)}{(5x-2)^2}$$

In this quotient, $u = x^3$ and $v = (5x - 2)$. The derivative of u with respect x is

$$\frac{du}{dx} = 3x^2$$

And the derivative of v with respect to x is

$$\frac{dv}{dx} = 5$$

Thus, the first component of the numerator is v multiplied du/dx. From that, you subtract the second component of the numerator, which is u multiplied by dv/dx, or

$$v\frac{du}{dx} - u\frac{dv}{dx} = (5x-2)3x^2 - x^3(5)$$

The denominator is v^2 or

$$v^2 = (5x-2)^2$$

Substituting everything into the quotient rule yields

$$\frac{dy}{dx} = \frac{v\frac{du}{dx} - u\frac{dv}{dx}}{v^2} = \frac{(5x-2)3x^2 - x^3(5)}{(5x-2)^2}$$

Chain rule

You're almost there, and I wonder whether you're thinking, "Not a moment too soon." Just one more rule is typically used in managerial economics — the chain rule.

For the chain rule, you assume that a variable z is a function of y; that is, $z = f(y)$. In addition, assume that y is a function of x; that is, $y = g(x)$. The derivative of z with respect to x equals the derivative of z with respect to y multiplied by the derivative of y with respect to x, or

$$z = f(y) \quad \text{and} \quad y = g(x) \quad \text{then} \quad \frac{dz}{dx} = \frac{dz}{dy} \times \frac{dy}{dx}$$

For example, if

$$z = y^2 \quad \text{and} \quad y = \left(3x^2 - 5x + 7\right)$$

Then

$$\frac{dz}{dy} = 2y \quad \text{and} \quad \frac{dy}{dx} = 6x - 5 \quad \text{so} \quad \frac{dz}{dx} = 2y \times \left(6x - 5\right)$$

Substituting $y = (3x^2 - 5x + 7)$ into dz/dx yields

$$\frac{dz}{dx} = 2\left(3x^2 - 5x + 7\right) \times \left(6x - 5\right) = 36x^3 - 90x^2 + 134x - 70$$

With this last substitution, I remove the third variable y from the derivative, and as a result, I have a function for dz/dx only in terms of x.

Holding most, but not all, things constant by using partial derivatives

You're not through with calculus yet. Get ready for a little variation called *partial differentiation*. This technique won't change any of the rules — thank goodness!

In most instances, two variable functions are too simplistic to describe a situation adequately.

When functions have three or more variables (two or more independent variables), economists frequently want to focus on how changes in one independent variable's value affect the dependent variable's value. Consider a situation where the quantity sold of your firm's product depends on the product's price, p, consumer incomes, Y, and the amount of money spent on advertising, A, or

$$q = f\left(p, Y, A\right)$$

You may be primarily interested in how your advertising affects the quantity sold.

In order to determine this relationship, you want to determine the incremental or marginal effect that advertising has on quantity, q, while holding everything else — the other independent variables — constant.

Obtain this information by taking the partial derivative of the function with respect to advertising.

You obtain a *partial derivative* by applying the rules for finding a derivative, while treating all independent variables, except the one of interest, as constants. Thus, in the example, you hold constant both price and income. And the great thing about constants is their derivative equals zero!

Assume the following equation describes the relationship between the quantity sold of a good and its price, consumer incomes, and the amount spent on advertising

$$q = 1,000 - 10p + 0.01Y + 0.2A - 0.01A \times p - 0.0001A^2$$

where q is the number of units sold per month, p is the price per unit in dollars, Y is average consumer income in dollars, and A is advertising expenditures in dollars.

In order to determine the partial derivative of quantity with respect to advertising, you should take the following steps:

1. **First, remember that both p and Y are treated as constants.** Therefore, you treat them exactly as you would a number when taking the derivative.

2. **To take the partial derivative of q with respect to A, start with the first term "1,000" and its derivative equals zero in the partial derivative.**

3. **The second term "$-10p$" has a partial derivative equal to zero because you treat the p like a constant or number.**

4. **The next term "$+0.01Y$" also has a partial derivative equal to zero because you treat the Y like a constant.**

5. **The derivative of the term "$0.2A$" equals 0.2, because you treat the A like a variable in this partial derivative.** You're interested in determining how changes in A's value affect q.

6. **The derivative of the term "$-0.01A \times p$" equals $-0.01p$.** Remember, you treat p the same as any number, while A is the variable.

7. **Finally, derivative of the term "$-0.0001A^2$" equals $-0.0002A$.**

   Putting each of these steps together yields a partial derivative of q with respect to A of

   $$\frac{\partial q}{\partial A} = 0.2 - 0.01p - 0.0002A$$

Similarly, the partial derivative of quantity with respect to price, $\delta q/\delta p$, and the partial derivative of q with respect to Y, $\delta q/\delta Y$, can be determined by treating any variables other than those specified in the partial derivative as constants. Those partial derivatives would be

$$\frac{\partial q}{\partial p} = -10 - 0.01A$$

and

$$\frac{\partial q}{\partial Y} = 0.01$$

Joining Derivatives and Optimization: An Ideal Partnership

A function's derivative yields an equation for the function's slope. This is especially useful because if the original function is at either a maximum or a minimum, its slope is zero. Thus, determining a maximum or minimum simply requires setting the derivative equal to zero and solving.

The relationship between your firm's total profit in dollars, π, and the quantity of output produced, q, is described by the following equation,

$$\pi = TR - TC = \left(150q - 0.002q^2\right) - \left(600,000 + 30q + 0.001q^2\right) = -600,000 + 120q - 0.003q^2$$

To determine the quantity of output that will maximize your profits, take the following steps:

1. **Take the derivative of total profit, π, with respect to quantity, q.**

$$\frac{d\pi}{dq} = 120 - 0.006q$$

2. **In order to find the quantity that maximizes profit, set the derivative or slope equal to zero.**

$$\frac{d\pi}{dq} = 120 - 0.006q = 0$$

3. **Solve the equation for q.**

$$120 = 0.006q \quad \text{or} \quad \frac{120}{0.006} = q \quad \text{or} \quad q = 20,000$$

4. **Substitute q equals 20,000 into the original equation to determine what the maximum profit equals.**

$$\pi = -600,000 + 120q - 0.003q^2 = -600,000 + 120(20,000) - 0.003(20,000)^2 = 600,000$$

Thus, profit equals $600,000.

I graph this function in Figure 3-2. The graph also indicates that profit is maximized at a quantity of 20,000 units.

Profit

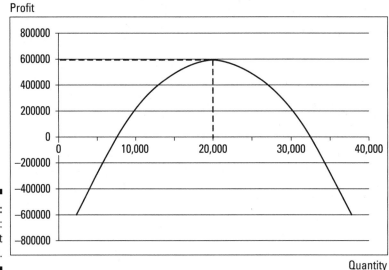

Figure 3-2:
Optimization:
Profit
maximization.

Quantity

Putting It All Together: Optimization, Constraints, and the Lagrangian Function

Business situations are further complicated by constraints — perhaps the business has signed a contract to produce 1,000 units of the good daily, or the business has certain inputs, such as the factory size, that can't be changed. Constraints limit the firm's options. In these situations, your goal is to optimize a function subject to the limitations or constraints. For example, your firm wants to minimize the cost of producing the 1,000 units of output daily as specified by a contract it has with a customer.

The *Lagrangian function* is a technique that combines the function being optimized with functions describing the constraint or constraints into a single equation. Solving the Lagrangian function allows you to optimize the variable you choose, subject to the constraints you can't change.

Identifying your objective (function)

The *objective function* is the function that you're optimizing. The dependent variable in the objective function represents your goal — the variable you want to optimize. Examples of objective functions include the profit function to maximize profit, the cost function to minimize costs, and the utility function for consumers to maximize satisfaction (utility).

Constraining functions: What you can't do

A *constraint function* represents a limitation on your behavior. The dependent variable in the constraint represents the limitation. Examples of constraint functions include the number of units you must produce in order to satisfy a contract, the production function for a given technology, and the budget available to a consumer.

Constructing the Lagrangian function

The technique for constructing a Lagrangian function is to combine the objective function and all constraints in a manner that satisfies two conditions. First, optimizing the Lagrangian function must result in the objective function's optimization. Second, all constraints must be satisfied. In order to satisfy these conditions, use the following steps to specify the Lagrangian function.

Assume u is the variable being optimized and that it's a function of the variables x and z. Therefore,

$$u = f(x, z)$$

In addition, there are two constraints, c_1 and c_2, that are also functions of x and z;

$$c_1 = g(x, z)$$

$$c_2 = h(x, z)$$

The following steps establish the Lagrangian function:

1. **Respecify the constraints so that they equal zero.**

   $c_1 - g(x, z) = 0$ and $c_2 - h(x, z) = 0$

2. **Multiply the constraints by the factors lambda one and lambda two, λ_1 and λ_2, respectively (more on these in a moment).**

   $\lambda_1[c_1 - g(x, z)]$ and $\lambda_2[c_2 - h(x, z)]$

3. **Add the constraints with the lambda term to the objective function in order to form the Lagrangian function £.**

   $£ = f(x, z) + \lambda_1[c_1 - g(x, z)] + \lambda_2[c_2 - h(x, z)]$

In this specification of the Lagrangian function, the variables are represented by x, z, λ_1, and λ_2. Taking the partial derivatives of the Lagrangian with respect to λ_1 and λ_2 and setting them equal to zero ensure that your constraints are satisfied, while taking the partial derivatives of the Lagrangian with respect to x and z and setting them equal to zero optimize your objective function.

Discovering the secret code: The Lagrangian Multiplier

One of the neat things about managerial economics is that it has a lot of useful shortcuts — if you know the secret. One of those shortcuts is the λ used in the Lagrangian function. In the Lagrangian function, the constraints are multiplied by the variable λ, which is called the *Lagrangian multiplier*. This variable is important because λ measures the change that occurs in the variable being optimized given a one-unit change in the constraint. So, if you're trying to minimize the cost of producing a given quantity of output, λ tells you how much total cost changes if you decide to produce one more unit of output. This shortcut enables you to quickly assess the relationships between constraints and the variable being optimized.

Suppose that your firm has a contract that requires it to produce 1,000 units of a good daily. The firm uses both labor and capital to produce the good. The quantity of labor employed, L, is measured in hours, and the wage is $10 per hour. The quantity of capital employed, K, is measured in machine-hours, and the price per machine hour is $40. Given this information, your firm's total cost, TC, equals

$$TC = 10L + 40K$$

The firm's production function describes the relationship between the amounts of labor and capital used and the quantity of the good produced

$$q = f(L, K) = 20L^{0.5}K^{0.5}$$

By contract, q must equal 1,000. You must determine the amount of labor and capital to use in order to minimize the cost of producing the 1,000 units of the good. And remember, at this point, you can use calculus to dazzle everyone!

The steps you take in order to dazzle everyone are the following:

1. **Create a Lagrangian function.** Recognize that the variable you're trying to optimize is total cost — specifically, you're trying to minimize total cost. So, your objective function is $10L + 40K$. Second, your constraint is that 1,000 units of the good have to be produced from the production function. So your constraint is

   $1,000 - 20L^{0.5}K^{0.5} = 0.$

Your Lagrangian function is

$$\mathcal{L} = 10L + 40K + \lambda \left(1000 - 20L^{0.5}K^{0.5} \right)$$

2. **Take the partial derivative of the Lagrangian with respect to labor and capital — L and K — and set them equal to zero.** These equations ensure that the objective function is being optimized — in this case, total cost is minimized.

$$\frac{\partial \mathcal{L}}{\partial L} = 10 - 0.5 \times 20L^{0.5-1}K^{0.5}\lambda = 10 - \frac{10K^{0.5}\lambda}{L^{0.5}} = 0$$

$$\frac{\partial \mathcal{L}}{\partial K} = 40 - 0.5 \times 20L^{0.5}K^{0.5-1}\lambda = 40 - \frac{10L^{0.5}\lambda}{K^{0.5}} = 0$$

3. **Take the partial derivative of the Lagrangian function with respect to λ and set it equal to zero.** This partial derivative ensures that the constraint — producing 1,000 units of the good daily — is satisfied.

$$\frac{\partial \mathcal{L}}{\partial \lambda} = 1,000 - 20L^{0.5}K^{0.5} = 0$$

4. **Solve the three partial derivatives simultaneously for the variables L, K, and λ to minimize the total cost of producing 1,000 units of the good.**

Rewriting the partial derivative of $\mathcal{L}$ with respect to L enables you to solve for λ.

$$10 - \frac{10K^{0.5}\lambda}{L^{0.5}} = 0 \quad \text{so} \quad 10 = \frac{10K^{0.5}\lambda}{L^{0.5}} \quad \text{or} \quad \frac{10L^{0.5}}{10K^{0.5}} = \frac{L^{0.5}}{K^{0.5}} = \lambda$$

Substituting the previous equation for λ in the partial derivative of $\mathcal{L}$ with respect to K yields

$$40 - \frac{10L^{0.5}\lambda}{K^{0.5}} = 40 - \frac{10L^{0.5}}{K^{0.5}}\lambda = 40 - \frac{10L^{0.5}}{K^{0.5}}\frac{L^{0.5}}{K^{0.5}} = 40 - \frac{10L}{K} = 0 \quad \text{or} \quad 40K = 10L$$

$$L = 4K$$

5. **Substitute $4K$ for L in the constraint (the partial derivative of L with respect to λ) to yield**

$$1,000 - 20L^{0.5}K^{0.5} = 1,000 - 20(4K)^{0.5}K^{0.5}$$
$$= 1,000 - 20 \times 2K^{0.5} \times K^{0.5} = 1,000 - 40K = 0 \qquad \text{or} \quad 40K = 1,000$$

Thus, your firm should use 25 machine hours of capital daily.

Because you earlier determined $L = 4K$

$$L = 4K = 4(25) = 100$$

Finally, you can solve for λ

$$\lambda = \frac{L^{0.5}}{K^{0.5}} = \frac{(100)^{0.5}}{(25)^{0.5}} = \frac{10}{5} = 2$$

Therefore, the combination 100 hours of labor and 25 machine-hours of capital minimize the total cost of producing 1,000 units of the good daily. In addition, λ equals 2. Remember that lambda indicates the change that occurs in the objective function given a one unit change in the constraint. Thus, in the example, if your firm wants to produce one more unit of the good, your total cost increases by $2.

Part II

Considering What Side You're On in the Decision-Making Process

The 5th Wave   By Rich Tennant

"This date has just exceeded its cost-benefit ratio."

In this part . . .

Consumers want low prices, and business owners want high prices. These fundamental truths are embodied in demand and supply. In this part, I break down the concepts of demand and supply. I start by examining demand — the decision-making process that you and I use when purchasing goods — and I explain how business owners can influence that process. I then turn to production and supply. Decision-making principles to reduce production costs through the right input combination and innovation are developed. Understanding these production decisions leads to an examination of the relationship between production costs and the quantity of output produced.

Chapter 4

Using the Elasticity Shortcut

*T*his chapter brings you up to speed on the concept of elasticity and how it works. It explains how elasticity determines a business's revenue side and tells you what price to charge, how much advertising to do, and how changes in other prices or income affect your sales. If you remember only one concept in managerial economics, elasticity is it. The fact that a single concept provides all this information makes it magical. Calculating an elasticity value is like pulling a rabbit out of a hat; one number tells nearly everything to the amazement of those watching (your coworkers). And when you combine elasticity and revenue information with production costs, you can determine how the firm will maximize its profit.

Using Elasticity Is The Key to Flexibility

The law of demand states that increasing a good's price reduces the good's *quantity demanded* (the amount of the good that customers purchase given its price). This relationship is important, but somewhat obvious. Similarly, demand reacts to changes in incomes, the price of related goods, and advertising efforts. *Elasticity* measures the responsiveness of one economic variable to another and is the concept you use to determine these relationships. For example, when the price of movie tickets goes up, you and other customers will buy fewer tickets. So, for the theater manager, the critical question is how much will the number of tickets sold decrease — will it be a little or a lot? Similarly, the theater manager needs to know how movie ticket demand reacts to changes in incomes, the price of popcorn at the concession stand, and advertising for the blockbuster movie.

Think of elasticity as a measure of flexibility. Elasticity tells you how flexible customers are to change. Generally, if customers are very flexible to a given change, they're considered *elastic*. If customers aren't very flexible to a change, they're *inelastic*.

As a general rule, you hope customers are inelastic. That way, when you increase price, they will still buy a lot of your product. But remember, general rules are just that — general. And there is a reason for the old saying, "The exception proves the rule."

Customers respond to many things, so focus on the things that are most important to them. The most important elasticity concepts describe how customers respond to changes in

- ✔ The good's price
- ✔ Income
- ✔ The prices of other goods
- ✔ Advertising

Managers typically control two of these factors: the good's price and advertising. Sometimes managers at least partially control a third factor, the prices of other goods. For example, a movie theater manager controls the ticket's price and the prices of concessions (although the manager doesn't control the prices other theaters charge). Finally, managers can't control the general level of customers' income, but demand is often affected by whether the general income level is increasing, a period of prosperity, or decreasing, a recession. A recession decreases movie ticket sales.

Knowing the Price Elasticity of Demand: The Fundamental Trade-Off

The *price elasticity of demand* measures the most important elasticity relationship — how much quantity demanded changes given a price change. In other words, the price elasticity of demand allows you to project how a price change impacts revenue. For example, if the price of movie tickets increases from $8 to $10, does quantity demanded decrease from 5,000 tickets per week to 4,500 or from 5,000 to 3,000? It really matters. In the first case, the movie theater's revenue increases from $40,000 ($8 × 5,000) to $45,000 ($10 × 4,500). In the second case, the theater's revenue decreases from $40,000 to $30,000 ($10 × 3,000).

Before changing price, you need to know if the result will be similar to the first or second situation, and the price elasticity of demand tells you which it will be.

Determining the price elasticity of demand: Formulas are your friend

Mastering managerial economics involves calculating values, with the ultimate goal of determining how to maximize profit. The usefulness of the price elasticity of demand depends upon calculating a specific value that measures how responsive quantity demanded is to a price change.

The formula used to calculate the price elasticity of demand is

$$\eta = \frac{(Q_1 - Q_0) \div (Q_1 + Q_0)}{(P_1 - P_0) \div (P_1 + P_0)}$$

The symbol η represents the price elasticity of demand. The symbol Q_0 represents the initial quantity demanded that exists when the price equals P_0. The symbol Q_1 represents the new quantity demanded that exists when the price changes to P_1.

In this formula, the price elasticity of demand will always be a negative number because of the inverse relationship between price and quantity demanded. As price went up, quantity demanded went down, or vice versa. When price goes down, quantity demanded goes up. Price and quantity demanded always move in opposite directions, hence the price elasticity of demand is always negative.

Suppose that you own a company that supplies vending machines. Currently, your vending machines sell soft drinks at $1.50 per bottle. At that price, customers purchase 2,000 bottles per week. In order to increase sales, you decide to decrease the price to $1, and sales increase to 4,000 bottles.

To calculate the price elasticity of demand with this information, here's what you do:

1. **Plug in the values for each symbol.**

   Because $1.50 and 2,000 are the initial price and quantity, put $1.50 into P_0 and 2,000 into Q_0. And because $1.00 and 4,000 are the new price and quantity, put $1.00 into P_1 and 4,000 into Q_1.

2. **Work out the expression on the top of the formula.**

   Start by dividing the expression on top of the equation. $(Q_1 - Q_0)$ equals 2,000, and $(Q_1 + Q_0)$ equals 6,000. Dividing 2,000 by 6,000 equals ⅓.

3. **Work out the expression in the bottom of the equation.**

   $(P_1 - P_0)$ equals –$0.50, and $(P_1 + P_0)$ equals $2.50. Dividing –$0.50 by $2.50 equals –⅕.

4. **Do the final division of the remaining values on the top and bottom of the equation.**

   Divide the top result, ⅓, by the bottom result, –⅕, to get the price elasticity of demand of –⅗ (or –1.67).

So the price elasticity of demand for soft drinks equals

$$\eta = \frac{(4,000 - 2,000) \div (4,000 + 2,000)}{(1.00 - 1.50) \div (1.00 + 1.50)} = -1.67$$

The price elasticity of demand is simply a number; it is not a monetary value. What the number tells you is a 1 percent decrease in price causes a 1.67 percent increase in quantity demanded. In other words, quantity demanded's percentage increase is greater than the percentage decrease in price. Thus, when you decrease the price of soft drinks, you will sell a lot more soft drinks, and your revenue will go up (from $3,000 to $4,000).

Whenever the absolute value of demand is greater than one, price decreases will increase revenue.

Recognizing degrees of flexibility with inelastic or elastic

Economists use the words inelastic and elastic to describe how responsive quantity demanded is to a price change. When demand is *inelastic*, quantity demanded changes very little when price changes. When the price elasticity of demand is between 0 and –1, demand is inelastic. In an extreme case, if demand is *perfectly inelastic* (the price elasticity of demand equals 0), quantity demanded doesn't change at all when price changes. This situation results in a vertical demand curve. Life-saving medicines may have a perfectly inelastic demand over large price ranges. In other words, even if the price of the medicine doubled, you'd still buy the same amount in order to save your life.

If quantity demanded changes a lot when price changes, demand is considered *elastic*, and the price elasticity of demand will be a negative number larger than -1. In an extreme situation, demand is *perfectly elastic* when the slightest change in price causes an incredibly large change in quantity demanded. Farmers often face a perfectly elastic demand. A farmer who tries to sell wheat at a price one cent higher than the market price won't sell any wheat. Buyers will go to any one of a million other wheat farmers and buy the wheat for a penny less. (And you know what Ben Franklin said: "A penny saved is a penny earned.") When that farmer lowers price by one cent to the market price, the farmer can sell all the wheat that is grown; a one cent decrease in price leads to an incredibly large change in quantity demanded.

Pitfalls of formula simplification

Sometimes, economists try to simplify the price elasticity of demand formula to

$$\eta = \frac{\%\Delta Q}{\%\Delta P}$$

This means the price elasticity of demand equals the percentage change in quantity demanded divided by the percentage change in price. But be careful; in this formula, where you start really matters. In the soft drink example, the initial price is $1.50, and the quantity demanded is 2,000. When the good's price decreases to $1, the quantity demanded increases to 4,000. In this case, a 33 percent decrease in price (from $1.50 to $1) caused a 100 percent increase in quantity (from 2,000 to 4,000). The price elasticity of demand equals –3.

However, if instead you start at the price of $1 and quantity demanded of 4,000, you get a different answer. If price increases 50 percent (from $1 to $1.50) and quantity demanded decreases 50 percent (from 4,000 to 2,000), the price elasticity of demand equals –1.

But don't make the mistake of thinking that the price elasticity of demand is different. These two points are the same on the demand curve; regardless of which direction price changes, the price elasticity of demand should be the same. And with the formula introduced in the text, the price elasticity of demand is the same.

As a manager, you hope the demand for your good is inelastic. You know that if you raise price, customers will buy less. But you hope they only buy a little less.

Influencing the price elasticity of demand

Four primary factors influence customers' reactions to price changes:

✔ **Substitutability:** The first factor affecting customer response to price increases is the number and closeness of substitute goods — what economists call *substitutability*. If you know of a small number of not-so-good substitutes available for your good, then the demand for your good is inelastic. Customers will find it difficult to switch to another good if you increase price. However, if a large number of close substitutes exist with a high degree of substitutability, when you increase price, your customers find it very easy to switch. As a result, the quantity demanded for your good goes down a lot with an elastic demand.

✔ **Luxury or necessity:** Whether your good is a luxury or necessity also influences how customers respond to price changes. If your good is a necessity, when you increase price, customers still have to have the good; their quantity demanded can't be very responsive to the price change, and demand is inelastic. If the good is a luxury, customers can do without, and quantity demanded will be very responsive to the price change. Demand for luxuries is elastic. (For more on this topic, see the section "Identifying necessities and luxuries," later in this chapter.)

✔ **Proportion of income spent:** Customers also respond to how much income they spend on a good. When you buy a new car, you tend to shop around. A 10 percent difference in price means a lot. For a $30,000 car, it means $3,000. In this case, your demand is elastic; you're very responsive to price differences. But a 10 percent difference in the price of a pizza might mean spending $11 rather than $10. This percentage difference is the same as for a car, but you're not likely to drive all over town trying to save a dollar. In this case, because pizza takes less of your income, you're not as responsive to the 10 percent price difference as with the car.

✔ **Time:** The longer the period of time since the price change, the easier it is to adjust your spending. When the price of gasoline increases, you can't do very much right away. The day after the price increases, you still have to get to work from where you live. Your demand is inelastic. But over a longer period of time, you may be able to join a car pool or move closer to work or find a new job. Thus, over a longer period of time, adjusting becomes easier, and your demand becomes more elastic.

These four factors determine whether customers respond to higher prices by purchasing a lot less, in other words, demand is elastic, or a little less, demand is inelastic.

Think about a local store trying to decide whether or not to raise the prices on the high-definition televisions it sells. How will customers respond? If a large number of other stores exist in the area, a high degree of substitutability occurs. Most customers are likely to think buying a new television is a luxury. Televisions are a big-ticket item; they tend to take a large proportion of your income. Finally, televisions are used over a very long period of time. You can wait for a sale before buying one. Each of these factors indicates that the demand for high-definition televisions will be elastic. Customers will buy a lot fewer televisions at the higher price.

Identifying the bottom line, almost: The price elasticity of demand and revenue

Total revenue equals the good's price multiplied by the quantity sold. Because the price elasticity of demand shows the relationship between price and quantity sold, the elasticity number captures all the information you need to anticipate changes in total revenue.

If demand is inelastic (the price elasticity of demand is between 0 and –1), the quantity sold does not change very much when price changes. As a result, a higher price causes a very small decrease in the quantity sold and total revenue increases. (The higher price you receive for the goods you sell more than offsets the slightly smaller number you sell.) On the other hand, charging a lower price does not cause much of an increase in quantity demanded; total revenue decreases.

As these situations illustrate, when demand is inelastic, price and total revenue change in the same direction; they both increase or decrease together.

For an elastic demand (the price elasticity of demand is bigger than –1), the opposite situation occurs; price and total revenue move in opposite directions. If the good's price increases, quantity demanded decreases a lot and total revenue decreases. (The higher price you receive isn't enough to offset the very large decrease in the amount of goods you sell.) If you decrease the good's price, a large increase occurs in quantity demanded, and total revenue increases.

Thus, when demand is elastic, price and total revenue change in opposite directions.

Say that your vending machine company initially charges a $1.50 per bottle and sells 2,000 bottles per week. Decreasing the price to $1 increases sales to 4,000 bottles. The price elasticity of demand equals –1.67; demand is elastic. The price decrease increases total revenue from $3,000 to $4,000 because the $0.50 decrease in price is more than offset by selling 2,000 more bottles. Thus, price and total revenue move in opposite directions given the elastic demand.

Another useful concept is *marginal revenue*, the change in total revenue that occurs when one additional unit of a good is sold. The formula describing the relationship between marginal revenue, MR, and the price elasticity of demand, η, is

$$MR = P\left(1 + \frac{1}{\eta}\right)$$

Use this formula with the point price elasticity of demand. (For information on how to calculate the point price elasticity of demand, see the section "Calculating Elasticity with Calculus (If You Must)," later in this chapter.)

If your good is currently selling at price P, and you know the point price elasticity of demand η, you can quickly determine how much your revenue changes if you lower price to sell one additional unit of the good.

Assume that your company charges a $1.25 per bottle of soft drink and the point price elasticity of demand is –⅗. To determine marginal revenue (the amount of revenue you add by selling one more bottle):

1. **Insert $1.25 for P and -⅗ for η.**

2. **Calculate the value in the parentheses.**

$$\left(1 + \frac{1}{-5/3}\right)$$

equals

$$\left(1-\frac{3}{5}\right)$$

or ⅖.

3. **Multiply \$1.25 by ⅖.**

The marginal revenue equals \$0.50.

So the marginal revenue received when an additional bottle is sold is

$$MR = \$1.25\left(1+\frac{1}{-5/3}\right) = \$0.50$$

Measuring the Income Elasticity of Demand

Elasticity measures consumer or customer flexibility — how responsive they are to changes in various factors. More precisely, elasticity measures the change in the quantity purchased given changes in other things. The most important of these relationships is the one between the good's price and the quantity demanded. But the beauty of elasticity is you can determine the relationship between demand or quantity purchased, and other factors in exactly the same way!

The *income elasticity of demand* measures the responsiveness of a good's demand to changes in income, just like the name suggests. So, one of the useful hints to note with elasticity is the term tells you what relationship you're examining. And although businesses can't control the general income level, it can have a strong effect on demand. For example, restaurants typically experience a decrease in demand during a recession. In recessions, incomes drop, and people eat out less. The restaurant owner can't change the income level or end the recession, but the owner must make adjustments based on how the recession affects the number of customers eating at the restaurant.

Determining the income elasticity of demand: Yet another formula friend

Calculating the income elasticity of demand is essentially the same as calculating the price elasticity of demand, except you're now determining how much the quantity purchase changes in response to a change in income.

The formula used to calculate the income elasticity of demand is

$$\eta_I = \frac{(Q_1 - Q_0) \div (Q_1 + Q_0)}{(I_1 - I_0) \div (I_1 + I_0)}$$

The symbol η_I represents the income elasticity of demand; η is the general symbol used for elasticity, and the subscript I represents income. In the formula, the symbol Q_0 represents the initial demand or quantity purchased that exists when income equals I_0. The symbol Q_1 represents the new demand that exists when income changes to I_1.

In this formula, the income elasticity of demand can be a positive or negative number, and it makes a real difference which it is. If the income elasticity of demand is negative, then the commodity is an inferior good. An *inferior good* is one whose demand decreases as incomes increase or demand increases as incomes decrease. (As an example, rice and potatoes are inferior goods.) In other words, an inverse relationship exists between demand and income, and the income elasticity of demand is negative. This relationship is unusual.

The opposite situation is a normal good — normal because you get the expected or normal relationship. For a *normal good,* as income increases, the good's demand increases. That's what you expect, and most goods are normal. As your income increases, your demand for movie tickets, restaurant meals, cars, and maybe even asparagus increases. And the opposite will happen if your income decreases. Therefore, normal goods have a direct relationship between income and demand, and the income elasticity of demand is positive.

Finally, the larger the number (either positive or negative) for the income elasticity of demand, the more responsive demand is to a change in income. A large number for the income elasticity of demand means a large change in demand occurs when income changes.

Say that you own a company that supplies vending machines. Currently, your vending machines sell soft drinks at $1.50 per bottle, and at that price, customers purchase 2,000 bottles per week. For your community, the weekly income is $600. Then a major employer in the community closes, and a number of workers lose their job. The average weekly income in the community falls to $400 and you note that your vending machine sales decrease to 500. You didn't change the price of soft drinks, but your sales decreased dramatically due to the change in income. The income elasticity of demand will tell you how responsive soft drink sales are to the change in income.

The method for calculating the income elasticity of demand is similar to the method used to calculate any elasticity. Here's what you do:

1. **Because $600 and 2,000 are the initial income and quantity, put $600 into I_0 and 2,000 into Q_0.**

Inferior is not Inferior

Economists use the term *inferior* to describe the relationship between income and demand, not quality. I love potatoes. When I was a student, my income was very low, and about twice a week, I had a baked potato with cheese as my dinner. Potatoes are cheap and pack a lot of nutrition — just the thing for a poor student. After I graduated and got a full-time job, my income increased. I could buy more expensive food like meat and fresh vegetables, especially asparagus. But as I bought more expensive food, my demand for potatoes decreased. Thus, as my income increased, my demand for potatoes decreased. My income elasticity of demand was negative for the very nutritious potato.

---

2. **Because $400 and 500 are the new income and quantity, put $400 into I_1 and 500 into Q_1.**

3. **Start by dividing the expression on top of the equation.**

   $(Q_1 - Q_0)$ equals −1,500, and $(Q_1 + Q_0)$ equals 2,500. Dividing −1,500 by 2,500 equals −⅗.

4. **Divide the expression in the bottom of the equation.**

   $(I_1 - I_0)$ equals −$200, and $(I_1 + I_0)$ equals $1,000. Dividing −$200 by $1,000 equals −⅕.

5. **Divide the top result, −⅗, by the bottom result, −⅕.**

   You get the income elasticity of demand 3.

So the income elasticity of demand for soft drinks equals

$$\eta_I = \frac{(500 - 2,000) \div (500 + 2,000)}{(400 - 600) \div (400 + 600)} = 3$$

The income elasticity value tells you a 1 percent decrease in income causes a 3 percent decrease in demand. Thus, because you sell fewer soft drinks when incomes decrease, soft drinks are a normal good.

Identifying necessities and luxuries

Inferior goods have an inverse relationship between income and demand, and normal goods have a direct relationship between income and demand (see preceding section). But you can subdivide normal goods into two groups:

  ✔ **Necessities** are goods you have to have. So, even if your income decreases, you will still purchase nearly the same amount, perhaps just a few less. As a result, the income elasticity of demand for necessities will be between 0 and 1.

 ✔ **Luxuries** are things you like, but you can do without. Thus, if your income decreases, you'll purchase a lot fewer luxuries. For example, you probably won't eat out so often. In the case of luxuries, the income elasticity of demand is greater than 1. The larger the value is, the greater the luxury.

Finally, a negative income elasticity of demand means the commodity is an inferior good.

Looking at the Cross-Price Elasticity of Demand

The *cross-price elasticity of demand* measures the responsiveness of a good's demand — say, the infamous brand *x* — to changes in the price of a second good, brand *y*. This relationship is crucial because the amount of your good customers purchase is influenced by the prices rival firms charge for similar or substitute goods. Also, the price you charge for one good — hamburgers, for example — influences the amount you sell of a second good, french fries.

Determining the cross-price elasticity of demand: Never enough friends or formulas

Calculating the cross-price elasticity of demand requires determining how good *x*'s demand changes in response to a different price for good *y*.

The cross-price elasticity of demand's formula is

$$\eta_{x,y} = \frac{(Q_{x1} - Q_{x0}) \div (Q_{x1} + Q_{x0})}{(P_{y1} - P_{y0}) \div (P_{y1} + P_{y0})}$$

Note how similar this formula is to other elasticity formulas. In this case, the symbol $\eta_{x,y}$ represents cross-price elasticity of demand. The *x* represents the good whose quantity is changing, and the *y* represents the good whose price is changing. So, in the formula, the symbol Q_{x0} represents the initial demand or quantity purchased for good *x* when the price of good *y* is P_{y0}. The symbol Q_{x1} represents good *x*'s new demand when good *y*'s price changes to P_{y1}.

As with all elasticity values, the larger the number (either positive or negative), the more flexible or responsive quantity is. For the cross-price elasticity of demand, a larger number indicates good x's demand will change a lot when good y's price changes.

Your vending machine company currently sells soft drinks at $1.50 per bottle, and at that price, customers purchase 2,000 bottles per week. At the same time, a local convenience store sells the same soft drinks for $1.25 per bottle. The convenience store decides to run a special and lowers the price of soft drinks to $1.00 per bottle. As a result, your sales decrease to 1,800 bottles per week. You didn't change the vending machine price for soft drinks, but your sales decreased due to the convenience store's sale. The cross-price elasticity of demand will tell you how responsive your vending machine soft drink sales are to the change in price at the convenience store.

Here's what you do to determine how much the convenience store's sale affects your demand:

1. **Because $1.25 is the initial price of soft drinks at the convenience store (good *y*), and 2,000 is quantity of soft drinks sold in vending machines (good *x*), put $1.25 into P_{y0} and 2,000 into Q_{x0}.**

2. **Because $1.00 and 1,800 are the new price for good *y* (convenience stores) and quantity for good *x* (vending machines), put $1.00 into P_{y1} and 1,800 into Q_{x1}.**

3. **Divide the expression on top of the equation.**

   $(Q_{x1} - Q_{x0})$ equals –200, and $(Q_1 + Q_0)$ equals 3,800. Dividing –200 by 3,800 equals $-\frac{1}{19}$.

4. **Divide the expression in the bottom of the equation.**

   $(P_{y1} - P_{y0})$ equals –$0.25, and $(P_{y1} + P_{y0})$ equals $2.25. Dividing –$0.25 by $2.25 equals $-\frac{1}{9}$.

5. **Divide the top result, $-\frac{1}{19}$, by the bottom result, $-\frac{1}{9}$.**

   You get the cross-price elasticity of demand $\frac{9}{19}$ or 0.474.

So the cross-price elasticity of demand for soft drinks equals

$$\eta_{x,y} = \frac{(1,800 - 2,000) \div (1,800 + 2,000)}{(1.00 - 1.25) \div (1.00 + 1.25)} = 0.474$$

The cross-price elasticity of demand tells you a 1 percent decrease in the price of good y, the convenience store soft drink, causes a 0.474 percent decrease in demand for soft drinks from vending machines. Vending machine sales are not affected very much by changes in convenience store prices.

Identifying substitutes and complements

Substitutes are goods that are used interchangeably — one is used in the place of another. Think of potato chips and pretzels. Thus, an increase in the price of one good, good *y,* causes an increase in the quantity consumed of the second good, good *x*. This change occurs because customers will tend to switch to the lower priced good. So, an increase in the price of potato chips, good y, means customers will switch and purchase more of good x, pretzels. Thus, a direct relationship exists between the price of good *y* and the demand for good *x,* and they are substitutes.

Complements are goods that are used together, such as coffee and cream. For complements, an inverse relationship exists between good *y*'s price and good *x*'s demand; if good *y*'s price increases, the demand for good *x* decreases and vice versa. So, if the price of coffee increases, good *y,* you drink less coffee, and your demand for cream, good *x,* decreases.

Finally, the larger the value, either positive or negative, for the cross-price elasticity of demand, the stronger the relationship between the two goods.

Finishing Up with the Advertising Elasticity of Demand

The *advertising elasticity of demand* measures the responsiveness of a good's demand to changes in spending on advertising. The advertising elasticity of demand measures the percentage change in demand that occurs given a 1 percent change in advertising expenditure.

The advertising elasticity of demand is calculated using the following formula:

$$\eta_A = \frac{(Q_1 - Q_0) \div (Q_1 + Q_0)}{(A_1 - A_0) \div (A_1 + A_0)}$$

The symbol η_A represents the advertising elasticity of demand. In the formula, the symbol Q_0 represents the initial demand or quantity purchased that exists when spending on advertising equals A_0. The symbol Q_1 represents the new demand that exists when advertising expenditures change to A_1.

The advertising elasticity of demand should be positive. (A negative value would indicate the more you spend on advertising, the lower your sales. That is a really bad ad! You should probably fire whomever is in charge of advertising.)

As with all elasticity values, the larger the number, the more responsive the good's demand is to a change in advertising.

Your vending machine company starts a new ad campaign, "Vend for Yourself." (Okay, I'll stick to economics rather than advertising.) Currently, your company sells soft drinks at $1.50 per bottle, and at that price, customers purchase 2,000 bottles per week. Initially, you spend $400 per week on advertising. After a month, you're spending $500 per week on advertising and, without changing the price of soft drinks, sales have increased to 3,000 bottles per week. The advertising elasticity of demand tells you how responsive your vending machine soft drink sales are to the change in advertising expenditures.

To determine the advertising elasticity of demand, follow the customary steps:

1. **Because $400 and 2,000 are the initial advertising expenditures and quantity sold, put $400 into A_0 and 2,000 into Q_0.**

2. **Because $500 and 3,000 are the new spending on advertising and sales, put $500 into A_1 and 3,000 into Q_1.**

3. **Divide the expression on top of the equation.**

   $(Q_1 - Q_0)$ equals 1,000 and $(Q_1 + Q_0)$ equals 5,000. Dividing 1,000 by 5,000 equals ⅕.

4. **Divide the expression in the bottom of the equation.**

   $(A_1 - A_0)$ equals $100, and $(A_1 + A_0)$ equals $900. Dividing $100 by $900 equals ⅑.

5. **Divide the top result, ⅕, by the bottom result, ⅑.**

   You get the advertising elasticity of demand equal to 9/5 or 1.8. Thus, the advertising elasticity of demand for soft drinks equals

   $$\eta_A = \frac{(3,000-2,000) \div (3,000+2,000)}{(500-400) \div (500+400)} = 1.8$$

You can conclude that a 1 percent increase in advertising expenditures increases demand 1.8 percent.

Calculating Elasticity with Calculus (If You Must)

The formulas throughout this chapter determine average elasticities for a range of values. For example, in the section "Determining the price elasticity of demand: Formulas are your friend," you calculate the price elasticity of demand for the range of values between P_0 and P_1. Similarly, you calculate the income elasticity of demand for the income range between I_0 and I_1 in the section "Determining the income elasticity of demand: Yet another formula friend." However, sometimes you need a more precise elasticity value. In these cases, you need to determine what is called the point elasticity, and calculus comes to your rescue.

The most important point elasticity is the point price elasticity of demand. This value is used to calculate marginal revenue, one of the two critical components in profit maximization. (The other critical component is marginal cost, which I introduce in Chapter 8.) As you can see in Chapter 9, profits are always maximized when marginal revenue equals marginal cost.

The formula to determine the point price elasticity of demand is

$$\eta = \frac{\partial Q}{\partial P} \times \frac{P_0}{Q_0}$$

In this formula, $\partial Q/\partial P$ is the partial derivative of the quantity demanded taken with respect to the good's price, P_0 is a specific price for the good, and Q_0 is the quantity demanded associated with the price P_0.

The following equation represents soft drink demand for your company's vending machines:

In the equation, Q represents the number of soft drinks sold weekly, P is the price per bottle from the vending machine in dollars, I is weekly income in dollars, P_C is the price at a convenience in dollars, and A is weekly advertising expenditures in dollars. Assume initially that P is $1.50, I is $600, P_C is $1.25, and A is $400. Substituting those values into the demand equation indicates that 2,000 bottles will be sold weekly.

$$Q = -1,500 - 4,000(1.5) + 7.5(600) + 800(1.25) + 10(400) = 2,000$$

To determine the point price elasticity of demand given P_0 is $1.50 and Q_0 is 2,000, you need to take the following steps:

1. **Take the partial derivative of Q with respect to P, $\partial Q/\partial P$.**

   For your demand equation, this equals –4,000.

2. **Determine P_0 divided by Q_0.**

   Because P is $1.50, and Q is 2,000, P_0/Q_0 equals 0.00075.

3. **Multiply the partial derivative, –4,000, by P_0/Q_0, 0.00075.**

   The point price elasticity of demand equals –3.

$$\eta = -4,000 \times \frac{1.50}{2,000} = -3$$

Therefore, at this point on the demand curve, a 1 percent change in price causes a 3 percent change in quantity demanded in the opposite direction (because of the negative sign).

In order to maximize profits, you need to know how much each additional unit you sell adds to your revenue, or in other words, you need to know marginal revenue. If you know the point price elasticity of demand, η, the following formula can enable you to quickly determine marginal revenue, MR, for any given price

$$MR = P\left(1 + \frac{1}{\eta}\right)$$

Assume your company charges a $1.50 per bottle of soft drink, and the point price elasticity of demand is –3. To determine how much revenue you add by selling an additional bottle:

1. **Determine (1 + 1/η).**

   Substituting –3 for η gives (1 + 1/[–3]) or (1 – ⅓) or ⅔.

2. **Multiply the price, $1.50, by ⅔.**

   The marginal revenue equals $1.00.

So the marginal revenue received when an additional bottle is sold is

$$MR = \$1.50\left(1 + \frac{1}{-3}\right) = \$1.00$$

If your cost of providing the extra bottle is less than $1.00, you will increase your profits by selling it.

Similarly, you can calculate point elasticities for the income elasticity of demand, cross-price elasticity of demand, and advertising elasticity of demand using the following formulas:

✔ **The point income elasticity of demand:**

$$\eta_I = \frac{\partial Q}{\partial I} \times \frac{I}{Q}$$

In this formula, $\partial Q/\partial I$ is the partial derivative of the quantity taken with respect to income, I is the specific income level, and Q is the quantity purchased at the income level I.

✔ **The point cross-price elasticity of demand:**

$$\eta_{x,y} = \frac{\partial Q_x}{\partial P_y} \times \frac{P_y}{Q_x}$$

In this formula, $\partial Q_x/\partial P_y$ is the partial derivative of good x's quantity taken with respect to good y's price, P_y is a specific price for good y, and Q_x is the quantity of good x purchased given the price P_y.

✔ **The point advertising elasticity of demand:**

$$\eta_{x,y} = \frac{\partial Q_x}{\partial P_y} \times \frac{P_y}{Q_x}$$

In this formula, $\partial Q/\partial A$ is the partial derivative of the quantity demanded taken with respect to advertising expenditures, A is the specific amount spent on advertising, and Q is the quantity purchased.

Chapter 5

Consumer Behavior: A Market for Anything?

In This Chapter

▶ Understanding what makes your customers happy

▶ Taking advantage of indifference

▶ Developing promotions to influence consumer choice

S uccessful businesses satisfy consumer desires. Knowing how consumers decide which desires to satisfy and which to leave unsatisfied is an important component in your managerial decision-making. Consumer theory describes how customers determine the purchases they make. By understanding consumer theory, you can influence customer behavior through pricing strategies such as coupons and gift cards.

Satisfying the Consumer

A famous line from the movie *Field of Dreams* is "If you build it, he will come." Well, that may have worked in the movie, but it doesn't work for businesses — "produce it and they will buy" isn't a certainty. Consumers compare the amount of satisfaction they receive from a good to its price to determine whether or not it's worth buying. Remember, ultimately the customer decides whether or not your product is a good deal.

Comparing apples and oranges: Utility as a common denominator

You've probably heard the expression "You can't compare apples and oranges." It's an absurd expression because of course you can compare apples and oranges, and you probably have. If you ever thought, "Oranges are really expensive this week; maybe I should buy apples instead," you just compared them. And the produce section manager also compares them all the time. At the very least, the manager has to decide how much space to allocate to displaying oranges and apples. And I suspect that the manager allocates more space to the one that makes the store more money.

It's crucial for you to recognize that consumers are always comparing different goods. Consumers must decide how much they're going to buy of each good — how many apples, how many oranges, how many tickets to the baseball game, how many new bicycles . . . the list is never ending.

How much you like apples, oranges, or any other good is based upon the amount of pleasure or satisfaction you get from the good. But instead of using terms like *pleasure* or *satisfaction,* economists use the term *utility.*

Utility is the amount of satisfaction an individual receives from consuming a good.

Economists like to measure everything — even satisfaction. They measure satisfaction using the idea of utils. Thus, an apple might give me 12 utils of satisfaction while an orange gives me 24 utils of satisfaction. Comparing the utils shows that I like the orange twice as much as the apple.

You don't have to measure everything as precisely as this example indicates. However, using utils makes consumer theory easier to understand.

Adding happiness — at a price

Typically, as you consume a greater quantity of a good, you get more satisfaction. You get satisfaction from the first scoop of ice cream you eat, and you get additional satisfaction from eating a second scoop of ice cream.

Economists call the additional satisfaction or change in satisfaction from an additional unit of the good *marginal utility.*

Economists also compare your additional satisfaction to the good's price.

Marginal utility per dollar spent simply equals the good's marginal utility divided by its price, or

$$MU \text{ per dollar} = \frac{MU}{P}$$

This equation indicates the amount of additional satisfaction you receive when you consume an additional dollar's worth of the good.

Getting less from more: The law of diminishing marginal utility

So, you really like ice cream. A one-scoop ice cream cone is good, and a two-scoop ice cream cone is better. Because you get additional satisfaction or utility from the second scoop of ice cream, your marginal utility is positive and your total utility increases. If you add a third scoop of ice cream, your total utility may continue to increase, but it's not likely to increase as much as with the second additional scoop. The third scoop of ice cream tastes good, but you also start to get full, and it starts to melt and make a mess. As a result, your additional satisfaction — your marginal utility — for the third scoop of ice cream is less than for the second scoop. Your marginal utility has begun to decrease. But although your marginal utility — additional satisfaction — has decreased, your total utility is still increasing.

Using utils in the ice cream example can illustrate this idea. Eating a one-scoop ice cream gives you 60 utils of satisfaction. Because this is the first scoop, the total utility and marginal utility are both 60. But one scoop is not quite enough; it leaves you wanting more. Adding a second scoop to your ice cream cone increases your total utility from 60 to 150. Therefore, the marginal utility or additional satisfaction of the second scoop is 90 utils — 150 – 60. To add a third scoop of ice cream increases your total utility to 200 utils. The third scoop tastes good, but it causes a mess. The change in total utility for the third scoop or the marginal utility of the third scoop is 50 — 200 – 150. Thus, the marginal utility of the third scoop, 50, is less than the marginal utility of the second scoop, 90, but the total utlity of the third scoop has increased from 150 to 200.

What happens in the ice cream situation happens with all goods. The first few units you consume tend to give you a lot of satisfaction, but eventually you reach a point where an additional unit gives less additional satisfaction.

This is called diminishing marginal utility and because it always happens, economists call this the *law of diminishing marginal utility*. The law states that as the quantity consumed of a good increases, eventually a point is reached where the marginal utility of an additional unit of the good decreases.

Suppose you've been working hard all day and you're really hungry. So, you decide to go out to eat rather than stay home and fix dinner. You go to a pizza restaurant with an all-you-can-eat buffet. What a great deal, especially given you're so hungry.

The first slice of pizza tastes great and you get 20 utils of satisfaction. The second slice tastes even better and you get 30 additional utils of satisfaction.

Your total utility is now 50 utils (20 + 30). The third slice of pizza also tastes good, but not quite as good as the second — your additional satisfaction is only 25 utils. At this point, diminishing marginal utility has set in, because 25 is less than 30. However, note that your total utility is still increasing. It is now 75 utils (20 + 30 + 25).

Diminishing marginal utility continues and by the time you reach the eighth slice of pizza, you're stuffed. The pizza still tastes good, but your stomach is starting to hurt from all the pizza. At this point, marginal utility becomes negative, and your total utility starts to decrease.

Table 5-1 illustrates this situation.

Table 5-1	Total and Marginal Utility	
Number of Pizza Slices	*Total Utility*	*Marginal Utility*
0	0	Marginal utility not yet established
1	20	20
2	50	30
3	75	25
4	95	20
5	110	15
6	120	10
7	125	5
8	120	−5

Note how the total utility for any given number of pizza slices equals the sum of the marginal utilities up to that slice. Also, note how the marginal utility is always the difference in total utility from one slice to the next.

Doing the Best You Can Given Consumer Constraints

Although you like both apples and oranges, you can't eat as many as you want because you're constrained by your income and the price of apples and oranges. The constraint imposed by income and the price of goods is called the *budget constraint.* The budget constraint is an equation that indicates that if you multiply the quantity of each good purchased by its price and then add those numbers up for all goods, the result must equal your income. Thus, the budget constraint would look like this for apples and oranges

$$I = (p_a \times q_a) + (p_o \times q_o)$$

In this equation, I is your income, p_a is the price of an apple, q_a is the quantity of apples purchased, p_o is the price of an orange, and q_o is the quantity of oranges purchased.

The slope of the budget constraint equals the price of the good on the horizontal axis divided by the price of the good on the vertical axis.

$$\text{Slope} = \frac{P_{\text{horizontal axis good}}}{P_{\text{vertical axis good}}}$$

Assume you budgeted $6.00 to purchase apples and oranges, and the price of an apple is $0.75 and the price of an orange is $0.50. In this case, your budget constraint is

$$6.00 = (0.75 \times q_a) + (0.50 \times q_o)$$

One possible combination of apples and oranges you can purchase with the $6.00 are 2 apples, requiring $1.50 ($0.75×2), and 9 oranges requiring $4.50 ($0.50 ×9). Other possible combinations of apples and oranges you can purchase include 0 apples and 12 oranges, 4 apples and 6 oranges, 6 apples and 3 oranges, or 8 apples and 0 oranges.

Maximizing Pleasure through Consumer Choice and Constrained Optimization

Choosing among the incredible number of goods available to you isn't difficult. Indeed, you do it all the time. You make these decisions based upon what gives you more happiness. You've maximized your happiness if you're indifferent to or less satisfied with any other combination of goods as compared to what you already have.

Identifying indifference

I don't care. You've probably said that phrase yourself. When I'm asked whether I want an apple or an orange, and I say "I don't care," it means I'm indifferent.

Indifference exists when the amount of utility you get in one situation exactly equals the amount of utility you get in another situation. So, "I don't care" simply means I receive the same total utility or satisfaction in both situations.

If I'm asked whether I'd like 3 apples and 8 oranges, or 4 apples and 6 oranges, or 5 apples and 5 oranges, and I say "I don't care," I've indicated indifference among all three of those possibilities. Each of those combinations gives me the same total utility.

Economists graph this situation with — are you ready — an indifference curve! An *indifference curve* shows all possible combinations of two goods that result in the same level of total utility. Figure 5-1 graphs my indifference curve for apples and oranges. This curve is labeled U_1.

Again, every point on the indifference curve U_1 gives me the same level of satisfaction or utility. But as was the case with ice cream earlier in this chapter, as I eat more apples, I experience diminishing marginal utility. The result of diminishing marginal utility is I become less willing to give up oranges for an additional apple. When I start with 3 apples, I'm willing to give up 2 oranges — going from 8 to 6 oranges — in order to get one more apple, or, in the example, to get a fourth apple. In Figure 5-1, I'm moving from point A to point B on the indifference curve. Once I have 4 apples, I'm only willing to give up 1 orange to get another apple, going from 4 to 5 apples. This is represented by moving from point B to point C in Figure 5-1. I'm not as willing to give up oranges for apples because an additional apple doesn't give me as much marginal utility. As a result of diminishing marginal utility, indifference curves are drawn convex to the origin on a graph. Convex to the origin is just a fancy term for the bowed shape the indifference curve has in Figure 5-1.

It's possible for me to get more satisfaction. If I get 6 apples and 6 oranges, that's better than my combination of 5 apples and 5 oranges because I'm getting both an extra apple and an extra orange. I get more utility from 6 apples and 6 oranges than I get from 5 apples and 5 oranges. Because 5 apples and 5 oranges are on my original indifference curve U_1, this new combination of apples and oranges will be on a new indifference curve — an indifference curve with higher utility or satisfaction. Thus, I move from point C on indifference curve U_1 to point D on indifference curve U_2 in Figure 5-2.

Indeed, I have lots of different indifference curves representing various levels of satisfaction. These indifference curves are illustrated on an indifference curve map like the one in Figure 5-2. As already mentioned, the indifference curve U_2 represents combinations of apples and oranges that give me more utility than combinations on indifference curve U_1. On the other hand, the indifference curve U_0 illustrates combinations of apples and oranges that give me less utlity than the combinations on indifference curve U_1.

Remember two things about indifference curves — every point on the same indifference curve has the same utility and higher indifference curves have higher utility.

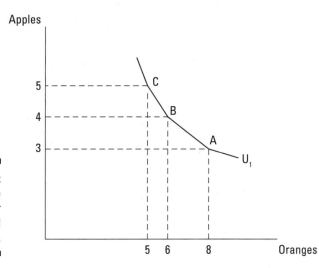

Figure 5-1:
Indifference
curve for
apples and
oranges.

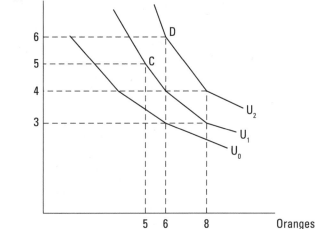

Figure 5-2:
Indifference
curve
map for
apples and
oranges.

Thinking at the margin: Just one more

As I tell you earlier in this chapter (see the earlier section "Adding happiness —
at a price"), marginal utility is the change in total utility that occurs when
one additional unit of a good is consumed. When you have an indifference
curve, the amount of utility that you gain from eating one more orange is
exactly offset by the amount of utility you lose by consuming fewer apples.
This doesn't mean you consume one less apple when you consume one more
orange (as indicated in Figure 5-1). To remain on the same indifference curve,
you keep eating fewer apples until the marginal utility you lose from eating
fewer apples is exactly offset by the marginal utility you gain from eating one
more orange.

Knowing the marginal rate of substitution

The *marginal rate of substitution* measures the change in the quantity of the good on the vertical axis of the diagram that is necessary per one unit change of the good on the horizontal axis of the diagram in order for the consumer to receive the same amount of total utility. Wow, that's a mouthful, even for an economist. In the case of the apple and orange example, it's the change in the quantity of apples consumed necessary given a one unit change in oranges for the same level of total utility. This is simply the slope of the indifference curve.

Now this is what you really have to remember: The slope of the indifference curve equals the marginal utility of the good on the horizontal axis divided by the marginal utility of the good on the vertical axis.

$$\text{Slope} = \frac{MU_{\text{horizontal axis good}}}{MU_{\text{vertical axis good}}}$$

Consuming within limits

Now, add the budget constraint to the diagram. Remember, you can only purchase combinations of goods on the budget constraint.

In the earlier section "Doing the Best You Can Given Consumer Constraints," I give an equation for my budget constraint in purchasing apples and oranges

$$6.00 = 0.75 \times q_a + 0.50 \times q_o$$

Adding this budget constraint to the indifference curve map graphed in Figure 5-2 generates the diagram in Figure 5-3.

Money can buy you happiness

There's an old saying, "Money can't buy you happiness." I won't get into the philosophical aspects of the saying, but as an economist, I can say money does buy satisfaction because money is used to purchase the goods that satisfy my wants and desires. On the other hand, I don't get any satisfaction from the money itself. I want to buy stuff — bicycles, vacations, good food, and lots of other stuff. I get satisfaction from the stuff I buy with money, not the money. As a

result, although you can purchase combinations of goods inside the budget constraint, you don't want to do that. You get satisfaction from consuming goods — not from money. If I gave you a one dollar bill and told you that you could never spend it, would you be any happier? Probably not. You want money in order to spend it — to buy as much stuff as possible. You save in order to buy more stuff in the future, not because you want money.

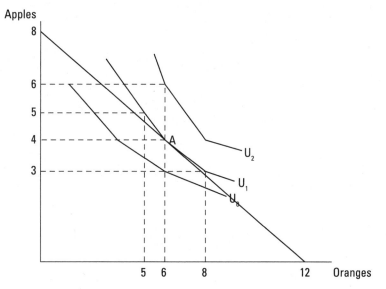

Figure 5-3:
Optimal
combina-
tion of
apples and
oranges.

Deciding what makes you happiest

Consumers want to get as much happiness as possible.

Higher indifference curves represent more happiness, so consumers want to get to the highest indifference curve possible given the budget constraint. In Figure 5-3, this combination is illustrated at point A — 4 apples and 6 oranges. Although the figure includes higher indifference curves, you can't reach those combinations of apples and oranges given the budget constraint.

Now for some magic. At the point where you're happiest given your budget constraint, the indifference curve and budget constraint are tangent with one another. This means the slopes of these two curves are equal. Therefore

$$\text{Indifference Curve Slope} = \frac{MU_{\text{horizontal axis good}}}{MU_{\text{vertical axis good}}} = \frac{P_{\text{horizontal axis good}}}{P_{\text{vertical axis good}}} = \text{Budget Constraint Slope}$$

Or, if you rearrange that equation

$$\frac{MU_{\text{horizontal axis good}}}{P_{\text{horizontal axis good}}} = \frac{MU_{\text{vertical axis good}}}{P_{\text{vertical axis good}}}$$

The preceding equation is an application of what economists call the *equimarginal principle*. By equating — "equi" — the marginal utilities per dollar spent (marginal) for all goods, you receive the maximum satisfaction or utility given your budget constraint.

You're happiest when the marginal utility per dollar spent on each good is equal for all goods.

Choosing to Use Calculus with Consumer Choice

Dangerous curves ahead. Really! This is the section where I show you how to maximize utility by using calculus and the Lagrangian function. Calculus does make indifference curves dangerous.

Measuring indifference

Indifference curves can be described by functions. For example

$$U = 8x^{0.5}y^{0.5}$$

shows the relationship between the quantity consumed of good x, the quantity consumed of good y, and total utility.

Constraining factors

Again, consumers face a budget constraint. For example, a consumer has a weekly budget of \$400 for goods x and y. The price of good x is \$10 and the price of good y is \$8. The budget constraint is

$$400 = 10x + 8y$$

where x and y are the quantities consumed of each good.

Lagrangians can make you happy

You'll recognize this as a constrained optimization problem — the consumer is trying to maximize utility, subject to a budget constraint. This situation is ideal for a Lagrangian. (Go to Chapter 3 for more information on the Lagrangian function and how to set it up.)

The consumer wants to maximize utility, subject to the budget constraint, based upon the functions I present earlier in this section. The steps you take in order to determine the quantity of x and y that maximize utility are the following:

1. **Create a Lagrangian function.** Recognize that the variable you're trying to maximize is total utility. So, your objective function is $8x^{0.5}y^{0.5}$. Second, your constraint is represented by the budget $400 - 10x - 8y = 0$. Your Lagrangian function $\mathcal{L}$ is

$$\mathcal{L} = 8x^{0.5}y^{0.5} + \lambda(400 - 10x - 8y)$$

2. **Take the partial derivative of the Lagrangian with respect to x and y, the commodities you're consuming, and set them equal to zero.** These equations ensure that total utility is being maximized.

$$\frac{\partial \mathcal{L}}{\partial x} = 0.5 \times 8x^{0.5-1}y^{0.5} - 10\lambda = \frac{4y^{0.5}}{x^{0.5}} - 10\lambda = 0$$

$$\frac{\partial \mathcal{L}}{\partial y} = 0.5 \times 8x^{0.5}y^{0.5-1} - 8\lambda = \frac{4x^{0.5}}{y^{0.5}} - 8\lambda = 0$$

3. **Take the partial derivative of the Lagrangian function with respect to λ and set it equal to zero.** This partial derivative ensures that the budget constraint is satisfied.

$$\frac{\partial \mathcal{L}}{\partial \lambda} = 400 - 10x - 8y = 0$$

Solving the three partial derivatives simultaneously for the variables x, y, and λ maximizes total utility, subject to the budget constraint.

Rewriting the partial derivative of $\mathcal{L}$ with respect to x enables you to solve for λ.

$$\frac{4y^{0.5}}{x^{0.5}} - 10\lambda = 0 \quad \text{so} \quad 10\lambda = \frac{4y^{0.5}}{x^{0.5}} \quad \text{or} \quad \lambda = \frac{4y^{0.5}}{10x^{0.5}}$$

Substituting the above equation for λ in the partial derivative of $\mathcal{L}$ with respect to y yields

$$\frac{4x^{0.5}}{y^{0.5}} - 8\lambda = \frac{4x^{0.5}}{y^{0.5}} - 8\left(\frac{4y^{0.5}}{10x^{0.5}}\right) = \frac{4x^{0.5}}{y^{0.5}} - \frac{32y^{0.5}}{10x^{0.5}} = 0 \quad \text{or} \quad \frac{4x^{0.5}}{y^{0.5}} = \frac{32y^{0.5}}{10x^{0.5}} \quad \text{or} \quad 40x = 32y$$

So

$$x = 0.8y$$

Finally, substituting $0.8y$ for x in the constraint (the partial derivative of $\mathcal{L}$ with respect to λ) yields

$$400 - 10x - 8y = 400 - 10(0.8y) - 8y = 400 - 8y - 8y = 400 - 16y = 0 \quad \text{or} \quad 400 = 16y$$

Thus, you should consume 25 units of good y.

Earlier you determined $x = 0.8y$.

$$x = 0.8y = 0.8(25) = 20$$

Finally, you can solve for λ.

$$\lambda = \frac{4y^{0.5}}{10x^{0.5}} = \frac{4(25)^{0.5}}{10(20)^{0.5}} = 0.447$$

Therefore, the combination 20 units of good x and 25 units of good y maximizes total utility given the budget constraint.

In addition, λ equals 0.447. Lambda is an awesome shortcut. Most decisions are affected by constraints, but constraints are not necessarily absolute. Often times, a constraint can be varied a little bit. Lambda, the Lagrangian multiplier, shows you the impact changing the constraint has on the objective function. Specifically, if you change the constraint one unit, lambda indicates how much the variable you're optimizing will change. Thus, in the example, if your income increases by $1 (you change the constraint by one unit) your total utility increases by 0.447 utils.

I graph this example in Figure 5-4.

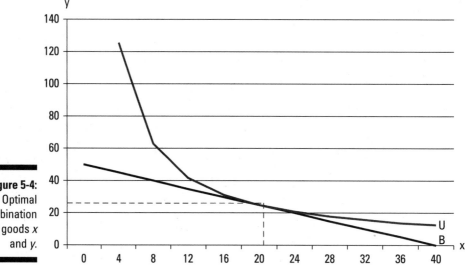

Figure 5-4:
Optimal
combination
of goods x
and y.

Influencing Consumer Choice

Understanding consumer behavior helps you in determining how to influence it. After all, your goal is to maximize profits, but to do that, you have to have customers purchase your product. The previous sections in this chapter illustrate a crucial point — consumers make decisions based upon satisfaction/ utility and price. And although you can influence satisfaction through things like advertising, you have complete control over price. Thus, how you price your product influences how much customers purchase, because changing the good's price changes the customer's budget constraint.

Buying one to get one free

One common pricing strategy is to offer customers who buy one unit of your product a second unit free. You may wonder how this strategy makes sense — if customers have already decided to buy one unit, why should you give them a second unit for free? But the point is that you don't know whether customers will buy one unit. The purpose of this pricing strategy is to get more customers to purchase the first unit.

The increase in the number of customers who buy the first unit occurs because this pricing strategy changes the slope of the budget constraint. Consider the situation where a customer is deciding where to go for lunch — the taco stand or your pizza restaurant. The taco stand sells tacos for $0.50 each while you sell pizza at $1.00 per slice. The customer plans to spend up to $3.00. The budget constraint for this situation is described in the first two columns of Table 5-2 and represented by the line B_a in Figure 5-5.

Table 5-2		Buy One, Get One Free	
Same Price Every Unit		**Buy One, Get One Free**	
Number of Pizza Slices	**Number of Tacos**	**Number of Pizza Slices**	**Number of Tacos**
0	6	0	6
1	4	1	4
2	2	2	4
3	0	3	2
		4	0

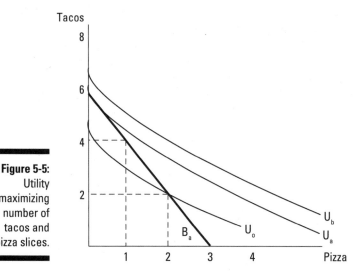

The customer's goal is to maximize utility by going to the highest indifference curve touched by the budget constraint B_a. For the indifference curve map in Figure 5-5, the highest indifference curve touched by the budget constraint B_a is U_a, which indicates the customer buys six tacos and zero slices of pizza.

Now, you decide to offer a special promotion: buy one slice of pizza and your second slice is free. Now, if customers buy one slice of pizza, they can still buy four tacos. And because the second slice of pizza is free, the customers can still buy four tacos with two slices of pizza. The resulting budget constraint is described in the last two columns of Table 5-2.

On the graph, this promotion has added a horizontal section to the budget constraint, shifting the budget constraint out at the point between one and two slices of pizza. (Remember, the second slice of pizza doesn't cost customers anything.) The new budget constraint for the customer is B_b in Figure 5-6.

Again, your customers want to maximize utility by finding the highest indifference curve touched by the new budget constraint. This is the indifference curve U_b in Figure 5-6 and it indicates that the customers now buy four tacos and two slices of pizza. You've gone from selling no pizza to this customer to selling two slices! And as an added bonus, your customer is getting even more satisfaction than before.

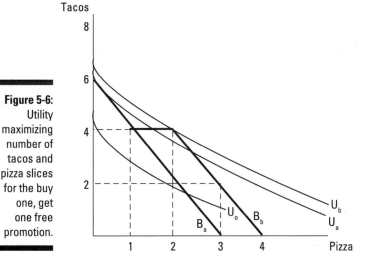

Figure 5-6:
Utility
maximizing
number of
tacos and
pizza slices
for the buy
one, get
one free
promotion.

Selling gift cards

Gift cards are used to bias customers toward your business over a competitor. Because the customer can use the gift card at only your business, gift cards affect the shape of the budget constraint.

Compare a situation where a customer has $50 in cash versus $25 in cash and a $25 gift certificate to your store. At first, these situations may seem essentially the same — but they're not. The gift certificate can be used at only your store, so the maximum that can be spent at your competitor is now only $25.

Figure 5-7 compares the two budget constraints. The budget constraint B_a is the budget constraint that exists if the customer can spend $50 cash at either your store or a competitor's store. (I assume a price of $1 per unit for the good being purchased.) Given $50 cash, the customer maximizes utility on indifference curve U_a, spending $38 at your competitor's store and $12 at your store.

If the customer has a $25 gift certificate at your store, the maximum he can spend at the competitor's store is $25, while he can spend a maximum of $50 at your store ($25 cash plus $25 gift certificate). The new budget constraint is B_b. Now the customer maximizes utility with indifference curve U_b, spending $25 at your competitor's store and $25 at your store. That's $13 more than he had previously spent at your store!

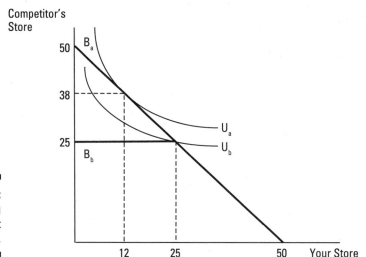

Figure 5-7:
Examining
the benefit
of gift cards.

Issuing coupons

As with gift cards, businesses use coupons to bias customers toward buying a particular good or from a specific business. By giving customers a discount, you effectively lower the product's price. An added advantage of coupons is that they allow you to differentiate between consumers with different price elasticities of demand — more on that in Chapter 13.

Back to your pizza restaurant (and you didn't even know you owned one). Instead of the buy one, get one free promotion you did earlier in this chapter, you decide to run a special — $0.25 off each pizza slice with coupon.

Before the coupon, your customers were deciding between tacos priced at $0.50 each and pizza priced at $1.00 per slice. The customer had $3.00 to spend. The budget constraint for this situation is described by B_a in Figure 5-8. In this situation, the customer maximizes utility by purchasing four tacos and one slice of pizza — the point where the indifference curve U_a is tangent to the budget constraint B_a.

If you now offer $0.25 off per slice of pizza, the effective price is $0.75 per slice. Now the customer can buy up to four slices of pizza. The new budget constraint is B_b in Figure 5-8. The pivot in the budget constraint reflects the lower after-coupon price of a pizza slice. As a result, the customer now purchases three tacos and two slices of pizza — the point where the indifference curve U_b is tangent to the new budget constraint B_b.

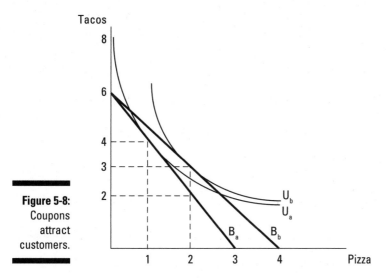

Figure 5-8:
Coupons
attract
customers.

As these examples indicate, understanding consumer theory gives you multiple options on pricing strategies that increase your sales.

Chapter 6

Production Magic: Pulling a Rabbit Out of the Hat

*E*conomics contains a lot of surprising and therefore magical conclusions. For example, you can increase your firm's revenues sometimes by lowering price and thus selling a lot more or other times by raising price if you sell only a few less. (See Chapter 4 on elasticity.) Similarly, in production, sometimes you're better off using a lot of machines, what economists call capital, to produce your good, and other times you're better off using more labor.

The amount you use of an input depends upon how much it costs and how much output it adds. The crucial thing to determine is what input combination minimizes the cost of producing a given quantity of output. And minimizing cost is mandatory if you want to maximize profits. Maximizing profits — now that's magical.

Producing Hats: Identifying the Types of Inputs and Timely Production

Any good magician needs a hat. That's where the rabbit comes from. Somebody has to produce the magician's hat, and I bet the producer wants to make a lot of money or profit. One way for the hat producer to make more profit is to choose inputs that minimize the cost of production. As an aside, I'll leave the description of rabbit production to somebody else.

Economists call inputs, or resources, factors of production. They are the factors used to produce your product or output.

Here are the four major factors of production:

- ✔ **Labor** refers to human effort
- ✔ **Capital** refers to machinery, equipment, and factories
- ✔ **Land** refers to resources taken from the earth
- ✔ **Entrepreneurial skills** refer to skills related to innovation and risk evaluation

As the manager, you have to decide what combination of these inputs minimizes your production cost.

So, you want to produce a hat. You'll need labor, felt (magicians use old felt top hats), thread, scissors, and a sewing machine. The quantity of some of these inputs can be changed fairly easily (labor), while the quantity of other inputs is harder to change (sewing machines). Economists distinguish between these types of inputs by calling them variable or fixed.

- ✔ **Variable inputs** are inputs whose quantities can be readily changed in response to changes in market conditions. Labor is typically a variable input. If you have a huge increase in the demand for felt top hats, working just a little longer, or perhaps hiring another worker, is easy to do.
- ✔ **Fixed inputs** are inputs whose quantities can't be readily changed in response to market conditions. Even if you have a huge change in the demand for felt top hats, it would take a fairly long period of time to adjust the size of the factory where you're making them in order to add more sewing machines.

Economists also create their own definition of time. Rather than use a clock or calendar like normal people, economists define time based upon whether or not the quantities employed of various inputs can be changed. Thus, instead of using hours, days, and weeks, economists talk about the short run and the long run.

Being limited in the short run

In the *short run,* some inputs are fixed and some inputs are variable. So, you can adjust some, but not all, of your inputs in order to change the quantity of output produced. With the increased demand for hats, you can change the labor in the short run — labor is a variable input — while you can't change the size of the factory — the factory is a fixed input.

Looking forward to the long run and life without limits

In the *long run,* all inputs can be changed and thus are variable. So in the long run, even building an entirely new factory is possible. But the relationship between the long run and your calendar varies from industry to industry. For a restaurant, you can probably start from scratch and have the restaurant open within six months. Thus, the long run in the restaurant industry is six months. For a power company, building a new power plant may take six years or more; thus, the long run is at minimum six years. Because all inputs are variable in the long run, your business can change anything it wants — you have no limits on what you can change.

Defining the Production Function: What Goes in Must Come Out

A *production function* specifies the relationship that exists between inputs and outputs for a given technology. In general terms, a production function is specified as

$$q = f(x_1, x_2, \ldots, x_n)$$

where x_1 through x_n represent the various inputs in the production process, and q represents the quantity of output produced. If you have only two inputs in the production process — labor, L, and capital, K — you write the production function as

$$q = f(L, K)$$

The specific function described by a general statement may have many forms. For example,

$$q = 2L + 5K$$

indicates a linear relationship between both labor and output and capital and output. In this equation, for every one-unit increase in labor, the quantity of output produced increases by two units, while a one-unit increase in capital leads to a five-unit increase in output. Alternatively, the production function may take the form

$$q = 4L^{0.5}K^{0.5}$$

This commonly used production function is called the Cobb-Douglas function. The Cobb-Douglas production function is widely used because it assumes some degree of substitutability between inputs, but not perfect substitutability. So, labor can be substituted for capital — dishes can be washed by hand at a restaurant or in a dishwasher — but labor is not a perfect substitute for capital.

Starting with Basics by Using Single Input Production Functions

Production functions typically have more than one input; however, in the case of a single input production function, you assume that the quantity employed of only one input can be varied. In other words, you have one variable input and all other inputs in the production process are fixed inputs — and you can't change the quantity of the fixed inputs.

You're a farmer trying to decide how much land you're going to plant in corn and how much you'll leave for hay. You've decided to treat the quantities of labor (you're the only one working) and machinery employed constant. In this situation, labor and capital (the machinery) are fixed inputs and land is a variable input.

The following equation describes the relationship between the amount of land you use and the quantity of corn produced

$$q = 180N^{0.9}$$

Where q is the number of bushels of corn grown and N is the amount of land used.

I know, the 0.9 power looks strange, but trust me, your computer can handle it. Nevertheless, Table 6-1 presents some of the land, output combinations that are possible.

Table 6-1	Land and Corn Production
Number of Acres of Land (N)	*Number of Bushels of Corn (q)*
50	6,086
99	11,255
100	11,357
150	16,359
200	21,193
250	25,907

I graph this equation in Figure 6-1.

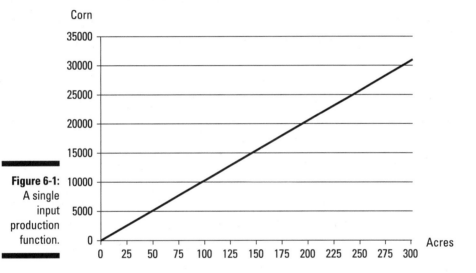

Figure 6-1:
A single input production function.

Corn

Distinguishing between average product and marginal product

You can examine the relationship between inputs and output in a number of different ways. You may be concerned with only the total amount of corn grown — what economists call *total product*. Alternatively, you may be interested in the average quantity of corn produced per acre of land, what farmers call yield, and economists call average product, or you may be interested in how much corn output increases when you plant one more acre, marginal product to economists. Each of these relationships is important, and each offers considerable insight into the production process.

- ✔ **Total product** refers to the entire quantity of output produced from a given set of inputs. In the equation, q represents total product. Therefore, if you plant 100 acres of corn, total product equals

$$q = 180N^{0.9} = 180(100)^{0.9} = 11,357$$

or 11,357 bushels of corn produced.

- ✔ **Average product** refers to the output per unit of input. For a production function that has a single variable input, average product equals the total product divided by the quantity of input used. Therefore,

$$AP_{land} = \frac{q}{N}$$

If you plant 100 acres of corn, the average product equals

$$AP_{land} = \frac{q}{N} = \frac{180N^{0.9}}{N} = \frac{180(100)^{0.9}}{100} = 113.57$$

or 113.57 bushels per acre.

- ✔ **Marginal product** is the change in total product that occurs when one additional unit of a variable input is employed. In Table 6-1, the marginal product of the 100th acre of land is 102 bushels of corn. The total product for 99 acres is 11,255 bushels, and the total product for 100 acres is 11,357 bushels. Thus, the difference or change between the two is 11,357 – 11,255 or 102 bushels of corn.

Marginal product is also determined with calculus.

To determine marginal product with calculus, take the following steps:

1. **Take the derivative of total product with respect to the input.** In the example, this is land (N).

$$MP_{land} = \frac{dq}{dN} = 0.9 \times 180N^{0.9-1} = 162N^{-0.1} = \frac{162}{N^{0.1}}$$

2. **Substitute in the appropriate value for the input.** So, to determine the marginal product of the 100th acre of land, substitute 100 for N and solve (with the help of your computer or calculator).

$$MP_{land} = \frac{162}{N^{0.1}} = \frac{162}{(100)^{0.1}} \approx 102$$

Thus, if you start at 100 acres, adding another acre of land increases output by 102 bushels.

Diminishing returns

The *law of diminishing returns* states that ceteris paribus, as the quantity employed of an input increases, eventually a point is reached where the marginal product of an additional unit of that input decreases.

The term *ceteris paribus* indicates that all other things — for example, the quantities employed of other inputs and technology — are held constant. Therefore, the law of diminishing returns indicates that after some point, additional units of a variable input aren't as productive as preceding units of the input.

Making Production More Realistic with Multiple Input Production Functions

Although single-input production functions are useful for illustrating many concepts, usually, they're too simplistic to represent a firm's production decision. Therefore, it's useful for you to understand the firm's employment decision when the quantities employed of two or more inputs are changed. In other words, you're dealing with two or more variable inputs.

Consider the production function $q = f(L,K)$, which indicates the quantity of output produced is a function of the quantities of labor, L, and capital, K, employed. The specific form of this function may be the following Cobb-Douglas function

$$q = 16L^{0.5}K^{0.5}$$

Table 6-2 illustrates the relationship between various values for labor and capital and a total product of 3,200 units for this equation.

Examining production isoquants: All input combinations are equal

The relationship between labor, capital, and the quantity of output produced in the previous equation is graphically described by using a production isoquant. A *production isoquant* shows all possible combinations of two inputs that produce a given quantity of output. Table 6-2 shows various combinations of labor and capital that produce 3,200 units of output.

Table 6-2	Two-Input Production Function	
Labor L	*Capital K*	*Total Product q*
25	1,600	3,200
50	800	3,200
75	533.3	3,200
100	400	3,200
125	320	3,200
150	266.7	3,200
175	228.6	3,200
200	200	3,200
225	177.8	3,200
250	160	3,200
275	145.5	3,200
300	133.3	3,200
325	123.1	3,200
350	144.3	3,200
375	106.7	3,200
400	100	3,200

Figure 6-2 illustrates the production isoquant, labeled q_1, derived from Table 6-2 and the equation

$$q = 3,200 = 16L^{0.5}K^{0.5}$$

In Figure 6-2, the curve labeled q_1 represents all combinations of capital and labor that produce 3,200 units of output.

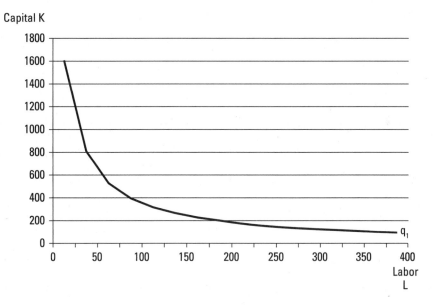

Figure 6-2:
This production isoquant shows all combinations of capital and labor that produce 3,200 units of output.

Thinking at the margin one more time

Earlier in this chapter, I define marginal product as the change in total product that occurs given one additional unit of an input. With a production isoquant, the amount of output you gain from using one more unit of labor is exactly offset by the amount of output you lose by using less capital.

Every input combination on the production isoquant produces the same level of output — output is constant. Capital can change by more or less than one unit. What is critical is that total product remains constant as you increase labor and decrease capital.

Knowing the marginal rate of technical substitution

The *marginal rate of technical substitution* measures the change in the quantity of the input on the vertical axis of the diagram that's necessary per one-unit change of the input on the horizontal axis of the diagram in order for total product to remain constant.

That's too technical of a definition, so remember this instead — the marginal rate of technical substitution is simply the production isoquant's slope. The production isoquant's slope equals the marginal product of the input on the horizontal axis divided by the marginal product the input on the vertical axis.

$$\text{Slope} = \frac{\text{MP}_{\text{horizontal axis input}}}{\text{MP}_{\text{vertical axis input}}}$$

Defining isocost curves: All input combinations cost the same

An important factor in your production decision is how much the inputs cost. If an additional worker (unit of labor) costs less than an additional unit of capital, but the worker produces the same quantity of output as the capital, it's a good deal to hire the additional worker. So, you need to add cost to your decision-making process.

The *isocost curve* illustrates all possible combinations of two inputs that result in the same level of total cost. The isocost curve is presented as an equation. For a situation with two inputs — labor and capital — the isocost curve's equation is

$$C = (p_L \times L) + (p_K \times K)$$

In this equation, C is a constant level of cost, p_L is the price of labor, L is the quantity of labor employed, p_K is the price of capital, and K is the quantity of capital employed.

On a graph, the isocost curve's slope equals the price of the input on the horizontal axis divided by the price of the vertical axis input.

$$\text{Slope} = \frac{\text{P}_{\text{horizontal axis input}}}{\text{P}_{\text{vertical axis input}}}$$

Assume your total cost is $4,000 a day, and labor costs $20 per hour, and capital costs $5 per machine-hour. Given this information, your isocost curve equation is

$$4{,}000 = (20 \times L) + (5 \times K)$$

Some possible combinations of labor and capital you can employ for a total cost of $4,000 are 50 hours of labor and 600 machine-hours of capital, 100 hours of labor and 400 machine-hours of capital, and 150 hours of labor and 200 machine hours of capital. Any combination of labor and capital that results in total cost being $4,000 would be on the same — $4,000 — isocost curve.

I illustrate the isocost curve for this equation in Figure 6-3.

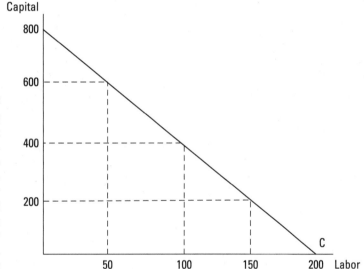

Figure 6-3:
An isocost curve showing possible combinations of labor and capital you can employ for $4,000.

Changes in input prices shift the isocost curve. If the input on the horizontal axis becomes cheaper, the isocost curve rotates out on that axis as illustrated in Figure 6-4. If the input on the vertical axis becomes cheaper, the isocost curve rotates as illustrated in Figure 6-5. More expensive inputs cause shifts in the opposite direction.

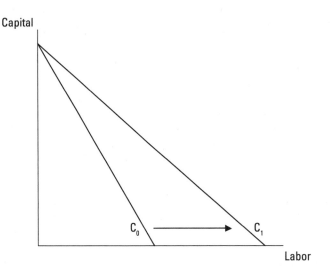

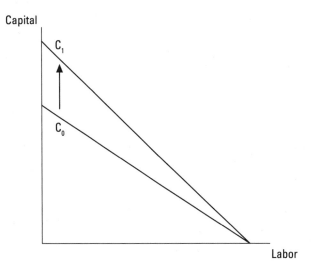

Making the most with the least: Cost minimization

In order to maximize profits, you must produce your output at the lowest possible cost.

The costs of producing a given quantity of output are minimized at the point where the production isoquant is just tangent — or, in other words, just touching — the isocost curve. This point is illustrated as point A in Figure 6-6. The cost-minimizing combination of labor and capital are the quantities L_0 and K_0.

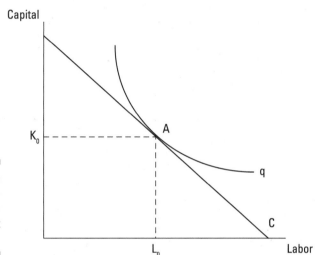

Figure 6-6:
Cost-
minimizing
input
combination.

Now comes the easy part. At the point where you minimize costs, the production isoquant and isocost curve are tangent. This means the slopes of these two curves are equal. Therefore

$$\text{Isoquant Slope} = \frac{MP_{\text{horizontal axis input}}}{MP_{\text{vertical axis input}}} = \frac{P_{\text{horizontal axis input}}}{P_{\text{vertical axis input}}} = \text{Isocost Slope}$$

Or, if you rearrange that equation

$$\frac{MP_{\text{horizontal axis input}}}{P_{\text{horizontal axis input}}} = \frac{MP_{\text{vertical axis input}}}{P_{\text{vertical axis input}}}$$

Thus, you minimize costs when the marginal product per dollar spent on each input is equal for all inputs. And this holds true no matter how many inputs you use!

Economists call the preceding concept the *least cost criterion,* and it's an application of the *equimarginal principle.* To produce goods with the lowest possible production cost, you equate the marginal product per dollar spent.

Minimizing Cost with Calculus (If You Want)

Dangerous intersection ahead. Not really, because a mathematician calls this a tangency, not an intersection. In this section, I show you how to determine the cost-minimizing input combination with calculus, but remember, use calculus only if you want to. Otherwise, simply use the least cost criterion in the previous section.

Cost minimization is another constrained optimization problem. In this situation, you want to minimize the cost of producing a given quantity of output. And with any constrained optimization problem, the Lagrangian function is the perfect tool. (Go to Chapter 3 for more information on the Lagrangian function and how to set it up.)

Your business decides to produce 3,200 units of product daily by using two variable inputs — labor, L, and capital, K. (This problem can have more than two variable inputs; the algebra is simply a little more complicated. See the steps for making a Lagrangian function in Chapter 3.) The relationship between your total product, 3,200, and the inputs of labor and capital is described by the following equation

$$q = 3,200 = 16L^{0.5}K^{0.5}$$

Assume the price of labor is $20 per hour and the price of capital is $5 per machine-hour. The resulting isocost curve is

$$C = (20 \times L) + (5 \times K)$$

Your goal is to minimize the cost of producing 3,200 units of output. The steps you take in order to determine the cost-minimizing amounts of labor and capital are as follows:

1. **Create a Lagrangian function.**

   Recognize that the variable you're trying to minimize is cost. So, your objective function is $20L + 5K$. Second, your constraint is represented by the desired output level, 3,200. The constraint based upon your production function is $3,200 - 16L^{0.5}K^{0.5}$. Your Lagrangian function is

   $$\mathcal{L} = 20L + 5K + \lambda\left(3,200 - 16L^{0.5}K^{0.5}\right)$$

2. **Take the partial derivative of the Lagrangian with respect to L and K, the inputs you're using, and set them equal to zero.**

These equations ensure that cost is minimized.

$$\frac{\partial \mathcal{L}}{\partial L} = 20 - \lambda\left(0.5 \times 16 L^{0.5-1} K^{0.5}\right) = 20 - \lambda \frac{8K^{0.5}}{L^{0.5}} = 0$$

$$\frac{\partial \mathcal{L}}{\partial K} = 5 - \lambda\left(0.5 \times 16 L^{0.5} K^{0.5-1}\right) = 5 - \lambda \frac{8L^{0.5}}{K^{0.5}} = 0$$

3. **Take the partial derivative of the Lagrangian function with respect to λ and set it equal to zero.**

   This partial derivative ensures that the production constraint is satisfied.

   $$\frac{\partial \mathcal{L}}{\partial \lambda} = 3{,}200 - 16 L^{0.5} K^{0.5} = 0$$

4. **Solve the three partial derivatives simultaneously for the variables L, K, and λ to minimize the cost of producing 3,200 units of output.**

   Rewriting the partial derivative of $\mathcal{L}$ with respect to L enables you to solve for λ.

   $$20 - \lambda \frac{8K^{0.5}}{L^{0.5}} = 0 \quad \text{so} \quad 20 = \lambda \frac{8K^{0.5}}{L^{0.5}} \quad \text{or} \quad \lambda = \frac{20 L^{0.5}}{8K^{0.5}} = \frac{2.5 L^{0.5}}{K^{0.5}}$$

   Substituting the previous equation for λ in the partial derivative of $\mathcal{L}$ with respect to K yields

   $$5 - \lambda \frac{8L^{0.5}}{K^{0.5}} = 5 - \left(\frac{2.5 L^{0.5}}{K^{0.5}}\right)\frac{8L^{0.5}}{K^{0.5}} = 5 - \frac{20L}{K} = 0 \quad \text{or} \quad 5 = \frac{20L}{K} \quad \text{or} \quad 5K = 20L$$

   so

   $$K = 4L$$

   Finally, substituting $4L$ for K in the constraint (the partial derivative of $\mathcal{L}$ with respect to λ) yields

   $$3{,}200 - 16 L^{0.5} K^{0.5} = 3{,}200 - 16 L^{0.5}\left(4L\right)^{0.5} = 3{,}200 - 16 L^{0.5} \times 2 L^{0.5}$$

   so $\quad 3{,}200 - 32L = 0 \quad$ or $\quad 3{,}200 = 32L$

   Therefore, you need to use 100 hours of labor.

   Earlier you determined $K = 4L$.

   $$K = 4L = 4\left(100\right) = 400$$

So you should use 400 machine-hours of capital.

Finally, you can solve for λ.

$$\lambda = \frac{2.5L^{0.5}}{K^{0.5}} = \frac{2.5(100)^{0.5}}{(400)^{0.5}} = \frac{2.5 \times 10}{20} = 1.25$$

Therefore, the combination 100 hours of labor and 400 machine-hours of capital minimizes the cost of producing 3,200 units of output. In addition, λ equals 1.25. Because lambda indicates the change that occurs in the objective function given a one-unit change in the constraint, it indicates that if you produce one more unit of output, your cost increases by $1.25. This is a great situation if you can receive more than an additional $1.25 in revenue from selling that extra unit.

Recognizing That More Isn't Always Better with Long-Run Returns to Scale

In the long run, all inputs can be changed. If you change all inputs by the same percentage or proportion, you need to know the amount output will change by. Economists call this relationship between output and all inputs returns to scale.

Returns to scale refers to the changes in output that occur when the scale of production changes. Changes in the scale of production indicate a proportional change in the quantity employed of *all* inputs.

Increasing returns to scale indicate that doubling the quantity employed of all inputs results in the quantity of output produced more than doubling. Increasing returns to scale can be caused by greater specialization within your company, or perhaps doubling your inputs allows you to build one large factory that's more efficient than two small factories. A number of factors lead to increasing returns to scale.

Decreasing returns to scale indicate that doubling the quantity employed of all inputs results in the quantity of output produced less than doubling. Decreasing returns to scale may result from the fact that larger business enterprises are harder to coordinate than smaller businesses. As a consequence, it's more difficult for you to convey your intent and to directly monitor the operation of specific areas of a larger business.

Constant returns to scale indicate that doubling the quantity employed of all inputs results in output also doubling. In the case of constant returns to scale, increasing and decreasing returns to scale essentially offset each other.

Determining Output Elasticity

Output elasticity is the percentage change in output that results from a one-percent change in the quantity employed of all inputs. Output elasticity, therefore, is related to returns to scale. If the output elasticity is greater than one, increasing returns to scale exist. An output elasticity equal to one indicates constant returns to scale, while an output elasticity of less than one indicates decreasing returns to scale.

Consider the Cobb-Douglas production function

$$q = 16L^{0.5}K^{0.5}$$

If you increase the quantity employed of both labor and capital by one percent, then

$$q = 16(1.01L)^{0.5}(1.01K)^{0.5}$$

Rearranging the equation results in

$$q = 16(1.01)^{.05}L^{0.5}(1.01)^{.05}K^{0.5} = 16(1.01)^{.05}(1.01)^{.05}L^{0.5}K^{0.5}$$

so $\quad q = 16(1.01)L^{0.5}K^{0.5}$

Therefore, a one-percent increase in both labor and capital results in a one-percent increase in output, as represented by the (1.01) in the equation. This situation indicates constant returns to scale.

One special feature of Cobb-Douglas production functions is that they always have constant returns to scale. Just a final little piece of production magic.

Chapter 7

Innovation and Technological Change: The Future Is Now

Creative destructionism isn't a term coined by Hollywood to describe the many ways global disaster occurs in the movies — earthquakes, asteroids, tsunamis, aliens, and so on. Economist Joseph Schumpeter used *creative destructionism* to refer to the constant technological revolution that affects business. Technological progress creates new products and new production techniques that destroy or replace established products and production techniques. Because of creative destructionism, you can't buy record players for music or VCRs for movies. The future also looks bleak for paper maps, landline telephones, and CDs.

One of life's guarantees is that things constantly change. Successful business decisions must recognize the inevitability of change. Consider that in its 116 year history, the Dow Jones Industrials (currently consisting of 30 companies) has been revised 48 times, and only General Electric remains from the original group of companies. Since 2008, there have been three revisions, with five companies dropped, including Honeywell, General Motors, and Citigroup.

In this chapter, I examine critical elements of technological change. Embracing technological change ensures that your business doesn't go the way of the dinosaurs or International Harvester (removed from the Dow in 1991).

Changing Everything: What Happened to the Good Old Days?

Long-term success and profitability depend upon your ability to introduce new products or develop new production processes that use resources more efficiently resulting in lower costs. These changes encompass technological change, and failure to make or adapt to these changes leads to the destruction part of Schumpeter's creative destructionism.

As a manager, you can fondly refer to the good old days; however, you can't allow your business to cling to them.

Defining Technological Change

Technological change alters the firm's production function by either changing the relationship between inputs and output or introducing a new product and therefore a new production function. An improvement in technology enables your firm to produce a given quantity of output with fewer inputs shifting the production isoquant inward.

This improvement in technology could be a new production technique, or it could result from organizational changes and improvements in management.

Technological change that introduces new products are difficult to view as a shift in the production function. The new product simply has a new production function. When they were first introduced, there weren't any goods comparable to computers, mircrowave ovens, and cellular telephones. When introduced, these new goods had their own, new production function.

Technological change has three components — invention, innovation, and diffusion.

Invention refers to a new device, method, or process developed from study and experimentation. According to the United States Patent and Trademark Office, an invention is "any art or process (way of doing or making things), machine manufacture, design, or composition of matter, or any new and useful improvement thereof, or any variety of plant, which is or may be patentable under the patent laws of the United States."

These definitions of invention exclude an important point. For business success, inventions must be economically viable — in other words, profitable.

An *innovation* is an invention that's applied for the first time. Although substantial evaluation occurs during the research and development process, innovation still entails a substantial degree of uncertainty regarding its profitability. This uncertainty can be removed only with the actual implementation of the innovation. After the innovation has been applied, reevaluation occurs based upon additional information obtained.

The two types of innovations are product innovations and process innovations.

- ✔ **Product innovation** refers to the introduction of new and improved goods. For many, Wikipedia represents an improvement on printed encyclopedias. Both provide general information but Wikipedia makes it easier — and less costly — for many people to access that information.

- ✔ **Process innovation** refers to the introduction of new and improved production processes. Typically, process innovations enable you to manufacture a product more cheaply. Thus, process innovations focus on how things are done. An example of a process innovation is Henry Ford's introduction of the assembly line in automobile production.

Diffusion examines the speed at which an innovation is adopted. Diffusion seeks to explain how, why, and at what rate innovations are adopted. As a result, diffusion introduces a time element in your decision-making.

Working hard: Measuring labor productivity

Determining the impact technological change has on your firm is important. Therefore, measuring technological change's impact is necessary. Two such measures, labor productivity and total factor productivity, are based upon a comparison between the quantity of output produced and the amount of input employed.

Technological change isn't the only thing that changes labor and total factor productivity. For example, as described in Chapter 6, changes in input prices change the relative amounts of inputs you employ to minimize production costs. These changes in input quantities due to new input prices also change labor and total factor productivity.

Labor productivity measures output per unit of input or, typically, output per labor-hour. An increase in labor productivity is frequently associated with an improvement in technology.

Again, be careful when measuring technological change by using labor productivity, because technological change isn't the only thing that influences labor productivity. For example, labor productivity is also affected by education, experience, motivation, and attitude of the worker.

Working harder: Calculating total factor productivity

An alternative measure of productivity is total factor productivity. *Total factor productivity* measures changes in output relative to changes in the quantity employed of all inputs. Use the following formula to calculate total factor productivity, represented by the symbol α:

$$\alpha = \frac{q}{p_1 I_1 + p_2 I_2 + p_3 I_3 + \ldots + p_n I_n}$$

where q represents the firm's quantity of output, I_1 through I_n represent the quantity employed of inputs 1 through n, and p_1 through p_n represent the prices of inputs 1 through n.

Suppose your firm produces 100,000 units of output. In order to produce that output, the firm uses 1,200 hours of labor, 600 machine-hours of capital, and 20,000 kilowatt-hours of electricity. If input prices are $10 per hour for labor, $5 per machine-hour for capital, and $0.04 per kilowatt-hour for electricity, you can use the following steps to calculate your firm's total factor productivity:

1. **Substitute the quantity of output, 100,000, for *q*.**

2. **For each input, insert the input price for *p* and the input quantity for *I* in the bottom of the equation.**

    In the example, p_1 is $10 and I_1 is 1,200; p_2 is $5 and I_2 is 600; and p_3 is $0.04 and I_3 is 20,000.

3. **Calculate the value in the bottom of the equation.**

4. **Divide the top of the equation by the bottom of the equation.**

    So, total factor productivity equals

$$\alpha = \frac{100,000}{10 \times 1,200 + 5 \times 600 + 0.04 \times 20,000} = \frac{100,000}{15,800} = 6.329$$

If prices are held constant over time, changes in total factor productivity represent changes in the firm's efficiency. Increases in total factor productivity represent improvements in a firm's efficiency that result from technological change.

Suppose that five years ago, your firm from the previous example produced 80,000 units of output by using 1,600 hours of labor, 500 machine-hours of capital, and 18,000 kilowatt-hours of electricity. If you hold input prices constant or the same as in the last example at $10 per hour for labor, $5 per machine-hour for capital, and $0.04 per kilowatt-hour for electricity, any change in the total factor productivity value results from changing input quantities. Using the same steps to calculate the firm's total factor productivity:

1. **Substitute the quantity of output, 80,000, for q.**

2. **For each input, insert the constant input price for p multiplied by the input quantity for I in the bottom of the equation.**

   So, p_1 is $10 and I_1 is 1,600; p_2 is $5 and I_2 is 500; and p_3 is $0.04 and I_3 is 18,000.

3. **Calculate the value in the bottom of the equation.**

4. **Divide the top of the equation by the bottom of the equation.**

   So, total factor productivity equals

   $$\alpha = \frac{80,000}{10 \times 1,600 + 5 \times 500 + 0.04 \times 18,000} = \frac{80,000}{19,220} = 4.162$$

Based on the two examples, total factor productivity in the last year is 152.1 percent (6.329/4.162) of the first year's value. Alternatively, total factor productivity increased 52.1 percent over the five-year period.

Spending on Research and Development

A business's research efforts are ultimately directed at making an invention, regardless of its source, into an economic success. However, the uncertain outcomes of research and development make it one of the riskier areas of corporate decision-making.

Research and development encompass a variety of efforts:

- **Basic research** refers to efforts that lead to the creation of new knowledge or inventions.

- **Applied research** covers efforts directed toward a practical payoff.

- **Development** puts research findings into practice.

The likelihood of success for research and development projects is a function of overcoming three major hurdles. First, the project must be a technical success. After it's a technical success, the research and development project must be a commercial success. Finally, the project must be an economic success; that is, it must be profitable for the firm.

In order to minimize wasted research and development resources, it's critical that an ongoing evaluation of the project's potential economic success be made. This economic success is dependent upon marketing realities as well as technical considerations. Therefore, for the firm's research and development projects to be consistently successful, you must incorporate marketing realities early in the project's conception and development.

Developing parallel efforts: Where two is less than one

Typically a new product or new production technique isn't successful. Because of the high risk and likelihood of failure, you can often reduce research and development costs by simultaneously working on several similar or parallel ideas. Ongoing evaluation of costs and potential benefits of the parallel efforts enables you to determine at what point you should abandon an effort in order to reduce research and development costs.

Your pharmaceutical company is developing two different drugs for the same medical condition. Each drug's development cost is influenced by a number of factors, such as potential side effects and other drug interactions. Because development costs are unknown, you develop best-case and worst-case scenarios that you assume are the same for both drugs. Your best-case scenario for either drug is that the development cost equals $20 million. Your worst-case scenario for either drug is that the development cost equals $75 million. Because you're unsure what the actual development cost will be for each drug, as a pessimist you assume a 30-percent chance for the best-case scenario and a 70-percent chance for the worst-case scenario. (Alternatively, you could be an optimist and use a higher probability for the best-case scenario, or you could base your probability on past experience.)

The *expected development cost,* EDC, for each drug equals the cost of a scenario, C_{bc} for the best-case scenario and C_{wc} for the worst-case scenario, multiplied by the probability of that scenario occurring, P_{bc} and P_{wc}, or

$$EDC = \left(C_{bc} \times P_{bc} \right) + \left(C_{wc} \times P_{wc} \right)$$

You use the following steps to calculate the expected development cost for a drug:

1. **First, substitute the values for C_{bc}, P_{bc}, C_{wc}, and P_{wc}.**
2. **For each scenario, multiply the cost by the probability.**

   For the best-case scenario, multiply $20 million by 0.3, and for the worst-case scenario, multiply $75 million by 0.7.

3. Add the resulting values for each scenario.

$$\text{EDC} = (\$20 \text{ million} \times 0.3) + (\$75 \text{ million} \times 0.7)$$
$$= \$6 \text{ million} + \$52.5 \text{ million} = \$58.5 \text{ million}$$

The expected development cost equals \$58.5 million.

Starting your research by developing both drugs at the same time can lower your expected development cost because partway through the process, you can decide to abandon one drug because its development costs are too high. If both drugs are developed in parallel, you have a 49-percent chance (0.7×0.7) that the development cost of each drug equals \$75 million. This is the probability of the worst-case scenario occurring for both drugs. You have a 9-percent chance (0.3×0.3) chance that the development cost of each drug equals \$20 million. This is your best-case scenario occurring for both drugs. Finally, you have a 42-percent chance that one of the two drugs has the best case scenario — a \$20 million development cost. This is the situation where one drug's development represents the best-case scenario and the other drug's development represents the worst-case scenario ($0.3 \times 0.7 + 0.7 \times 0.3$).

Because you ultimately complete the development of only one drug — remember, both drugs are for the same condition — you'll choose the cheapest drug to develop. Thus, you have a 51-percent chance — the 9-percent chance of best-case for both drugs, plus the 42-percent chance of best-case for one of the two drugs — that the development cost equals \$20 million. Note how 51 percent is better than the 30 percent chance of the best-case scenario's \$20 million development cost if you develop only one drug.

Now comes a critical step. If the actual development cost of each drug can be determined with certainty after $C have been spent, and only the drug with the lowest development cost is developed after that point, the expected development cost equals

$$\text{EDC} = (C_{bc} \times P_{bc}) + (C_{wc} \times P_{wc}) + C$$

In the example, you know that you can determine the actual development cost for each drug after spending \$8 million. (This value varies from situation to situation and must be determined in advance, usually by past experience.) Thus, your expected development cost of parallel efforts equals

$$\text{EDC} = (\$20 \text{ million} \times 0.51) + (\$75 \text{ million} \times 0.49) + \$8 \text{ million}$$
$$= \$10.2 \text{ million} + \$36.75 \text{ million} + \$8 \text{ million} = \$54.95 \text{ million}$$

In this situation, your parallel efforts have lowered the expected development cost by \$3.55 million from the initial \$58.5 million to \$54.95 million.

Time is money

An important factor influencing research and development costs is how much time you take for the project's completion. A shorter time frame tends to increase research and development cost because you require more resources and false starts resulting in wasted effort are more likely. Thus, an inverse relationship exists between time and research and development costs. The *time-cost trade-off function* describes this relationship between time and development cost.

In addition to the time-cost trade-off in development cost, a project's potential net revenue is also influenced by time. Because other firms also innovate, there is the possibility that their innovation makes your research and development project obsolete. Therefore, a development project of short duration is likely to have higher net revenue.

Based upon these two elements, you need to determine the optimal time frame for the project's completion. The optimal time maximizes profit — the difference between net revenue and the time-cost trade-off function.

I describe the relationship between development cost, net revenue, and time in Figure 7-1. You want to choose a time span (t) for the project that maximizes profit — the difference between net revenue (R_n) and development cost (C). The optimal time span in Figure 7-1 is represented by t_0 as it maximizes the difference between net revenue (R_n) and development cost (C). These is shown by the large gap or vertical difference between these two lines.

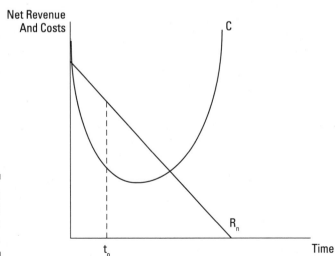

Figure 7-1:
Optimal
project time
span.

The expected net revenue, R_n, from your research and development project equals

$$R_n = 128 - 8t$$

where R_n represents net revenue in millions of dollars and t is time measured in years.

Your time-cost trade-off function is

$$C = 140 - 16t + t^2$$

where C is development cost in millions of dollars and t is again time.

In order to determine the optimal time frame for the project's completion, take the following steps:

1. **Note that the expected profit, π, from the project equals net revenue minus the development cost represented by the time-cost trade-off function.**

   Thus,

   $$\pi = R_n - C = 128 - 8t - \left(140 - 16t + t^2\right) = -12 + 8t - t^2$$

2. **In order to maximize profit, take the derivative of profit, π, with respect to time, t.**

   This derivative equals

   $$\frac{d\pi}{dt} = 8 - 2t$$

3. **Set the derivative equal to zero and solve for t.**

   $$\frac{d\pi}{dt} = 8 - 2t = 0 \quad \text{or} \quad 8 = 2t \quad \text{or} \quad t = 4$$

   Thus, the project's optimal time frame is four years. Substituting t equals 4 into the expected profit equation indicates that the expected profit is $4 million.

   $$\pi = -12 + 8t - t^2 = -12 + 8(4) - (4)^2 = -12 + 32 - 16 = 4$$

Evaluating projects

Ongoing review of research and development projects requires that you have criteria for project selection. These criteria vary from firm to firm and situation to situation; however, an evaluation process must include a precise specification of assumptions.

Keep two items in mind when evaluating research and development projects. First, research and development expenditures essentially represent a method of obtaining information. Therefore, even "unsuccessful" projects may provide valuable information for the firm. Second, because project managers have a self-interest in the project's continuation, their forecasts and assumptions may be overly optimistic.

Spreading Diffusion

The diffusion of new technology introduces a crucial time element into managerial decision-making. You may be interested in how an innovation is going to affect your firm's production costs over time. Or you may be interested in determining how diffusion occurs within your firm's industry. Learning curve and diffusion models examine the relationship between time and technological change and provide you perspective on how technological change evolves.

Getting better with the learning-by-doing concept

Adopting an innovation doesn't necessarily result in an immediate reduction in production costs. Often on-the-job experience is necessary before you can take full advantage of the innovation. *Learning-by-doing* results in decreasing production cost per unit as the cumulative output produced increases, and firms use the innovation more efficiently. The relationship between cumulative output and production cost per unit is described by a *learning curve*.

It's easy to mistakenly believe the new innovation's adoption immediately leads to impressive gains in productivity and output. The day before the innovation, workers are using the old, inferior production method. The next day, the new production method leads to dramatic increases in productivity and lower production costs. But many productivity gains are only realized after an extended period of time. With the passage of time, further improvements in production techniques occur as greater experience is gained. This accumulated learning leads to additional refinements in both production and organization that support additional productivity gains that further reduce production costs.

Given the learning curve, you may want to accept short-term losses in order to gain experience in producing a product. Setting a lower price encourages greater demand for the firm's product, resulting in increased production. The learning-by-doing associated with the increased production results in lower per-unit cost on subsequent units produced, ultimately resulting in greater profits. By accepting an initial loss through low prices and high production, you can take advantage of the learning curve in a shorter period of time, ultimately resulting in greater profits overall.

Watching developments by modeling diffusion

The speed with which an innovation is adopted by firms in an industry is influenced by a number of factors. The most profitable innovations are adopted first. In addition, innovations requiring a small investment are typically adopted more readily than innovations requiring a substantial investment. Also, innovations that have already been adopted by a large number of firms are more likely to be adopted by other firms due to increased information and competition.

The relationship between diffusion, as measured by the percent of firms using an innovation, and time is often described by an S-shaped diffusion curve. Edwin Mansfield's logistic curve often is used to describe this diffusion process. The formula for Mansfield's logistic curve is

$$P(t) = \frac{1}{1 + e^{-(\alpha + \beta t)}}$$

where $P(t)$ represents the percentage of firms using the innovation at time t. The symbol e (Euler's number) approximates to 2.718. The parameters α and β describe the diffusion process, and they vary among innovations. The function described by the logistic curve is illustrated in Figure 7-2.

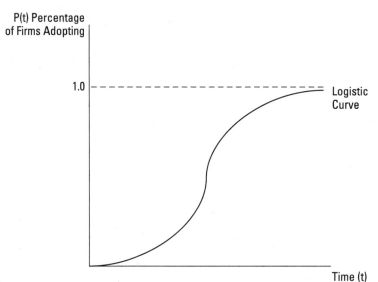

P(t) Percentage
of Firms Adopting

1.0 — — — — — — — — — — — — — — — — —   Logistic
                                          Curve

Time (t)

Figure 7-2:
Diffusion
(logistic)
curve.

After you obtain data on the adoption of an innovation for previous years, you can estimate the logistic curve. After you estimate the curve, use it to predict the future diffusion path of the innovation. Firms have found that this technique has generated useful forecasts for the diffusion of a variety of innovations.

Mansfield's logistic curve

In his early research on diffusion using the logistic curve, Edwin Mansfield examined several innovations, including continuous mining machines and railroad locomotives. Based upon this research, Mansfield concluded that several factors lead some firms to adopt innovations more quickly than other firms. For example, innovations tend to be adopted more rapidly by larger firms than smaller firms. However, Mansfield also concluded that technical leadership and a firm's financial health aren't important factors influencing how they adopt innovations. In other words, the same firms don't consistently lead in the adoption of innovations. Finally, and not surprisingly, firms that find an innovation is more profitable tend to adopt it more quickly.

Chapter 8

Production Costs: Where Less Is More

*P*roduction requires costs, and obviously you want to keep those costs as low as possible. Lower costs mean more profit, and profit is ultimately your goal. Before examining the various types of costs, recognize every cost associated with production. Costs that are often ignored include the cost of the business owner's time and the money the owner has invested in the business.

In addition, recognize that not all costs are the same. Some costs can be changed very quickly, while other costs can't be changed for a long time. Some costs factor into business decision-making, while other costs are ignored. Thus, you need a clear understanding of costs before you're able to maximize profit.

Because your ultimate goal is to produce the profit-maximizing quantity of output, in this chapter I focus on the relationship between production costs and the quantity of output produced. The relationship between the production costs and output assumes that you're using the cost-minimizing combination of inputs to produce any particular level of output. (See Chapter 6 for an overview of inputs and cost minimization.) Furthermore, the relationship between costs and output includes the opportunity costs of all inputs used in the production process.

Determining the Cost of Everything: Opportunity Costs

Everything!? To produce goods, you must decide how to use scarce resources. Using those resources for one thing means they can't be used for something else. Economists define production costs in terms of what's forgone or given-up. Therefore, the cost of using resources to produce one good is based upon the value of the next best alternative for those resources. This is the concept of *opportunity cost*.

The importance of opportunity costs is emphasized in the distinction between explicit and implicit costs:

- **Explicit costs** represent the costs of using resources contributed by non-owners of the firm. Explicit costs include the wages and salaries paid to workers, the interest paid on debt, and payments made to suppliers. Typically, these costs require a direct cash expenditure.

- **Implicit costs** are the opportunity costs of resources contributed by the firm's owners. Implicit costs include the value of your time, the opportunity cost of the financial resources you contribute to the firm, and depreciation on the firm's machinery, equipment, and factories. Often no immediate direct cash outlay is associated with the implicit costs.

Accountants and business owners normally don't include implicit costs. When determining whether or not your business is profitable, you need to include the opportunity costs of the time you contributed. You also must include the opportunity costs of the money you invested. At the very least, you could have invested that money and earned interest. Be very careful that you include every cost associated with production, regardless of whether or not it involves an immediate cash outlay.

Purchasing Inputs

Because your goal is profit, inputs — and the goods produced with those inputs — are simply a means to your goal. But just like you've heard about your health — you are what you eat — what you produce and its cost are determined by the inputs you use. The product you produce reflects the inputs you choose.

Changing inputs in response to changing market conditions is influenced by the timeframe you have to adjust. An increased demand for your product may lead you to immediately hire additional workers. Over a longer period of time, you may decide to expand by building a new facility or renovating an existing facility to produce more. When examining production costs, recognize that some inputs aren't easily changed due to the timeframe available.

Inputs that are changed easily are called *variable inputs,* while inputs that are more difficult to change — that is they can be changed only over a long period of time — are called *fixed inputs.*

Recognizing Different Short-Run Production Costs

The short run involves a period of time during which some inputs can be changed, while other inputs are fixed. A *fixed input* is an input whose quantity can't be readily changed in response to changes in market conditions. In the short run, fixed inputs can't be changed, and thus the cost of these inputs becomes a fixed cost or a constant. A factory and many types of machinery are examples of fixed inputs.

A *variable input* can be readily changed in response to changes in market conditions. Thus, variable inputs can be changed in the short run. Changing variable inputs leads to changes in variable costs in the short run. Labor is typically a variable input.

Total cost

Total cost is the production cost that results from the use of all inputs — fixed and variable — in the production process. Therefore, total cost includes implicit, as well as explicit, costs.

A *total cost function* illustrates the relationship between total cost and the quantity of output produced or

$$TC = f(q)$$

where *TC* represents total cost and *q* represents the quantity of output produced or total product.

A specific functional form specifies the relationship between total cost and the quantity of output

$$TC = 5,600 + 27q - 6q^2 + 0.5q^3$$

Given this functional form, if the quantity of output produced equals 20, total cost in dollars equals

$$TC = 5,600 + 27(20) - 6(20)^2 + 0.5(20)^3$$
$$= 5,600 + 27(20) - 6(400) + 0.5(8,000) = 7,740$$

or $7,740.

In the short run, total cost is divided into two components — total variable cost and total fixed cost.

Fixed costs

Total fixed cost is the component of total cost that results from the use of fixed inputs in the short run. Because the quantity employed of the fixed inputs can't be changed in the short run, total fixed cost is constant.

Even if your firm decides to shut down in the short run, it still incurs the fixed cost. Thus, if you shut down, in the short run your losses equal your total fixed cost. An example is signing a 12-month lease to rent a location for a restaurant. If you decide to close down after seven months, you still have to make monthly lease payments for another five months. These lease payments are a fixed cost.

Given the total cost function

$$TC = 5,600 + 27q - 6q^2 + 0.5q^3$$

The total fixed cost corresponds to the equation's constant or $5,600.

Variable costs

Total variable cost is the component of total cost associated with the use of variable inputs in the short run. Because the quantity of variable inputs employed in the short run can be changed, total variable cost can also change. Therefore, total variable cost equals zero if there are no variable inputs employed and increases as the quantity of inputs employed increases.

Changing the quantity of variable inputs used changes the quantity of output produced. Thus, any component of the total cost function that contains q is part of the total variable cost function.

If the total cost function is

$$TC = 5,600 + 27q - 6q^2 + 0.5q^3$$

The total variable cost equation is

$$TVC = 27q - 6q^2 + 0.5q^3$$

The wages paid to labor are typically part of your total variable cost. If your firm wants to increase production, you simply hire more workers, incurring the variable cost of the additional wages. Similarly, if you want to cut back production, you lay off workers, with an associated reduction in wages and total variable cost.

Figure 8-1 illustrates the graphical relationships for total cost, total fixed cost, and total variable cost. As indicated in Figure 8-1, at output q_a the total cost is C_a and the total fixed cost is TFC_a. At the output level q_b, total fixed cost is the exact same amount as it was at q_a, TFC_a.

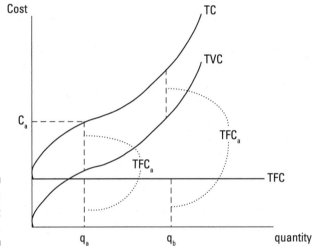

Figure 8-1:
Total cost
curves.

Marginal cost

Marginal cost is the change in total cost that occurs when one additional unit of output is produced.

Marginal cost is often determined by using calculus. To find marginal cost, you simply take the derivative of total cost with respect to the quantity of output produced. For the total cost equation

$$TC = 5{,}600 + 27q - 6q^2 + 0.5q^3$$

marginal cost equals

$$MC = \frac{dTC}{dq} = 27 - 12q + 1.5q^2$$

> # PSI powers down
>
> Public Service Company of Indiana started construction of the Marble Hill nuclear power plant near Hanover, Indiana, in 1977. Construction was stopped on three separate occasions during the summer of 1979 to investigate and correct the growing number of reports of poor construction. After spending $2.5 billion in construction costs, PSI halted construction of the power plant in 1984. PSI decided to abandon Marble Hill because it estimated that another $4 billion was required to complete the project. PSI's decision wasn't based upon what it had already spent — the $2.5 billion was a sunk cost. Instead, PSI made its decision based upon the $4 billion that was still required to complete the project.

It Is What It Is: Ignoring Sunk Costs

Don't live in the past. As a decision-maker you need to focus on what can be changed and what can't be changed. Sunk costs are costs that have already been incurred and can't be recovered or changed. Because nothing can be done to change sunk costs, they don't affect decision-making. If you can't change it, you must ignore it.

Determining Average Costs

Frequently you want to know the cost per unit associated with producing a good, because you can use this information to establish your product's price and determine your profit per unit. If you want to know cost per unit, average cost is what you need to know.

Average total cost

Average total cost (ATC) is the total cost per unit of output. It's determined by dividing the total cost equation by the quantity of output. Using the total cost equation

$$TC = 5,600 + 27q - 6q^2 + 0.5q^3$$

average total cost equals

$$ATC = \frac{TC}{q} = \frac{5,600 + 27q - 6q^2 + 0.5q^3}{q} = \frac{5,600}{q} + 27 - 6q + 0.5q^2$$

where q is the quantity of output produced.

Marginal cost always intersects the minimum point on the average total cost curve. Thus, average total cost initially decreases, and then begins to increase, resulting in a U-shaped curve.

Average total cost has two components — average fixed cost and average variable cost. As an equation,

$$ATC = AFC + AVC$$

Average fixed cost

Average fixed cost (AFC) is fixed cost per unit of output and is determined by dividing total fixed cost by the quantity of output. In the total cost equation

$$TC = 5,600 + 27q - 6q^2 + 0.5q^3$$

total fixed cost is $5,600, so averaged fixed cost is

$$AFC = \frac{TFC}{q} = \frac{5,600}{q}$$

Because the numerator of average fixed cost is a constant, while the denominator is the quantity of output produced, average fixed cost always decreases as the quantity of output produced increases.

Average variable cost

Average variable cost (AVC) represents variable cost per unit of output and equals total variable cost divided by the quantity of output. Given total variable cost equals

$$TVC = 27q - 6q^2 + 0.5q^3$$

average variable cost equals

$$AVC = \frac{TVC}{q} = \frac{27q - 6q^2 + 0.5q^3}{q} = 27 - 6q + 0.5q^2$$

Typically, average variable cost initially decreases, and then begins to increase, resulting in a U-shaped curve. Marginal cost intersects the minimum point on the average variable cost curve.

Figure 8-2 illustrates the average total cost, average fixed cost, average variable cost, and marginal cost curves. Note that the average fixed cost curve is always decreasing and also note that the difference between average total cost and average variable cost is average fixed cost — so AFC_b at q_b is less than AFC_a at q_a. Therefore, as you produce more output, average variable cost and average total cost get closer to one another. Finally, marginal cost intersects the minimum points on the average variable and average total cost curves.

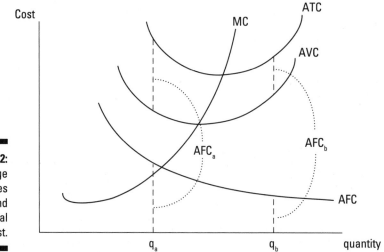

Figure 8-2:
Average cost curves and marginal cost.

Deriving Cost Concepts with Calculus (Ignore if You Want)

Equations provide an excellent means of determining the exact cost associated with a given quantity of output. In addition, taking the derivative of an equation provides an opportunity to easily determine the minimum levels of various costs, including marginal cost, average variable cost, and average total cost.

Linking short-run cost functions to production isoquants

Chapter 6 presents production theory. Production costs are directly derived from production theory. In production theory, you determine the cost-minimizing input combination for a specific quantity of output. If you determine the cost-minimizing input combination for every output level, you have the points comprising the total cost function. Thus, the total cost function is derived from production theory.

Figure 8-3 illustrates a series of production isoquants and isocost curves. Because a production isoquant represents a fixed quantity of output, the cost of producing that quantity of output is minimized at the point where the isocost curve is tangent to the isoquant. For the production isoquant q_a, production cost is minimized by employing K_a of capital and L_a of labor. (See Chapter 6 for a more detailed explanation.) This results in the cost level C_a. So, one point on your total cost curve corresponds to output q_a and total cost C_a. (See Figure 8-1.) Other points on your total cost curve are derived through the remaining production isoquants and isocost curve combinations.

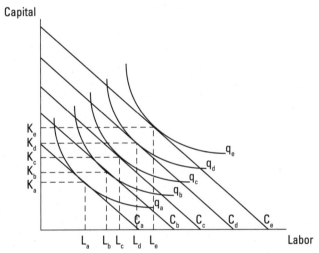

Figure 8-3:
Production
isoquants
and total
cost.

Your firm's production isoquant is

$$q = 0.25K^{0.5}N^{0.25}L^{0.5}$$

where q is the quantity of output produced, K is the quantity of capital employed in machine-hours, N is the quantity of land employed in acres, and L is the quantity of labor employed in hours. Capital and land are both fixed inputs. The quantity of capital is fixed at 400 machine-hours, and the quantity of land is fixed at 625 acres. Your input prices are $50 per machine-hour of capital, $40 per acre of land, and $25 per hour for labor.

To convert the production isoquant into a total cost equation, take the following steps:

1. **Using the given input prices, write the equation for total cost.**

$$TC = (p_K \times K) + (p_N \times N) + (p_L \times L) = 50K + 40N + 25L$$

2. **Substitute 400 for K and 625 for N in the equation for total cost.**

Because capital and land are fixed, they're your fixed inputs, and they determine your fixed costs.

$$TC = 50K + 40N + 25L = 50(400) + 40(625) + 25L = 45,000 + 25L$$

3. **Substitute 400 for K and 625 for N in the production isoquant.**

Total cost needs to be expressed as a function of total product, q, instead of labor, L. You use the production isoquant to make this substitution.

$$q = 0.25K^{0.5}N^{0.25}L^{0.5} = 0.25(400)^{0.5}(625)^{0.25} L^{0.5}$$
$$= 0.25(20)(5)L^{0.5} = 25L^{0.5} \quad \text{or} \quad q = 25L^{0.5}$$

4. **Rearranging the equation to solve for L gives you**

$$25L^{0.5} = q \quad \text{or} \quad L^{0.5} = \frac{q}{25}$$

5. **Squaring both sides of the equation leaves you with**

$$L = \left(\frac{q}{25}\right)^2 = \frac{q^2}{(25)^2} = \frac{q^2}{625} = 0.0016q^2$$

6. **Substitute the equation in Step 5 for L in the total cost function.**

$$TC = 45,000 + 25L = 45,000 + 25(0.0016q^2) = 45,000 + 0.04q^2$$

By using your production isoquant, you generate an equation for total cost that's expressed as a function of the quantity of output produced.

Hoping for less by minimizing per-unit costs

You can also use calculus to determine various minimum costs, such as the minimum average total cost, minimum average variable cost, and minimum marginal cost. To determine each of these minimums, you simply take the derivative of the appropriate function, set it equal to zero, and determine the quantity of output that minimizes that concept.

As I indicate in the earlier sections, "Marginal cost" and "Determining Average Costs," the total cost function

$$TC = 5,600 + 27q - 6q^2 + 0.5q^3$$

results in the following functions for marginal cost (*MC*), average variable cost (*AVC*), and average total cost (*ATC*)

$$MC = 27 - 12q + 1.5q^2$$

$$AVC = 27 - 6q + 0.5q^2$$

$$ATC = \frac{5,600}{q} + 27 - 6q + 0.5q^2$$

To minimize each of these costs, you simply take the derivative of the function and set it equal to zero.

For marginal cost, follow these steps:

1. **Take the derivative of marginal cost with respect to quantity.**

   $$\frac{dMC}{dq} = -12 + 3q$$

2. **Set the derivative equal to zero and solve for *q*.**

   $$-12 + 3q = 0$$

   The quantity of output that minimizes marginal cost is 4. This is also the quantity of output at which diminishing returns begin.

Use a similar process to minimize average variable cost:

1. **Take the derivative of average variable cost with respect to quantity.**

   $$\frac{dAVC}{dq} = -6 + q$$

2. **Set the derivative equal to zero and solve for *q*.**

   $$-6 + q = 0$$

   Average variable cost is minimized at 6 units of output.

Finally, to minimize average total cost, follow these steps:

1. **Take the derivative of average total cost with respect to quantity.**

Remember, the term $5,600/q$ can also be written as $5,600q^{-1}$, so its derivative is $-5,600q^{-2}$ or $-5,600/q^2$.

$$\frac{dATC}{dq} = -\frac{5,600}{q^2} - 6 + q$$

2. **Set the derivative equal to zero.**

$$-\frac{5,600}{q^2} - 6 + q = 0$$

3. **Multiply both sides of the equation by q^2.**

$$-5,600 - 6q^2 + q^3 = 0$$

4. **Solve for q.**

This step is a little tricky with q raised to the third power, but your calculator or computer should be able to handle it. Average total cost is minimized at 20 units of output.

Marginal cost always equals the minimum values of average variable cost and average total cost.

Identifying Long-Run Production Costs

In the long run, none of your inputs are fixed. You can choose any input combination to produce a given quantity of output. This decision ultimately leads to the selection of some inputs that become fixed after their initial selection. For example, when considering whether or not to produce the Saturn, General Motors could have chosen a variety of configurations for the factory. Each configuration General Motors evaluated had its own short-run average-total-cost curve. After a configuration was chosen, it became a fixed input, and General Motors subsequently operated on the short-run average-total-cost curve associated with that configuration. Therefore, General Motors' long-run decision amounted to choosing the best possible short-run average-total-cost curve from a variety of possibilities.

Putting costs in the envelope curve

Because there are no fixed inputs in the long run, the long-run total cost function doesn't have a constant. Therefore, if you decide to produce zero units of output in the long run, your total cost equals zero.

The *long-run average-total-cost curve* is derived by dividing the long-run total-cost function by the quantity of output. Another way to view long-run average total cost is to keep in mind that a short-run average-total-cost curve is associated with a given level of fixed inputs. If you choose a different level of fixed inputs, you get a different short-run average-total-cost curve. The long-run average-total-cost curve reflects the set of fixed inputs that yields the lowest possible cost of producing each output level. Therefore, the long-run average-total-cost curve links the short-run average-total-cost curves associated with the minimum cost of producing any output level. Or, the long-run average-total-cost curve is the envelope that holds all the short-run possibilities.

Figure 8-4 illustrates a long-run average-total-cost curve. The lowest per-unit cost associated with producing the output level q_b is ATC_b. This cost results when the fixed inputs associated with the short-run average-total-cost curve $SRATC_b$ are chosen. Similarly, the fixed inputs associated with $SRATC_a$ result in the production of q_a with the lowest per-unit cost ATC_a, and the fixed inputs associated with $SRATC_c$ result in the production of q_c with the lowest per-unit cost ATC_c.

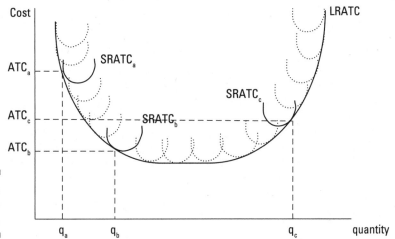

Figure 8-4:
The enve-
lope curve.

Going as far as you can with economies of scale

Economies of scale exist when long-run average total cost decreases as the quantity of output produced increases. Economies of scale result from many different factors, including increasing returns to scale, quantity discounts on input prices, and the ability to spread management and overhead costs over a larger quantity of output.

In Figure 8-5, economies of scale are associated with the downward-sloping portion of the long-run average-total-cost curve.

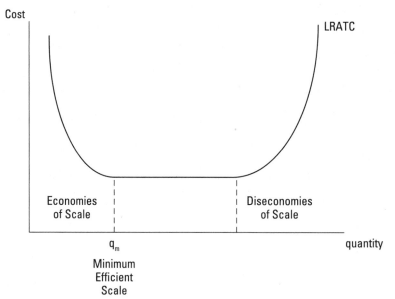

Figure 8-5:
Economies
and
diseconomies
of scale.

Avoiding diseconomies of scale: An output level too far

Diseconomies of scale occur when long-run average total cost increases as the quantity of output produced increases. Diseconomies of scale may result from decreasing returns to scale or managerial limitations resulting from the firm's large size. Larger firms become increasingly complex, making it more difficult to coordinate necessary activities.

In Figure 8-5, diseconomies of scale correspond to the upward-sloping segment of the long-run average-total-cost curve.

Diseconomies of scale indicate that your cost per unit increases as you produce more output. This isn't just higher per-unit cost for the additional units — it's higher cost for *all* units.

Identifying the minimum efficient scale

The *minimum efficient scale* is the output level at which economies of scale cease. Therefore, it's the smallest output quantity that results in minimum cost per unit. Any production scale below this minimum efficient scale is at a disadvantage relative to other scales, because its per-unit production costs are higher than this.

Comparing economies of scale and returns to scale

Chapter 6 defines returns to scale, and the earlier section "Going as far as you can with economies of scale" defines economies of scale. These terms are very closely related; however, they aren't interchangeable. Returns to scale describe the relationship between the quantity of inputs employed and the quantity of output produced given the firm's production function. On the other hand, economies of scale describe the relationship between the quantity of output produced and production costs. Production costs are determined not only by the firm's production function, but also by input prices. Therefore, it's possible for a firm to be simultaneously experiencing decreasing returns to scale and economies of scale. This situation could occur if the firm receives price discounts for using larger amounts of the inputs that offset the decreasing returns to scale.

In Figure 8-5, the minimum efficient scale occurs at the output level q_m.

Estimates of long-run average total cost for various industries typically indicate the presence of economies of scale at small output levels — long-run average total cost is decreasing for these output levels. After economies of scale are exhausted, however, research has generally indicated that long-run average total cost becomes constant, implying that the long-run average-total-cost curve is horizontal. Therefore, diseconomies of scale, or increasing long-run average total cost, is rarely observed in actual commodity production.

Recognizing that Two Can Be Less Than One with Economies of Scope

Economies of scope exist when the cost of producing two or more goods together is less than the cost of producing each good separately. Economies of scope can result if two or more products share the same production facilities. For example, General Motors produces different car models that use the same engines and transmissions. Economies of scope can also arise through marketing, such as Proctor and Gamble having a large number of home and beauty products that they market in similar ways. Thus, marketing strategies, product branding, and product design costs are spread over a large number of products. Finally, economies of scope arise from reduced distribution cost.

Economies of scope are determined with the following formula

$$S = \frac{C(q_a) + C(q_b) - C(q_a + q_b)}{C(q_a + q_b)}$$

In the formula, $C(q_a)$ is the cost of producing the quantity q_a of good a separately, and $C(q_b)$ is the cost of producing the quantity q_b of good b separately. The term $C(q_a + q_b)$ is the cost of producing the same quantities of good a and good b together. Economies of scope, S, measures the percentage cost saving that occurs when the goods a and b are produced together. Thus, S is greater than zero when economies of scope exist, and the larger the positive value for S, the greater the economies of scope.

Your firm produces both face cream and hand lotion. The cost of separately producing 2,000,000 jars of face cream is $0.75 each or $1.5 million. If 4,000,000 bottles of hand lotion are produced separately, the cost is $0.60 each or $2.4 million. If 2,000,000 jars of face cream and 4,000,000 bottles of hand lotion are produced together, the total cost is $3 million.

To determine the economies of scope, you take the following steps.

1. **In the top of the equation, substitute $1.5 million for $C(q_a)$, $2.4 million for $C(q_b)$, and $3 million for $C(q_a + q_b)$.**

   Remember that $C(q_a)$ is the cost of producing one product, face cream, separately; $C(q_b)$ is the cost of producing the second product, hand lotion, separately; and $C(q_a + q_b)$ is the cost of producing the two products together.

2. **In the bottom of the equation, substitute $3 million for $C(q_a + q_b)$.**

3. **Calculate the value in the top of the equation.**

   $$S = C(q_a) + C(q_b) - C(q_a + q_b) = 1.5 + 2.4 - 3 = 0.9$$

4. **Divide the top of the equation by the bottom of the equation and your economies of scope, S, equals 0.3 or 30%.**

   Thus the cost of producing face cream and hand lotion together is 30% less than the cost of producing them separately.

   $$S = \frac{1.5 + 2.4 - 3}{3} = \frac{0.9}{3} = 0.3$$

Part III

Recognizing Rivals: Market Structures and the Decision-Making Environment

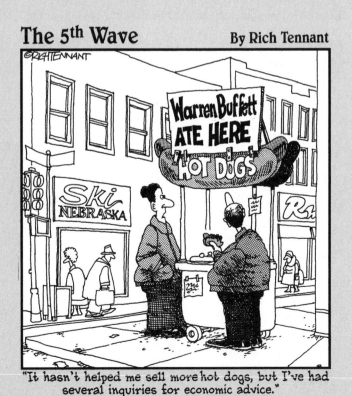

"It hasn't helped me sell more hot dogs, but I've had several inquiries for economic advice."

In this part . . .

The most important factor business owners control is the ability to set their product's price. The price business owners set determines the quantity of the product they sell. However, the ability to set price is not unconstrained; business owners have to consider consumer demand for their product and the behavior of rival firms providing the same or a similar product. In this part, I present theories for determining price based upon the number of rivals — degree of competition — a firm has. Rivals necessitate strategic decision-making, so I cover game theory as well as additional special situations for price determination.

Chapter 9

Limited Decision-Making in Perfect Competition

*B*aseball player Yogi Berra once said, "If the world was perfect, it wouldn't be." That quote actually fits the economist's idea of perfect competition — please forgive me — perfectly.

When economists use the term *perfect competition,* they don't refer to competition at all. Indeed, perfect competition is the least competitive business environment there is. In perfect competition, you can't set your product's price and you have no incentive to advertise or innovate. You don't compete with other firms. (However, you still have an incentive to minimize your production costs.) See, Yogi Berra is a lot smarter than you think — maybe he would have been an even better economist than he was a baseball player.

What perfect competition really refers to is a special outcome. As the owner of a firm in perfect competition, you choose to produce the quantity of output that maximizes profit; however, you can't determine price. Price is determined by market forces that are outside your control. Ultimately, perfectly competitive markets reach a long-run equilibrium where the product's price equals minimum cost per unit. For you as a business owner, this means zero profit — not what you hope for. For consumers, however, this represents the lowest price that continues to result in the product being available.

This chapter provides an overview of perfect competition, and as Yogi Berra would say, "It ain't over 'til it's over."

Identifying the Characteristics of Perfect Competition

Perfect competition has four primary characteristics:

- ✔ **A large number of firms:** Your firm is one of a large number of firms, so it produces a negligible amount of the total quantity of the commodity provided in the market. Therefore, if you decide to produce and sell a greater quantity of the commodity in the market, your decision (and extra production) doesn't substantially alter market conditions.

- ✔ **Standardized commodity:** All firms produce a standardized or homogeneous commodity, which means the commodity produced by your firm is no different from the commodity produced by any other firm. An example of a standardized commodity is wheat. If you're a farmer, the wheat you grow is no different from the wheat grown by any other farmer, so consumers don't care who grows the wheat that's in the bread they purchase.

- ✔ **Easy entry and exit:** There are no barriers to entry in perfect competition. Therefore, new firms can easily establish themselves in the market, and similarly, existing firms can easily exit the market. Typically, this easy entry and exit occurs because perfectly competitive firms have relatively small fixed costs.

- ✔ **Perfect information:** The good's price and quality are known to all buyers and sellers.

Given these characteristics, a perfectly competitive firm is a price taker. The firm can't set price; rather, the firm "takes" the price established by the market's supply and demand.

The best examples of perfectly competitive markets are markets for agricultural commodities, such as wheat, corn, and soybeans. In these markets, a large number of firms — farmers — produce a standardized commodity — corn is the same no matter who grows it — in a market characterized by relatively easy entry and exit — farmland is bought and sold rather easily — and perfect information — such as on the Chicago Board of Trade.

Making an Offer the Firm Can't Refuse: Market Price

As a result of perfect competition's characteristics, each firm is a *price taker*. When a firm is a price taker, price is established through supply and demand in the market. The perfectly competitive firm must then sell its product at the market-established price. The firm's owner can't set price! Under these conditions, you can determine only the quantity of output to produce in order to maximize profits, and what inputs to use to minimize costs.

If an individual firm attempts to charge a price that's higher than the market price, consumers will buy the product from one of the large number of rival firms who sell the product at the lower market price. Because the firm charging a higher price provides a negligible amount of the total market output, all consumer demand is easily satisfied by the other firms. Therefore, the firm charging the higher price is unable to sell any of its product.

On the other hand, the firm won't want to charge a price lower than the market price. If the firm can sell everything it produces at the market price, charging a lower price simply means lower revenue and profit.

Because the individual firm can sell any quantity of output at the prevailing market price, the demand for an individual firm's output is perfectly elastic or horizontal. Therefore, each additional unit of the commodity the firm sells adds the prevailing market price to total revenue, or, marginal revenue equals price.

Competing with Advertising

Advertising's purpose is to enable the firm to sell more product at a higher price. In a perfectly competitive market, advertising is a waste of money. The perfectly competitive firm doesn't gain anything through advertising; indeed, the firm loses money if it advertises.

Because the perfectly competitive firm is a price taker, advertising doesn't enable it to charge a higher price, and because the firm can already sell any quantity of output it produces, it has no need to advertise to sell more.

Although this market structure is called perfect competition, it includes no competition among firms.

Sprinting to Maximum Short-Run Profit

Given the perfectly competitive firm is a price taker, the firm simply determines the quantity of output to produce in order to maximize profits. The firm can't determine the product's price; hence, the idea of limited decision-making. In addition, the firm can't change its fixed cost in the short run. Therefore, the firm must choose the level of variable inputs that results in the profit-maximizing output level.

Determining price is out of your control

Given the perfectly competitive firm is a price taker, price is determined through the interaction of supply and demand in the market. Markets always move toward equilibrium, so the market-determined price ultimately is the price that makes quantity demanded equal to quantity supplied.

The market demand curve for the good you produce is

$$Q_d = 2,600,000 - 15,000P$$

where Q_d is the market quantity demanded and P is the market price in dollars.

The market supply curve is

$$Q_s = -200,000 + 20,000P$$

where Q_s is the market quantity supplied and P is the market price in dollars.

In order to determine the equilibrium price, you take the following steps:

1. **Set quantity demanded equal to quantity supplied.**

$$Q_d = Q_s$$
$$2,600,000 - 15,000P = -200,000 + 20,000P$$

2. **Combine similar terms.**

$$2,800,000 = 35,000P$$

3. **Divide both sides of the equation by 35,000 to solve for *P*.**

$$\frac{2,800,000}{35,000} = 80 = P$$

Thus the market-determined equilibrium price is $80.00. This is the price your firm must charge in a perfectly competitive market. If you charge $80.01, nobody will buy your product because they can purchase it from any one of a large number of other firms for $80.00. And you don't want to charge $79.99, because you can sell everything you produce for $80.00. You have no need to settle for a penny less.

Maximizing profit with total revenue and total cost

Total revenue equals price multiplied by the quantity sold, or

$$TR = P \times q$$

In this equation, *P* represents the commodity's price as determined by supply and demand in the market. For a perfectly competitive market, this price is a constant — it doesn't change regardless of the quantity of output produced by your firm. You must determine the quantity of output, q_0, that maximizes your firm's profit given the market price *P*.

In Figure 9-1, total revenue is illustrated as an upward-sloping straight line. Because your firm is a price taker in perfect competition, the slope of the total revenue function is a constant and corresponds to the market-determined price.

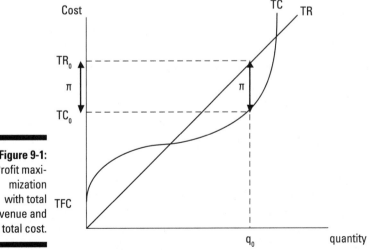

Figure 9-1:
Profit maxi-
mization
with total
revenue and
total cost.

As I explain in Chapter 8, total cost has two components — total fixed cost and total variable cost. Total fixed cost is a constant, so even if your firm shuts down and produces zero units of output, it still incurs total fixed cost. In Figure 9-1, total fixed cost corresponds to the point where the total cost curve intersects the vertical axis at TFC.

As the quantity of output produced increases, total cost increases at a decreasing rate. This fact indicates the total cost curve is becoming flatter due to diminishing returns. Inevitably, however, total cost begins increasing at an increasing rate; or, in other words, the total cost curve becomes steeper, as illustrated in Figure 9-1.

Total profit equals total revenue minus total cost, or

$$\pi = \text{TR} - \text{TC}$$

Total profit is maximized at the output level where the difference between total revenue and total cost is greatest. In Figure 9-1, this occurs at the output level q_0. At the output level q_0, total revenue equals TR_0, total cost equals TC_0, and total profit is the difference between them. On the graph, total profit, π, is the vertical distance between TR_0 and TC_0, and this vertical distance is at its greatest at q_0.

Economists use the terms *profit* and *economic profit* interchangeably. *Economic profit* is defined as the difference between total revenue and the explicit plus implicit costs of production. (See Chapter 8 for the discussion of explicit and implicit costs.) As an equation

$$\text{Economic Profit} = \text{Total Revenue} - (\text{Explicit Costs} + \text{Implicit Costs})$$

The explicit costs plus implicit costs include every cost associated with production, including the opportunity cost of your time and financial investment. Therefore, if economic profit equals zero, you stay in business. Zero economic profit means you're receiving exactly as much income in this situation as you will in your next best alternative.

Zero economic profit is okay. Positive economic profit is even better. Negative economic profit is always bad.

Maximizing total profit with calculus

You can also determine maximum profit by using calculus. In this case, you simply take the derivative of total profit with respect to quantity in order to determine the profit-maximizing quantity of output. Using equations and calculus to maximize profit enables you to avoid "eyeballing" a graph, trying to determine where the difference between total revenue and total cost is greatest.

The market-determined price for your good is $80. Therefore, your total revenue equals

$$TR = 80q$$

Your total cost function is

$$TC = 12{,}500 + 10q + 0.05q^2$$

Therefore, your total profit equation is

$$\pi = TR - TC = 80q - \left(12{,}500 + 10q + 0.05q^2\right)$$
$$= 80q - 12{,}500 - 10q - 0.05q^2 = -12{,}500 + 70q - 0.05q^2$$

In order to determine the profit maximizing quantity, you take the following steps:

1. **Take the derivative of total profit with respect to quantity.**

$$\frac{d\pi}{dq} = 70 - 0.1q$$

2. **Set the derivative equal to zero and solve for *q*.**

$$\frac{d\pi}{dq} = 70 - 0.1q = 0 \quad \text{or} \quad 70 = 0.1q$$

3. **Divide both sides of the equation by 0.1.**

$$\frac{70}{0.1} = 700 = q$$

Thus, 700 units of the good is the profit-maximizing quantity.

4. **To determine total profit, simply substitute 700 for *q* in the total profit equation.**

$$\pi = -12{,}500 + 70q - 0.05q^2$$
$$= -12{,}500 + 70(700) - 0.05(700)^2 = 12{,}000$$

Total profit equals $12,000.

Maximizing profit as a marginal decision

To maximize profit by using marginal revenue and marginal cost, you focus on the contribution one additional unit of output makes to your revenue relative to its contribution to your cost.

Marginal revenue is the change in total revenue that occurs when one additional unit of output is produced. Thus,

$$MR = \frac{\Delta TR}{\Delta q}$$

This equation indicates that marginal revenue is the slope of the total revenue function.

As I note in Chapter 8, *marginal cost* is the change in total cost that occurs when one additional unit of output is produced.

$$MC = \frac{\Delta TC}{\Delta q}$$

So, marginal cost is the slope of the total cost equation.

In order to maximize profit, you want to maximize the difference between total revenue and total cost. Thus, if your marginal revenue is greater than your marginal cost (MR>MC), an additional unit of output adds more to your firm's revenue than it adds to your firm's cost, and the additional unit earns you more profit.

On the other hand, if your marginal revenue is less than your marginal cost (MR<MC), then the additional unit adds less to your revenue than it adds to your cost, and your profit decreases.

In order to maximize profit, you want to produce the quantity of output that corresponds to marginal revenue equals marginal cost (MR=MC).

Figure 9-2 indicates the profit-maximizing quantity of output by using marginal revenue equals marginal cost.

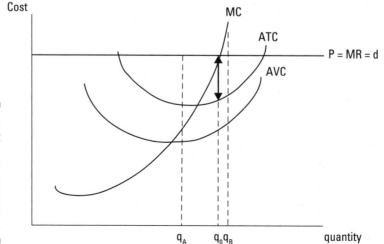

Figure 9-2: Profit maximization with marginal revenue and marginal cost.

The marginal revenue curve in Figure 9-2 is horizontal because you can sell every unit you produce at the prevailing market price. Thus, price equals marginal revenue or

$$P = MR$$

This equation also represents the firm's demand curve, d, because if the firm charges a price one cent higher than P nobody will buy its product and the quantity demanded equals zero. However at the price P, the firm can sell everything it produces.

The firm's marginal cost curve is eventually upward-sloping, passing through the minimum points on the average-variable-cost and average-total-cost curves. (For a detailed explanation of these relationships, see Chapter 8.)

The output level where marginal revenue and marginal cost intersect, q_0, is the profit-maximizing quantity of output. This output level is exactly the same as the output level q_0 determined in Figure 9-1 by using total revenue and total cost.

Because marginal revenue represents the slope of the total revenue function and marginal cost represents the slope of the total cost function, profit is maximized at the output level where the slopes of total revenue and total cost are the same. Thus, the output level represented by q_0 in Figure 9-2 is exactly the same as the output level represented by q_0 in Figure 9-1. Regardless of whether you maximize profit using total revenue and total cost or marginal revenue and marginal cost, you get the same answer for the profit-maximizing quantity of output.

If your firm produces output at a level less than q_0, such as q_A, those units add more to your revenue than they add to your cost because marginal revenue is greater than marginal cost. Those units, by adding more to your revenue than they add to your cost, cause your profit to increase. Therefore, you want to increase production and move toward q_0.

If your firm produces output beyond q_0, say q_B, those units add more to your cost than they add to your revenue because marginal cost for those units is greater than marginal revenue. By adding more to your cost than they add to your revenue, those units cause your profit to be lower. So, you want to decrease production and move back toward q_0.

Using calculus to find marginal revenue equals marginal cost

You can determine marginal revenue and marginal cost with calculus. Marginal revenue is the change in total revenue; thus it's represented as the derivative of total revenue taken with respect to the quantity of output or

$$MR = \frac{d\text{TR}}{dq}$$

Similarly, marginal cost is the change in total cost, so it's represented as the derivative of total cost taken with respect to the quantity of output produced

$$MC = \frac{d\text{TC}}{dq}$$

As previously indicated in Figure 9-2, the profit-maximizing quantity of output is determined where marginal revenue equals marginal cost.

The market-determined price for your good is $80. Therefore, your total revenue equals

$$TR = 80q$$

Marginal revenue equals the derivative of total revenue taken with respect to quantity or

$$MR = \frac{d\text{TR}}{dq} = 80 = P$$

Again note that marginal revenue and price are the same in perfect competition.

If your total cost function is

$$TC = 12,500 + 10q + 0.05q^2$$

Marginal cost equals

$$MC = \frac{d\text{TC}}{dq} = 10 + 0.1q$$

In order to determine the profit-maximizing quantity of output, you simply set marginal revenue or price equal to marginal cost and solve for q.

1. **Set marginal revenue equal to marginal cost.**

$$MR = \frac{d\text{TR}}{dq} = \frac{d\text{TC}}{dq} = MC$$
$$80 = 10 + 0.1q$$

2. **Solve for q.**

$$70 = 0.1q \quad \text{or} \quad q = 700$$

The profit maximizing quantity of output is 700 units. Note this is the same answer you obtain when you maximize the total profit equation by using calculus.

Two methods enable you to maximize total profit. First, you can maximize total profit by using total revenue and total cost. Alternatively, you can use marginal revenue and marginal cost to maximize profit.

Calculating economic profit

After you determine the profit-maximizing quantity of output, you want to determine how much profit you make. Using total revenue and total cost, your total profit is easily calculated by subtracting total revenue from total cost. However, determining the profit-maximizing quantity of output by using marginal revenue and marginal cost doesn't directly provide you with a measure of total profit.

In this situation, total profit is determined by first calculating your profit per unit of output and then multiplying that amount by the profit-maximizing quantity of output. *Profit per unit* equals price minus average total cost, or

profit per unit $= \pi/\text{unit} = P - \text{ATC}$

Total profit is determined by multiplying profit per unit by the quantity of output produced

$$\pi = (P - \text{ATC})q$$

In Figure 9-2, profit per unit is represented by the double-headed arrow between price and average total cost at the output level q_0.

The total revenue and total cost equations from previous examples in this chapter are

$$\text{TR} = 80q$$

and

$$\text{TC} = 12{,}500 + 10q + 0.05q^2$$

Given these equations, you determine the profit-maximizing quantity is 700 units of the good given the market-determined price of \$80. In order to determine the profit per unit and total profit, you take the following steps:

1. **Determine the average total cost equation.**

   Average total cost equals total cost divided by the quantity of output.

   $$\text{ATC} = \frac{\text{TC}}{q} = \frac{12{,}500 + 10q + 0.05q^2}{q} = \frac{12{,}500}{q} + 10 + 0.05q$$

2. **Substitute the profit-maximizing quantity of 700 for q to determine average total cost.**

$$\text{ATC} = \frac{12{,}500}{q} + 10 + 0.05q = \frac{12{,}500}{(700)} + 10 + 0.05(700) = 62.857$$

3. **Calculate profit per unit.**

$$\pi/\text{unit} = P - \text{ATC} = 80 - 62.857 = 17.143$$

or profit per unit equals $17.143.

4. **Determine total profit by multiplying profit per unit by the profit-maximizing quantity of output.**

$$\pi = (P - \text{ATC})q = (80 - 62.857)700 = 12{,}000$$

or total profit equals $12,000.

Making the best of a bad situation by minimizing losses

To this point, I've used situations where the firm is earning positive profit. Of course it isn't always the case that the firm's profit is positive. Nevertheless, firms may continue producing in the short run in order to minimize losses. It's important to remember that firms who shut down in the short run still have production costs — total fixed cost can't be changed. Thus, if a firm loses less money than total fixed cost by producing in the short run, the firm should continue production in order to minimize losses.

Figure 9-3 illustrates a situation where a firm minimizes losses by producing in the short run. The profit-maximizing quantity of output is still determined by equating marginal revenue and marginal cost. The firm produces the profit-maximizing quantity of output q_0 at that point. However, because price is less than average total cost at q_0, the firm loses money. Its loss per unit equals price minus average total cost. This loss per unit is represented by the double-headed arrow in Figure 9-3.

If instead of producing q_0 the firm shuts down, it loses total fixed cost. As I indicate in Chapter 8, total fixed cost equals average fixed cost multiplied by the quantity of output, and average fixed cost equals average total cost minus average variable cost. Thus, in Figure 9-3, the difference between average total cost, ATC_0, and average variable cost, AVC_0, represents the fixed cost per unit at q_0. This difference between average total cost and average variable cost is clearly larger than the difference between price and average total cost. Thus, shutting down and losing your fixed costs is a greater loss than occurs if you produce q_0.

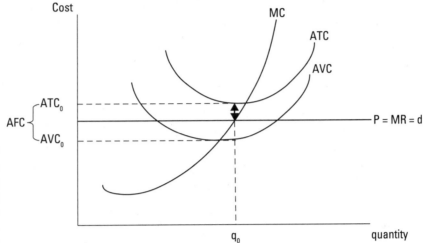

Figure 9-3:
Producing
with
economic
losses.

Assume the market-determined price for your good is \$6.80. Therefore, your total revenue equals

$$TR = P \times q = 6.8q$$

Marginal revenue equals the derivative of total revenue taken with respect to quantity or

$$MR = \frac{dTR}{dq} = 6.8 = P$$

If your total cost function is

$$TC = 5{,}625 + 8q - 0.005q^2 + 0.0000025q^3$$

Marginal cost equals

$$MC = \frac{dTC}{dq} = 8 - 0.01q + 0.0000075q^2$$

In order to determine the profit-maximizing quantity of output, you simply set marginal revenue or price equal to marginal cost and solve for q.

1. **Set marginal revenue equal to marginal cost.**

$$MR = \frac{dTR}{dq} = \frac{dTC}{dq} = MC$$

$$6.8 = 8 - 0.01q + 0.0000075q^2$$

2. **Solve for *q*.**

   Use either a calculator or the quadratic formula.

   $$0.0000075q^2 - 0.01q + 1.2 = 0$$

   $$\frac{-b \pm \sqrt{b^2 - 4ac}}{2a} = \frac{-(-0.01) \pm \sqrt{(-0.01)^2 - 4(0.0000075)(1.2)}}{2(0.0000075)}$$

   $$= \frac{0.01 \pm \sqrt{0.0001 - 0.000036}}{0.000015} = \frac{0.01 \pm \sqrt{0.000064}}{0.000015} = \frac{0.01 \pm 0.008}{0.000015}$$

   $$= 1,200$$

   The profit maximizing quantity of output is 1,200 units.

3. **Determine the average total cost equation.**

   Average total cost equals total cost divided by the quantity of output.

   $$\text{ATC} = \frac{\text{TC}}{q} = \frac{5,625 + 8q - 0.005q^2 + 0.0000025q^3}{q}$$

   $$= \frac{5,625}{q} + 8 - 0.005q + 0.0000025q^2$$

4. **Substitute the profit-maximizing quantity of 1,200 for *q* to determine average total cost.**

   $$\text{ATC} = \frac{5,625}{q} + 8 - 0.005q + 0.0000025q^2$$

   $$= \frac{5,625}{(1,200)} + 8 - 0.005(1,200) + 0.0000025(1,200)^2 = 10.2875$$

5. **Calculate profit per unit.**

   $$\pi/\text{unit} = P - \text{ATC} = 6.8 - 10.2875 = -3.4875$$

   or profit per unit equals –$3.4875.

6. **Determine total profit by multiplying profit per unit by the profit-maximizing quantity of output.**

   $$\pi = (P - \text{ATC})q = (6.8 - 10.2875)1,200 = -4,185$$

   or total profit equals –$4,185. Your firm is losing $4,185. But note that if you immediately shut down, your losses equal total fixed cost, which is $5,625. Losing $4,185 is a bad situation, but losing $5,625 is even worse. Continuing production makes the best of a bad situation.

Giving up and shutting down

There is a point where you should immediately give up and shut down. But first remember that going out of business in the short run doesn't mean that your losses go to zero. Because some of the inputs you employ are fixed, going out of business in the short run means you lose your fixed costs. Therefore, if you can make enough revenue to cover all your variable costs (see the previous section), you should stay in business in the short run in order to minimize your losses. However, given your goal is to maximize profits — or, in a bad situation, minimize losses — you should immediately shut down if your revenue doesn't cover your variable costs. Producing when your revenue is less than your variable costs means that your losses associated with the profit-maximizing quantity of output are greater than your fixed costs. You're better off shutting down and losing only your fixed costs.

In Figure 9-4, the profit-maximizing quantity of output, based on marginal revenue equals marginal cost, is q_0. If you produce this quantity of output, your loss per unit equals price minus average total cost or the distance represented by the double-headed arrow in Figure 9-4. However, your fixed cost is represented by the vertical distance between average total cost, ATC_0, and average variable cost, AVC_0. Because this distance is less than the loss represented by the double-headed arrow, you'll lose less money by shutting down — producing zero units of output — and limiting your losses to total fixed cost.

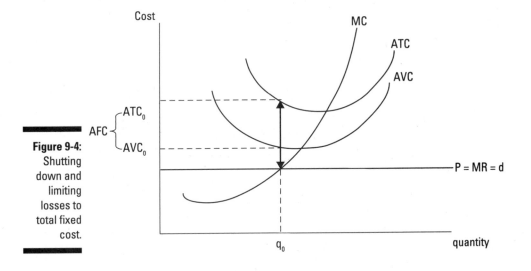

Figure 9-4:
Shutting down and limiting losses to total fixed cost.

Assume the market-determined price for your good is $4.80. Therefore, your total revenue equals

$$TR = P \times q = 4.8q$$

Marginal revenue equals the derivative of total revenue taken with respect to quantity, or

$$MR = \frac{dTR}{dq} = 4.8 = P$$

If your total cost function is

$$TC = 5,625 + 8q - 0.005q^2 + 0.0000025q^3$$

Marginal cost equals

$$MC = \frac{dTC}{dq} = 8 - 0.01q + 0.0000075q^2$$

Again, to determine the profit-maximizing quantity of output, set marginal revenue or price equal to marginal cost.

1. **Set marginal revenue equal to marginal cost.**

$$MR = \frac{dTR}{dq} = \frac{dTC}{dq} = MC$$

$$4.8 = 8 - 0.01q + 0.0000075q^2$$

2. **Solve for _q_ by using the quadratic formula.**

$$0.0000075q^2 - 0.01q + 3.2 = 0$$

$$\frac{-b \pm \sqrt{b^2 - 4ac}}{2a} = \frac{-(-0.01) \pm \sqrt{(-0.01)^2 - 4(0.0000075)(3.2)}}{2(0.0000075)}$$

$$= \frac{0.01 \pm \sqrt{0.0001 - 0.000096}}{0.000015} = \frac{0.01 \pm \sqrt{0.000004}}{0.000015} = \frac{0.01 \pm 0.002}{0.000015}$$

$$= 800$$

The profit-maximizing quantity of output is 800 units.

3. **Determine the average-total-cost equation.**

Average total cost equals total cost divided by the quantity of output.

$$ATC = \frac{TC}{q} = \frac{5,625 + 8q - 0.005q^2 + 0.0000025q^3}{q}$$

$$= \frac{5,625}{q} + 8 - 0.005q + 0.0000025q^2$$

4. **Substitute the profit-maximizing quantity of 800 for *q* to determine average total cost.**

$$\text{ATC} = \frac{5{,}625}{q} + 8 - 0.005q + 0.0000025q^2$$

$$= \frac{5{,}625}{(800)} + 8 - 0.005(800) + 0.0000025(800)^2 = 12.63125$$

5. **Calculate profit per unit.**

$$\pi/\text{unit} = \text{P} - \text{ATC} = 4.8 - 12.63125 = -7.83125$$

or profit per unit equals –$7.83125.

6. **Determine total profit by multiplying profit per unit by the profit-maximizing quantity of output.**

$$\pi = (\text{P} - \text{ATC})q = (4.8 - 12.63125)800 = -6{,}265$$

or total profit equals –$6,265. By producing 800 units of output where marginal revenue equals marginal cost, your firm is losing $6,265. But note that if you immediately shut down, your losses equal total fixed cost, which is only $5,625. Losing $5,625 is a bad situation, but losing $6,265 is even worse. Shutting down immediately becomes your best option for minimizing your losses.

Disappearing Profit in the Long Run

The long run is a period of time in which all inputs you employ are variable. Therefore, the perfectly competitive firm operating in the long run can change the quantity employed of any input — fixed inputs don't exist.

Perfect competition has two important characteristics that influence the long-run equilibrium: easy entry and exit and the firm is a price taker.

✔ **Easy entry and exit:** Firms have no difficulty moving into or out of a perfectly competitive market.

✔ **Price taker:** Individual firms can't set price, but they can sell everything they produce at the price established by the market.

Motivating entry and exit: Where did all your profit go?

Remember that economic profit is based on all production costs; therefore, zero economic profit represents a normal rate of return for your business. If economic profit is greater than zero, your business is earning something greater than a normal return. This profit attracts other firms to enter the market. Similarly, if initial economic losses (negative economic profit) exist, firms leave the market. In the long run, economic profit ultimately equals zero.

Zero economic profit means that price equals average total cost.

Determining the long-run equilibrium

Profit maximization depends on producing a given quantity of output at the lowest possible cost, and the long-run equilibrium in perfect competition requires zero economic profit. Therefore, firms ultimately produce the output level associated with minimum long-run average total cost. In Chapter 8 I tell you that marginal cost must pass through the minimum point of average total cost. Therefore, in the long-run equilibrium, price equals three costs: minimum long-run average total cost, $LRATC$; the minimum point on one short-run average-total-cost curve, $SRATC$; and marginal cost, MC.

Figure 9-5 illustrates the long-run equilibrium in perfect competition. The left diagram in Figure 9-5 illustrates the equilibrium price, P_E, being determined by the intersection of demand and supply in the market. The perfectly competitive firm is a price taker, so this price is the firm's marginal revenue curve, $P = MR = d$, in the right diagram. This price also corresponds to minimum long-run average total cost to ensure zero economic profit in the long run. Thus, new firms have no incentive to enter the market, and existing firms have no incentive to leave the market. Price or marginal revenue equals marginal cost at q_0, ensuring that profit is maximized.

Assume the short-run average-total-cost function associated with minimum long-run average total cost is

$$\text{SRATC} = \frac{\text{TC}}{q} = \frac{12{,}500 + 10q + 0.05q^2}{q} = \frac{12{,}500}{q} + 10 + 0.05q$$

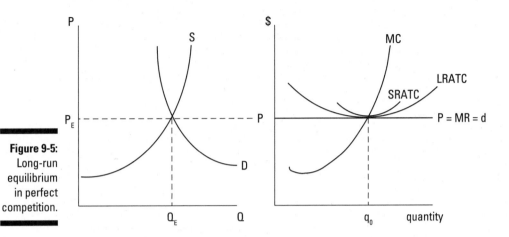

Figure 9-5:
Long-run
equilibrium
in perfect
competition.

The long-run equilibrium requires that both average total cost is minimized and price equals average total cost (zero economic profit is earned). In order to find the long-run quantity of output produced by your firm and the good's price, you take the following steps:

1. **Take the derivative of average total cost.**

   Remember that $12{,}500/q$ is rewritten as $12{,}500q^{-1}$ so its derivative equals $-12{,}500q^{-2}$ or $12{,}500/q^2$.

   $$\frac{d\mathrm{SRATC}}{dq} = -\frac{12{,}500}{q^2} + 0.05$$

2. **Set the derivative equal to zero and solve for _q_.**

   $$-\frac{12{,}500}{q^2} + 0.05 = 0 \quad \text{or} \quad -12{,}500 + 0.05q^2 = 0 \quad \text{or} \quad 0.05q^2 = 12{,}500$$

   $$q^2 = 250{,}000 \quad \text{or} \quad q = 500$$

   or average total cost is minimized at 500 units of output.

3. **Determine the long-run price.**

   Remember that zero economic profit means price equals average total cost, so substituting 500 for _q_ in the average-total-cost equation equals price.

   $$\mathrm{SRATC} = \frac{12{,}500}{q} + 10 + 0.05q = \frac{12{,}500}{(500)} + 10 + 0.05(500) = 60$$

The long-run equilibrium price equals $60.00. So the firm earns zero economic profit by producing 500 units of output at a price of $60 in the long run.

Firms have no difficulty moving into or out of a perfectly competitive market. If economic profit is greater than zero, your business is earning something greater than a normal return. This profit attracts other firms to enter the market. This situation is illustrated in Figure 9-6. At the initial price P_A, your firm maximizes profits at q_A based on marginal revenue equals marginal cost. At q_A, your firm earns positive profit because price is greater than average total cost. This profit provides incentive for new firms to enter the market, increasing the market supply from S_A to S_{LR}. The entry of new firms results in a lower equilibrium price for the good, P_{LR}. As price decreases, your profit-maximizing quantity moves to q_{LR} and your economic profit moves toward zero because price now equals average total cost. When economic profit reaches zero, no one has any incentive for entry or exit.

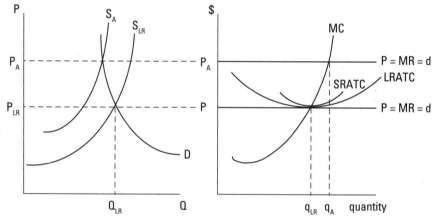

Figure 9-6:
Moving from
positive to
zero profit.

Similarly, if initial economic losses — negative economic profit — exist, firms leave the market, moving the perfectly competitive market to its long-run equilibrium. This situation is illustrated in Figure 9-7. The loss of firms decreases supply from S_B to S_{LR}, resulting in upward pressure on price, from P_B to P_{LR}. With the increase in price, your firm's profit-maximizing quantity increases from q_B to q_{LR}, and zero economic profit is reached because the price P_{LR} now equals average total cost.

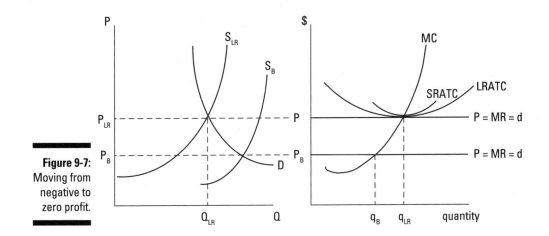

Figure 9-7:
Moving from
negative to
zero profit.

So no matter where you start, in perfect competition your economic profit ultimately becomes zero. And at this point, Yogi Berra might say it's over.

Chapter 10

Monopoly: Decision-Making Without Rivals

. . . .

In This Chapter

▶ Identifying the source of monopoly power

▶ Separating demand and marginal revenue

▶ Determining the profit-maximizing quantity and price

▶ Minimizing cost with multiple factories

. . . .

*P*arker Brothers' popular board game Monopoly has it all wrong. The board game doesn't describe monopoly at all. The board game has 22 properties — not counting railroads and utility companies — that you can buy, sell, and rent. That's way too much competition. In the market structure of monopoly, there's only one firm, and because a single firm produces the good, monopoly has a very low degree of competition. In fact, monopolists have no direct rivals.

This situation may give the misimpression that a monopolist has unlimited power. That isn't the case. The monopolist is constrained by whether or not consumers are willing to buy the monopolist's product at a given price. Also, a monopolist can face indirect competition from other firms that produce something that addresses the same needs. For example, the firm providing natural gas and the firm providing electricity are monopolies. As a consumer, you can choose either natural gas or electricity to operate your home's oven and stove.

In this chapter, I start by examining monopoly characteristics and their impact on decision-making, especially price setting. These characteristics give the monopolist the ability to set price. After identifying the source of monopoly power, I summarize how a monopolist determines the short-run profit-maximizing quantity, price, and amount of profit by using two approaches — the first based on total revenue and total cost, and the second based on marginal revenue and marginal cost. After considering the short-run situation, I explain how things evolve in the long run. Finally, I conclude the chapter by examining how monopolies profitably produce the same good in two or more factories. And after you understand these concepts, you'll feel like you own both Park Place and Boardwalk. Now, that's a really profitable monopoly.

Standing Alone: Identifying the Sources of Monopoly Power

If you possess monopoly power, you're able to set your good's price. Thus, as manager, you must now determine both the profit-maximizing quantity of output and the good's price. You really have to mind your p's and q's in monopoly.

Monopolies have the following characteristics:

- ✔ **A single firm:** Your firm is the only one that produces the good. Therefore, the entire quantity of the good sold in the market is produced by your firm.

- ✔ **No close substitutes:** In addition to being the only firm producing the good, there are no close substitutes for the good you produce. No other firm provides a similar or directly substitutable good. As a consequence, no direct competition between firms exists.

- ✔ **Barriers to entry:** Barriers to entry ensure the continued existence of the monopoly. Barriers to entry also enable the monopolist to maintain positive economic profit, or returns in excess of the normal rate of return, in the long run. Barriers to entry can take many forms, including economies of scale, government regulation, patents, and control of specific natural resources.

Because a single firm produces the good's entire market output, the firm is a price setter — the monopolist determines the price it charges for the good. The demand for the monopolist's product is the same as the market demand because only one firm is producing the good. However, this situation has its pros and cons. On the pro side, you get to set price, and you have no direct rivals. On the con side, if you want to sell more of the good, you have to lower price. In perfect competition (see Chapter 9), you could sell as much as you wanted without having to change price. This isn't the case in monopoly.

The reason you have to lower price to sell more of the good is a monopolist's ability to set price is constrained by consumer demand — consumers will buy more of the product only if you lower its price.

Also, the absence of close substitutes for the monopolist's product ensures the monopolist's ability to set price without direct competition. However, to the extent imperfect substitute goods exist, they influence consumer demand and the monopolist's ability to set price. Therefore, the monopolist doesn't take into account rival firm behavior when it determines its short-run profit-maximizing quantity and price. But over an extended period of time, or in the long run, the monopolist's profits are affected by indirect competition.

Unable to Charge as Much as You Want: Relating Demand, Price, and Revenue

There is little doubt that monopoly has a bad reputation. At the word *monopoly,* consumers typically picture a large firm that charges any price it wants. It's a firm with virtually unlimited power. But consumers are wrong!

The ultimate source of power in a market is the consumer. As a consumer, you get to decide whether you're willing and able to purchase a good at a given price. In theory, the monopolist can charge any price it wants, but practically, the monopolist can't charge too high of a price or you won't buy the good. The monopolist is constrained by your willingness to pay the price it charges.

For example, economists consider De Beers a resource monopoly because it effectively controls the world's supply of diamonds. And although diamonds are very popular, if De Beers keeps raising its price, consumers will start substituting other precious gems, such as rubies and emeralds, for diamonds. Thus, as diamond prices increase, the quantity of diamonds consumers purchase will decrease.

The monopolist's pricing decision is subject to the constraint imposed by consumer demand. If the monopolist charges too high of a price, nobody wants to buy its product. So, if the monopolist wants to sell more product, it must lower price as indicated by the market demand curve.

The inverse relationship between price and quantity demanded is the critical element in monopoly price setting. Because a single firm provides the entire quantity of the commodity in the market, the demand for the monopolist's product, represented by a lower-case *d* in Figure 10-1, is the same as the market demand, represented by a capital *D* in Figure 10-1. The market demand possesses the usual characteristics; an inverse relationship between price and quantity demanded and changing price elasticity of demand along the demand curve. In order to sell more of its product, the monopolist must lower its price, not only for the additional unit but for every other unit as well.

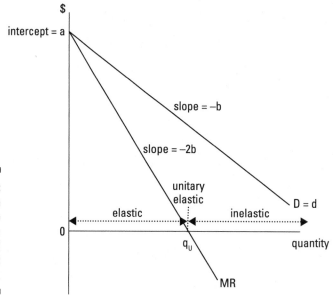

Figure 10-1:
The
relationship
between
demand and
marginal
revenue.

Figure 10-1 also illustrates the relationship between a monopolist's demand and marginal revenue. Remember that marginal revenue is the change in total revenue that occurs when one additional unit of a good is produced and sold. Because the monopolist's demand curve is identical to the market demand curve, the monopolist can sell an additional unit of output only by lowering the product's price. Assuming no price discrimination (charging different customers different prices for the same good), this lower price is charged for all units of the commodity sold. As a consequence, the firm's marginal revenue curve lies below its demand curve. Marginal revenue is less than price.

Marginal revenue — the change in total revenue — is below the demand curve.

Marginal revenue is related to the price elasticity of demand — the responsiveness of quantity demanded to a change in price. As I indicate in Chapter 4, when marginal revenue is positive, demand is elastic; and when marginal revenue is negative, demand is inelastic. The output level at which marginal revenue equals zero corresponds to unitary elasticity. This occurs at the quantity q_u in Figure 10-1.

A linear demand curve has the form

$$P = a - bq$$

where P is the good's price in dollars and q is the quantity demanded. Constants in the equation are represented by a and b — a is the intercept of the demand curve (where the demand curve intersects the vertical axis) and b is the demand curve's slope.

Total revenue, *TR*, equals price times quantity or

$$TR = P \times q = (a - bq)q = aq - bq^2$$

Marginal revenue, *MR*, equals the derivative of total revenue taken with respect to quantity

$$MR = \frac{d TR}{d q} = a - 2bq$$

If you compare the marginal revenue equation with the demand equation, you see that both equations have an intercept represented by *a*. The slope of the demand equation is represented by –*b*, while the slope of the marginal revenue equation is –*2b*. Thus, for a linear demand curve, the marginal revenue curve starts at the same intercept as the demand curve, but its slope is twice as steep. This is represented in Figure 10-1.

Engaging in Advertising and Non-Price Competition

Monopolists don't have direct rivals. However, monopolists still have incentive to engage in advertising and other forms of non–price discrimination, such as innovation. Because the monopolist is constrained by consumer demand, anything that increases demand increases the monopolist's revenues. Thus De Beers — who essentially monopolizes the market for diamonds — extensively advertises diamonds for special occasions in order to increase its demand. The result is that engagement rings have diamonds, although I prefer emeralds.

Maximizing Short-Run Profit

Like every other firm, regardless of how much competition exists in the market, the monopolist wants to maximize profit — the difference between its total revenue and total cost. Basic cost theory, as I describe in Chapter 8, isn't affected by the amount of competition that exists. So what's the big difference that more or less competition has on a firm? Competition affects the revenue side of the firm's decision. In the case of monopoly, the market demand is the same as the firm's demand, and marginal revenue lies below the demand curve. This is the critical difference in monopoly as compared to other markets with a higher degree of competition.

A monopoly can't force you to buy its product. Thus, a monopoly must determine the profit-maximizing quantity and price given the constraint imposed by consumer demand.

Maximizing profit with total revenue and total cost

Total profit equals total revenue minus total cost. In order to maximize total profit, you must maximize the difference between total revenue and total cost. The first thing to do is determine the profit-maximizing quantity. Substituting this quantity into the demand equation enables you to determine the good's price. Alternatively, dividing total revenue by quantity enables you to determine price.

Graphically, the total revenue and total cost curves appear as illustrated in Figure 10-2. The total revenue curve increases but at a decreasing rate — the curve becomes flatter. Eventually, total revenue begins to decrease. This relationship between total revenue and quantity reflects the fact that as a monopolist, you need to charge a lower price in order to sell more output. The lower price leads to smaller increases and eventually decreases in total revenue.

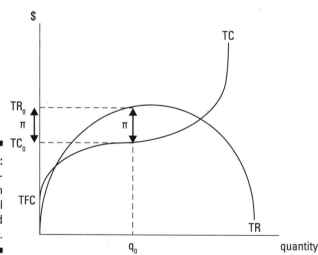

Figure 10-2: Profit maximization with total revenue and total cost.

The nonlinear relationship, or increasing at a decreasing rate, also reflects the changing price elasticity of demand along the demand curve. The region where total revenue is increasing corresponds to the elastic region of the market demand curve. In Figure 10-1, this is the region where marginal revenue is greater than zero, and thus total revenue is increasing. Decreasing total revenue as output increases reflects the inelastic region of market demand where marginal revenue is negative. Producing more in this region means less revenue because in order to sell more of the good you have to lower price on every unit you sell. The lower price on every other unit you sell decreases your revenue by more than you gain through the one extra unit you're now able to sell. The point where total revenue is maximized corresponds to unitary elasticity. This is the point where marginal revenue equals zero in Figure 10-1.

Remember that even when you produce nothing in the short run, you're stuck with fixed costs. So at zero units of output, the monopoly's total fixed cost equals *TFC* in Figure 10-2. As the quantity of output produced increases, total cost initially increases at a decreasing rate. This situation occurs until diminishing returns begin. After diminishing returns start — and they must start at some point — total cost increases at an increasing rate. That is, the total cost curve becomes steeper, as illustrated in Figure 10-2.

Total profit is represented by the vertical difference between the total revenue and total cost curves. The monopolist determines the output level at which total profit is maximized or the difference between total revenue and total cost is greatest. In Figure 10-2 this corresponds to q_0 of output. At q_0, your total revenue equals TR_0 and your total cost equals TC_0. Your total profit equals total revenue minus total cost and is represented by the double-headed arrow labeled π in Figure 10-2.

For output levels less than or greater than q_0, total profit, as represented by the difference between total revenue and total cost is less than the total profit π at q_0.

Deriving maximum profit with derivatives

You can use calculus to maximize the total profit equation. Because total revenue and total cost are both expressed as a function of quantity, you determine the profit-maximizing quantity of output by taking the derivative of the total profit equation with respect to quantity, setting the derivative equal to zero, and solving for the quantity.

The market demand curve for the good your monopoly produces is

$$q = 10,000 - 200P$$

where q is the market and firm's quantity demanded, and P is the market price in dollars.

Using the demand equation to derive total revenue as a function of q requires the following steps:

1. **Add 200P to both sides of the demand equation.**

   $q + 200P = 10{,}000 - 200P + 200P$

   $q + 200P = 10{,}000$

2. **Subtract q from both sides of the equation.**

   $q + 200P - q = 10{,}000 - q$

   $200P = 10{,}000 - q$

3. **Divide both sides of the equation by 200.**

   $\dfrac{200P}{200} = \dfrac{10{,}000 - q}{200}$ or $P = 50 - 0.005q$

4. **To determine total revenue, multiply both sides of the demand equation by q.**

   $TR = P \times q = (50 - 0.005q) \times q = 50q - 0.005q^2$

This equation tells you how much total revenue equals given any value for quantity, q. Thus, total revenue is a function of q.

If your total cost equation is

$TC = 12{,}000 + 20q + 0.0025q^2$

total profit, π, is determined by subtracting total cost from total revenue, or

$\pi = TR - TC = (50q - .005q^2) - (12{,}000 + 20q + 0.0025q^2) = -12{,}000 + 30q - 0.0075q^2$

After you have the total profit equation, the following steps enable you to determine the profit-maximizing quantity and price:

1. **Take the derivative of the total profit equation with respect to quantity.**

   $\dfrac{d\pi}{dq} = 30 - 0.015q$

2. **Set the derivative equal to zero and solve for q.**

   This is your profit-maximizing quantity of output.

   $\dfrac{d\pi}{dq} = 30 - 0.015q = 0$ or $30 = 0.015q$ or $q = 2{,}000$

3. **Substitute the profit-maximizing quantity of 2,000 into the demand equation and solve for *P*.**

$$P = 50 - 0.005q = 50 - 0.005(2,000) = 40$$

Or you should set a price of $40 for the good.

4. **Finally, total profit is determined by substituting 2,000 for *q* in the total-profit equation.**

$$\pi = -12,000 + 30q - 0.0075q^2 = -12,000 + 30(2,000) - 0.0075(2,000)^2 = 18,000$$

Your total profit equals $18,000.

Maximizing profit with a marginally better method

Quite often it's easier to determine the profit-maximizing quantity of output by focusing on the last unit you produce, or the marginal unit. In order to add to your profit, an additional or marginal unit of the good must add more to your revenue than it adds to your cost. In other words, marginal revenue is greater than marginal cost. As long as an additional unit adds more to your revenue than it adds to your cost, your profit is increasing. At the output level that maximizes profit, an additional unit of output doesn't add any more to your total profit. This occurs when marginal revenue equals marginal cost. Stop at this output level because if you go beyond this point and continue to produce more, marginal cost is greater than marginal revenue — so you're adding more to your cost than you're adding to your revenue, and your total profit is decreasing.

In monopoly, only one firm is producing the good. Therefore, any customer who wants to buy the good must buy it from the monopoly. Thus, the demand for the firm's product is the market demand.

In Figure 10-3, the monopolist's downward-sloping demand curve *d* is the same as the market demand curve *D*, or *D* = *d*. As previously described in the section "Unable to Charge as Much as You Want: Relating Demand, Price, and Revenue," given the linear demand curve, the marginal revenue curve has the same intercept on the vertical axis and is twice as steep as the demand curve. Marginal revenue is represented by the curve labeled *MR*.

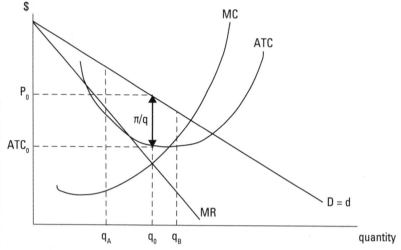

Figure 10-3:
Profit
maximiza-
tion with
marginal
revenue and
marginal
cost.

Marginal cost, *MC*, is upward-sloping and passes through the minimum point on average total cost, *ATC*.

To maximize profits, you produce the output level associated with marginal revenue equals marginal cost, or the output level q_0 that corresponds to the point where the marginal revenue and marginal cost curves intersect.

Marginal revenue equals marginal cost maximizes total profit.

To find the price you charge, go from the profit-maximizing quantity of output, up to the demand curve and across. The profit-maximizing price corresponds to P_0.

The fact that price is determined by the point where q_0 hits the demand curve emphasizes the constraint that market demand places on the monopolist's ability to set price. If advertising increases demand — shifts the demand curve to the right — you're able to set a higher price.

If you produce less than q_0 output, for example q_A, those units still add more to your revenue than they add to your cost. For those units, marginal revenue is greater than marginal cost. You increase profits by producing more output moving toward q_0.

If you produce output beyond q_0, such as q_B, those units add more to your cost than they add to your revenue because marginal cost is greater than marginal revenue. These units reduce your profit so you should cut back production to q_0.

As is the case for any firm, a monopolist determines profit per unit by subtracting average total cost from price. In Figure 10-3, profit per unit is represented by the double-headed arrow labeled π/q. Total profit is determined by multiplying profit per unit by the number of units sold, q_0.

Maximizing profit with calculus

Figure 10-3 indicates that profit is maximized at the quantity of output where marginal revenue equals marginal cost. Marginal revenue represents the change in total revenue associated with an additional unit of output, and marginal cost is the change in total cost for an additional unit of output. Therefore, both marginal revenue and marginal cost represent derivatives of the total revenue and total cost functions, respectively. You can use calculus to determine marginal revenue and marginal cost; setting them equal to one another maximizes total profit.

Earlier in this chapter, in the section "Deriving maximum profit with derivatives," I noted that the monopolist's demand curve

$$P = 50 - 0.005q$$

generated the total revenue equation.

$$TR = 50q - 0.005q^2$$

Also assume your total cost equation is

$$TC = 12,000 + 20q + 0.0025q^2$$

Given these equations, the profit-maximizing quantity of output is determined through the following steps:

1. **Determine marginal revenue by taking the derivative of total revenue with respect to quantity.**

$$MR = \frac{d TR}{d q} = 50 - 0.01q$$

2. **Determine marginal cost by taking the derivative of total cost with respect to quantity.**

$$MC = \frac{d TC}{d q} = 20 + 0.005q$$

3. **Set marginal revenue equal to marginal cost and solve for *q*.**

$$MR = MC$$

$$50 - 0.01q = 20 + 0.005q \text{ or } 30 = 0.015q \text{ or } q = 2{,}000$$

4. **Substituting 2,000 for q in the demand equation enables you to determine price.**

$$P = 50 - 0.005q = 50 - 0.005(2{,}000) = 40$$

Thus, the profit-maximizing quantity is 2,000 units and the price is $40 per unit.

The profit-maximizing quantity and price are the same whether you maximize the difference between total revenue and total cost or set marginal revenue equal to marginal cost.

Calculating economic profit and the profit-per-unit fallacy

Economic profit per unit equals price minus average total cost, or

$$\pi/\text{unit} = P - ATC$$

In Figure 10-3, economic profit per unit is illustrated by the double-headed arrow labeled π/q.

Total profit equals profit per unit multiplied by the number of units sold, or

$$\pi = (\pi/\text{unit}) \times q_0 = (P - ATC) \times q_0$$

Using the same information in the previous example, the monopolist's demand curve is

$$P = 50 - 0.005q$$

And the monopolist's total cost equation is

$$TC = 12{,}000 + 20q + 0.0025q^2$$

Given this information, the profit-maximizing quantity is 2,000 units at a price of $40 per unit.

In order to determine the monopolist's economic profit per unit and total profit, you take the following steps:

1. **Determine the average total cost equation by dividing the total cost equation by the quantity of output q.**

$$\text{ATC} = \frac{\text{TC}}{q} = \frac{12,000 + 20q + 0.0025q^2}{q} = \frac{12,000}{q} + 20 + 0.0025q$$

2. **Substitute q equals 2,000 in order to determine average total cost at the profit-maximizing quantity of output.**

$$\text{ATC} = \frac{12,000}{q} + 20 + 0.0025q = \frac{12,000}{(2,000)} + 20 + 0.0025(2,000) = 31$$

Thus, the average total cost is $31 at the profit-maximizing quantity of 2,000 units.

3. **Calculate profit per unit.**

$$\pi/\text{unit} = P - \text{ATC} = 40 - 31 = 9$$

Profit per unit equals $9.

4. **Determine total profit by multiplying profit per unit by the profit-maximizing quantity of output.**

$$\pi = (\pi/\text{unit}) \times q_0 = (P - \text{ATC}) \times q_0 = (40 - 31) \times 2,000 = 18,000$$

Total profit equals $18,000.

Don't confuse maximizing total profit with maximizing profit per unit. You're willing to accept less profit per unit if you sell a lot more units. For example, if your profit per unit was $11 and you sold 1,265 units of output, your total profit equals $13,915.

$$\pi = (\pi/\text{unit}) \times q_0 = 11 \times 1,265 = 13,915$$

On the other hand, if your profit per unit is only $9 but you're now able to sell 2,000 units because you charge a lower price, your total profit equals $18,000.

$$\pi = (\pi/\text{unit}) \times q_0 = 9 \times 2,000 = 18,000$$

Remember, your goal is always to maximize total profit.

Minimizing losses to make the best of a bad situation

In the short run, monopolies can incur economic losses. In the case of economic losses, the price associated with the marginal revenue equals marginal cost output level is less than average total cost. Figure 10-4 indicates a situation where the monopoly earns negative economic profit.

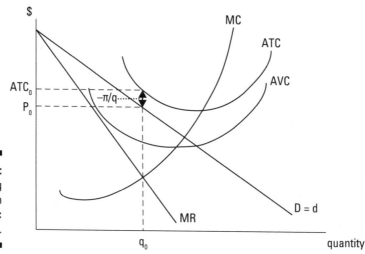

Figure 10-4:
Producing
with
economic
losses.

In Figure 10-4, note the monopolist's demand and marginal revenue curves have the same shape as in situations I describe earlier in this chapter. The demand curve is downward-sloping, indicating that the monopolist must lower price to sell a greater quantity of output, and marginal revenue lies below the demand curve. Average total cost, average variable cost, and marginal cost all have the usual shapes. Marginal cost is upward-sloping, reflecting diminishing returns. Average variable cost and average total cost are both U-shaped, and marginal cost passes through the minimum point on both curves.

Given its demand curve and cost curves, this monopolist maximizes profits — minimizes losses — by producing the quantity of output q_0 that corresponds to the intersection of marginal revenue and marginal cost. Price is determined by going from q_0 up to the demand curve and across to P_0.

Economists use the term *maximize profits* even when they're minimizing losses. Maximizing profits means the highest possible profit. In the case of a firm that loses money, the highest possible profit is the smallest loss.

The firm's economic loss equals the difference between price and average total cost. It's a loss because price is less than average total cost, so

$$\pi = P - ATC < 0$$

The loss per unit is represented by the double-headed arrow labeled $-\pi/q$ in Figure 10-4.

Shutting down

In the short run, if you immediately shut down, you still lose money because of your fixed costs. Shutting down means you produce zero output, earn zero revenue, and incur zero variable costs. However, because you can't change your fixed inputs, you still have fixed costs. Thus, your short-run losses equal total fixed cost.

In order for an immediate shutdown to make sense, the shutdown has to maximize profits, or, in this case, minimize losses. For that to happen, the economic losses resulting from the production of the output level associated with marginal revenue equals marginal cost are greater than total fixed costs. This is the case if the price determined off the demand curve is less than your average variable cost. Thus, you should immediately shut down if the profit-maximizing price is less than average variable cost. If price is less than average variable cost, you not only lose fixed costs, you're not even able to pay all your variable costs.

Anticipating the Long Run

The long run allows you to change any input — fixed inputs don't exist in the long run. But the long run also usually allows other firms to enter profitable markets. However, this doesn't happen in monopolistic markets due to barriers to entry.

Keeping others out with barriers to entry

A critical characteristic of monopoly is the presence of barriers to entry. However, different barriers to entry exist. The different barriers to entry lead to different types of monopoly.

✓ **Natural Monopoly:** Natural monopolies exist due to economies of scale. As the consequence of the economies of scale, the monopoly provides the commodity at much lower cost per unit than potential entrants, discouraging new firms from establishing themselves in the market. Electric companies are an example of a natural monopoly.

✓ **Legal Monopoly:** Legal monopolies exist due to government legislation and protection. Typically, legal monopolies are privately-owned companies that are granted a monopoly by the government. The legal monopoly is established to protect consumers' interests. An example of a legal monopoly is local cable television service. In this situation, a local government grants a monopoly in order to eliminate unnecessary duplication of costs that leads to higher prices for customers. For example, two cable television companies have to lay twice as much cable, construct two transmission facilities, and so on. The consequence is a doubling in cost. In addition, these two companies would split the market, resulting in each company serving half as many customers as a monopolist. The inevitable result is higher prices for consumers.

✓ **Government Monopoly:** A government monopoly is a monopoly that's owned and operated by government. The primary difference between a government monopoly and a legal monopoly is that the government monopoly is publicly owned while the legal monopoly is privately owned. Examples of government monopolies include garbage collection in some cities and public water companies.

✓ **Patent Monopoly:** Protection of an invention under the patent laws results in a patent monopoly. This protection's purpose is to encourage research and development by ensuring a period of time over which the potential for monopoly profit exists. Such protection, however, is temporary; therefore, patent monopolies have a limited lifespan as a monopoly. Examples of patent monopolies are numerous, ranging from Xerox's patents on components of copying technology to Lego's patent on the interlocking feature of plastic toy building blocks.

✓ **Resource Monopoly:** A single firm's virtual control of an entire resource's supply results in a resource monopoly. The best current example of a resource monopoly is De Beers's control of diamonds.

Enjoying the long run

Because of barriers to entry, monopolies are able to maintain positive economic profit in the long run. Therefore, the conditions of the short-run equilibrium that I describe in previous sections also describe the long-run equilibrium with one caveat. In order to stay in business in the long run, the monopoly must earn at least zero economic profit.

Polaroid and bankruptcy

If you have substantial profits in the long run, other firms try to offer similar substitutes in order to receive some of those profits. For example, you may remember Polaroid. Polaroid had a patent monopoly on instant-developing film. Introduced in 1948, instant-developing film and the camera it required were Polaroid's flagship products for over half a century.

Because of the great profits Polaroid received, however, other companies started developing substitutes. One result of this innovative process is the digital camera that allows you to even take pictures with your phone. Who needs instant-developing film now? Evidently, Polaroid thought the answer was nobody. In October 2001, Polaroid filed for Chapter 11 bankruptcy, and the reorganized company stopped producing the camera in 2007 and the film in 2009.

Zero economic profit is the same as a normal rate of return. As the monopoly's owner, you're receiving exactly as much income as you would in your next-best alternative. Zero profit doesn't mean zero income.

Producing with Multiple Facilities

Monopolists, as is the case for many other firms, often produce their product in more than one factory. In order to maximize profits, the monopolist must determine how to allocate production among these factories. In determining this allocation, the monopolist's goal is to produce additional units at the lowest cost. Therefore, the monopolist produces additional units of the product in the factory that has the lowest marginal cost. As a result, the monopolist minimizes the total cost of producing the total amount of the product.

Getting each facility's best

If the marginal cost of producing an additional unit of output in one factory is higher than the marginal cost of producing the additional unit of output in a second factory, you're not minimizing total production costs. Your total costs are lower if you switch production from the factory with the higher marginal cost to the factory with the lower marginal cost.

Cost minimization requires that the marginal cost of the last unit produced in each factory is equal for all factories. Figure 10-5 illustrates cost minimization for a monopoly with two factories. The marginal cost curve in the far right diagram labeled ΣMC is the horizontal summation of the marginal cost curves for each factory. Figure 10-5 shows two factories, A and B. Thus, marginal cost equals MC^* is associated with the output level q_{A1} in factory A and the output level q_{B2} in factory B. For the monopoly, it produces the output level q^* at a marginal cost MC^*. The output q^* simply is the horizontal summation of the quantities each factory produces given MC^*, or

$$q^* = q_{A1} + q_{B2}$$

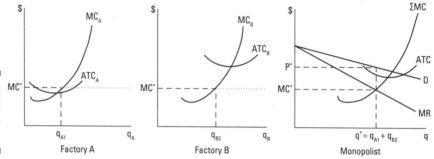

Figure 10-5:
Producing
with multi-
ple facilities.

Note in Figure 10-5 the monopolist wants to produce the output level q^* and charge the price P^* in order to maximize profits, because marginal revenue, MR, equals marginal cost, MC, in the far right diagram. In order to minimize the cost of producing q^*, the monopolist must produce the output level in each factory that corresponds to MC^*. Thus, q_1 units are produced in factory A and q_2 units are produced in factory B.

Calculating the best allocation with calculus

Calculus precisely determines the amount of output to produce in each factory — something that is difficult to determine graphically. Profit-maximizing production with multiple factories requires the satisfaction of the following equation

$$MR = \left(MC_A = MC_B = \dots = MC_i \right)$$

In other words, profit maximization requires that the monopolist's overall marginal revenue, MR, equals the marginal cost of production at each of its factories — factory A, factory B, and out to factory I — however many factories there are.

Assume the following equations describe a monopolist's demand, total revenue, and marginal revenue curves:

$$P = 190 - 0.01q$$

$$TR = p \times q = 190q - 0.01q^2$$

$$MR = 190 - 0.02q$$

The firm has two factories. Factory A's total cost and marginal cost equations are

$$TC_A = 150,000 + 40q_A + 0.01q_A^2$$

$$MC_A = \frac{dTC_A}{dq_A} = 40 + 0.02q_A$$

Factory B's total cost and marginal cost equations are

$$TC_B = 125,000 + 20q_B + 0.02q_B^2$$

$$MC_B = \frac{dTC_B}{dq_B} = 20 + 0.04q_B$$

As indicated, profit-maximization requires

$$MR = MC_A = MC_B$$

By solving this set of equations simultaneously, the monopolist's profit-maximizing quantity of output is determined, as well as the quantity of output that's produced in each factory.

1. **Set $MC_A = MC_B$ and solve for q_A as a function of q_B.**

$$MC_A = MC_B$$
$$40 + 0.02q_A = 20 + 0.04q_B$$

$$0.02q_A = -20 + 0.04q_B$$

$$q_A = \frac{-20 + 0.04q_B}{0.02} = -1,000 + 2q_B$$

2. **Set $MR = MC_B$.**

$$MR = 190 - 0.02q = 20 + 0.04q_B = MC_B$$

3. **Substitute $q_A + q_B$ for q.**

Because the total quantity of output the monopolist sells, q, is produced in some combination from factories A and B, the quantities produced in each factory added together must equal the quantity sold by the monopolist.

$$MR = 190 - 0.02q = 190 - 0.02(q_A + q_B)$$

$$MC_B = 20 + 0.04q_B$$

$$MR = 190 - 0.02(q_A + q_B) = 190 - 0.02q_A - 0.02q_B = 20 + 0.04q_B = MC_B$$

4. **Substitute $q_A = -1,000 + 2q_B$ from Step 1 for q_A in Step 3's equation.**

$$MR = 190 - 0.02q_A - 0.02q_B = 190 - 0.02(-1,000 + 2q_B) - 0.02q_B = 20 + 0.04q_B = MC_B$$
$$= 190 + 20 - 0.04q_B - 0.02q_B = 210 - 0.06q_B = 20 + 0.04q_B$$

5. **Solve for q_B.**

$$210 - 0.06q_B = 20 + 0.04q_B \quad \text{or} \quad 190 = 0.1q_B \quad \text{or} \quad q_B = 1,900$$

6. **Using the equation from Step 1, solve for q_A.**

$$q_A = -1,000 + 2q_B = -1,000 + 2(1,900) = 2,800$$

7. **Solve for q, the total quantity of output the monopolist sells.**

$$q = q_A + q_B = 2,800 + 1,900 = 4,700$$

8. **Solve for P, the price the monopolist establishes.**

P is determined by using the demand equation I give at the beginning of the example.
$$P = 190 - 0.01q = 190 - 0.01(4,700) = 143$$

9. **The monopolist's total profit is determined by subtracting the total cost of producing the given output in each factory from total revenue.**

$$\pi = TR - TC_A - TC_B$$
$$= (P \times q) - (150,000 + 40q_A + 0.01q_A^2) - (125,000 + 20q_B + 0.02q_B^2)$$
$$= (143 \times 4,700) - (150,000 + 40[2,800] + 0.01[2,800]^2) -$$
$$(125,000 + 20[1,900] + 0.02[1,900]^2)$$
$$= (672,100) - (340,400) - (235,200) = 96,500$$

So, the monopolist's total profit is $96,500. Knowing how to minimize cost when producing in two or more facilities is even better than collecting $200 when you pass "Go" in the board game Monopoly.

Chapter 11

Oligopoly: I Need You

· ·

In This Chapter

▶ Competing with a few rivals

▶ Recognizing mutual interdependence

▶ Developing theories for anticipating rival behavior

▶ Prospering in the long run

· ·

I Need You is a popular song first performed by the Beatles. The lyrics describe how one person doesn't realize how much he needs another with one lyric being "see just what you mean to me." Well, in oligopoly, rival firms make decisions that impact or mean something to one another. Oligopolies need rivals.

Oligopolies have a small number of firms. As a result, you know that your rivals and their actions directly impact you and everybody else's firm operating in that market. The result is mutual interdependence among firms. You need to understand how your rivals respond to your decisions, and responses can vary. Because anticipating reactions is difficult, no single theory describes oligopolistic markets. Several theories are needed to cover the range of possible behaviors.

In this chapter, I start by describing the characteristics of oligopoly. Understanding these characteristics helps you recognize when you must anticipate rival behavior. Next, I develop different models describing how various reactions affect your decisions and profits. For each of these models, I summarize the circumstances that make it the appropriate explanation for firm behavior helping you to choose when to use the model. I finish the chapter by examining how you maintain profit over an extended period of time.

So, as the song says, I need you. But I don't want to need too many others, because keeping the number of rivals small enables me to enjoy profit for a long time.

Managing with a Few Rivals in Oligopoly

Oligopolistic markets are easily recognized by the small number of firms that dominate the market. Because there are very few rivals, everybody knows everything about everybody else. It's sort of like living in a small town. Although this description may seem a little extreme, I'm not exaggerating by much. Examples of oligopolistic markets include the airline, steel, and automobile industries.

Identifying oligopolies

Oligopolies have two major characteristics.

- **Small number of firms:** Oligopolistic markets are dominated by a small number of firms. Each firm provides a fairly large percentage of the total quantity of the good available in the market. Therefore, individual firms have some degree of monopoly power and are able to set the good's price.

- **Barriers to entry:** Barriers to entry ensure the continued dominance of a small number of firms. Barriers to entry also enable oligopolistic firms to maintain positive economic profit, or returns in excess of the normal rate of return, in the long run. Barriers to entry typically result from economies of scale. The presence of economies of scale leads to larger firms having lower production cost per unit. Smaller new firms with fewer customers and lower production levels find it difficult to match the lower per-unit production costs of the existing firms.

The type of commodity produced by oligopolies isn't an important characteristic. Oligopolistic firms can produce either standardized — that is identical — or differentiated goods.

Living with mutual interdependence

Because of their small number, oligopolistic firms regard themselves as *mutually interdependent.* The actions of any one firm influence all other firms operating in the market. Oligopolistic firms must take into account how rivals respond to their actions.

Yikes! Mutual interdependence means you have to take into account how your rivals respond to your decisions, and there are only about a gazillion ways they might respond. This potential number of responses isn't a big problem for economists. They don't mind developing a gazillion theories. But for you it's a problem — unless, of course, you don't mind learning a gazillion theories.

The key point is that oligopolistic markets can't be described with a single theory like perfect competition and monopoly. (See Chapters 9 and 10 for details on perfect competition and monopoly, respectively.) Thus, I present several different theories that describe firm profit-maximizing behavior. With each of these theories, pay close attention to the way rivals respond to your decisions. Your understanding of rivals and how they respond determines which theory is appropriate.

Finally, mutual interdependence introduces the possibility of *collusion* among oligopolistic firms. Collusion occurs when firms act jointly in setting price and quantity. It typically isn't legal to collude in the United States, although a few exceptions, such as Major League Baseball, exist.

Engaging in advertising and non-price competition

Another method of discouraging entry to the market is to increase advertising. Advertising not only increases visibility and brand loyalty for an existing firm's product, but it also makes it more difficult for new firms to attract potential customers. Advertising enables you to increase the demand for your product by attracting new customers and "stealing" current customers from rival firms.

Oligopolies also innovate to separate themselves from rivals. Innovations that improve product quality or result in a better product to satisfy the same consumer desires increase the firm's demand and profits. Innovation can also increase profit by lowering the firm's production costs.

Modeling Oligopoly Behavior

In this section, I present six theories for oligopoly behavior. I know six is a lot, so you may want to skip some. But also, remember, I'm trying to anticipate how rivals respond and guessing how others react is risky business.

Sticking with sticky prices

The theory of the *kinked demand curve* is used to explain price inflexibility in an oligopolistic market. This theory is used when prices change very rarely — or in other words, prices are sticky.

The theory stresses mutual interdependence by describing how firms respond to any price change your firm may make. If your firm lowers price, the theory assumes that everyone lowers price to avoid losing customers and market share. So, if you lower price, you won't sell much more. On the other hand, if you raise price, none of your rivals will raise price. As a result, many of your customers will switch to one of your rivals. You'll lose a lot of sales.

Figure 11-1 portrays the situation that exists with a kinked demand curve. The top panel of the graph illustrates the demand curve your firm faces. The current profit-maximizing quantity and price are q_0 and P_0, respectively. Note that the profit-maximizing quantity corresponds to marginal revenue intersects marginal cost, and price is determined based upon where the quantity q_0 hits the demand curve.

If your firm decreases price, you assume that all your rivals will also decrease their price in order to avoid losing customers. The portion of your firm's demand curve associated with a price decrease is less elastic. Your demand curve is steeper and quantity demanded is less responsive to a decrease in price. That's because your firm is unable to steal customers from rival firms that also lower their product's price. This less-elastic demand is represented by the steeper curve labeled d_B in the upper panel of Figure 11-1. Because this demand curve is relevant only for price decreases and quantities above q_0, it's a solid line only for prices below P_0. (The dotted section of the line for prices above P_0 isn't relevant.)

The marginal revenue curve associated with d_B is the steeper curve labeled MR_B. Again, only the portion of the marginal revenue curve above q_0 is relevant and illustrated with a solid line.

For a linear, straight-line demand curve, marginal revenue always begins at the same point on the vertical axis and is twice as steep as the demand curve.

If your firm increases price, you assume none of your rivals increase their prices. Your customers are likely to switch to buying the product from your rivals that are relatively cheaper after your price increase. The portion of your firm's demand curve above P_0 is likely to be more elastic; quantity demanded is more responsive to a price increase. This segment of the firm's demand curve is represented by the flatter line d_A above P_0 and to the left of q_0.

The marginal revenue curve associated with d_A is the flatter curve labeled MR_A.

The kink in the firm's demand curve at P_0 and q_0 introduces a discontinuity in the marginal revenue curve. The solid segments of the marginal revenue curves MR_A and MR_B don't touch. This discontinuity is connected by the solid vertical segment in the marginal revenue curve.

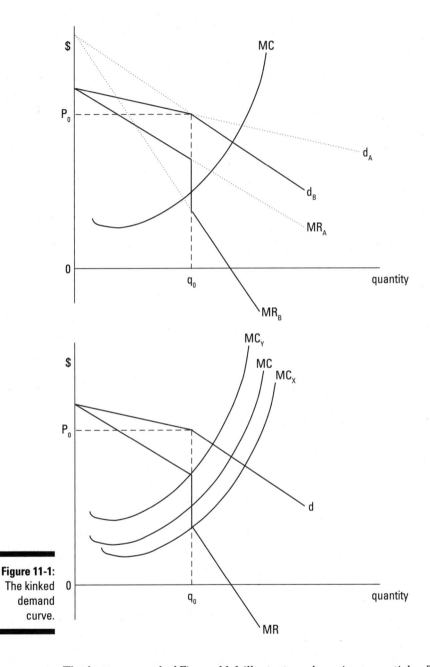

The bottom panel of Figure 11-1 illustrates why prices are sticky. The kinked demand curve and its resulting marginal revenue curve are the same as derived in the upper panel. The profit-maximizing quantity based on marginal revenue intersects marginal cost is q_0 and going from that quantity up to the demand curve leads to the profit-maximizing price P_0.

What's critical to note is that the marginal revenue curve resulting from the kinked demand curve has a vertical region. Thus, if marginal cost shifts anywhere in that vertical region — anywhere between the marginal cost labeled MC_x to the curve labeled MC_Y — the profit-maximizing quantity and price don't change. Price doesn't change in response to shifts in the marginal cost curve — hence price is sticky. Given price's inflexibility, firms in this situation must rely more heavily on non-price competition.

When rivals follow price decreases but ignore price increases, you have great difficulty in changing your price even when marginal cost changes.

Reacting to rivals in the Cournot model

Oligopolies commonly compete by trying to steal market share from one another. Thus, rather than compete by lowering price — the kinked demand curve (see the previous section) indicates that this tactic doesn't work because everyone lowers price — firms often compete on the other factor that directly affects profit — the quantity of the good they sell.

The Cournot model is used when firms produce identical or standardized goods and don't collude. Each firm assumes that its rivals make decisions that maximize profit.

The Cournot duopoly model offers one view of firms competing through the quantity produced. *Duopoly* means two firms, which simplifies the analysis. The *Cournot model* assumes that the two firms move simultaneously, have the same view of market demand, have good knowledge of each other's cost functions, and choose their profit-maximizing output with the belief that their rival chooses the same way. With all these assumptions, you may wonder why not just assume the right answer. Unfortunately, it doesn't work that way. On the other hand, you may think that these assumptions are unrealistic. However, research has shown that decision-makers operating in the same market over an extended period of time tend to have similar views of market demand and good knowledge of one another's cost structure.

Given these assumptions, one firm reacts to what it believes the other firm will produce. In other words, if firm B produces q_B of output, what quantity should I have my firm — firm A — produce? The *Cournot reaction function* describes the relationship between the quantity my firm produces and the quantity my rival produces. Here's how it works.

The market demand curve faced by Cournot duopolies is:

$$P = 120 - 0.5Q_D$$

where Q_D is the market quantity demanded and P is the market price in dollars.

Assuming firm A has a constant marginal cost of $20 and firm B has a constant marginal cost of $34, the reaction function for each firm is derived by using the following steps:

1. **Note that the market quantity demand, Q_D, must be jointly satisfied by firms A and B.**

   Thus,

   $$Q_D = q_A + q_B$$

2. **Substituting the equation in Step 1 for Q_D in the market demand curve yields**

   $$P = 120 - 0.5(q_A + q_B) = 120 - 0.5q_A - 0.5q_B$$

3. **For firm A, total revenue equals price multiplied by quantity.**

   $$TR_A = P \times q_A = (120 - 0.5q_A - 0.5q_B) \times q_A = 120q_A - 0.5q_A^2 - 0.5q_Bq_A$$

4. **Firm A's marginal revenue is determined by taking the derivative of total revenue, TR_A, with respect to q_A.**

   Remember to treat q_B as a constant because firm A can't change the quantity of output produced by firm B.

   $$MR_A = \frac{dTR_A}{dq_A} = 120 - q_A - 0.5q_B$$

5. **Firm A maximizes profit by setting its marginal revenue equal to marginal cost.**

   Firm A's marginal cost equals $20.

   $$MR_A = 120 - q_A - 0.5q_B = 20 = MC_A$$

6. **Rearranging the equation in Step 5 to solve for q_A gives firm A's reaction function.**

   $$120 - 20 - 0.5q_B = 100 - 0.5q_B = q_A$$

7. **Repeat Steps 3 through 6 to determine firm B's reaction function.**

   Remember that firm B's marginal cost equals $34.

   $$TR_B = P \times q_B = (120 - 0.5q_A - 0.5q_B) \times q_B = 120q_B - 0.5q_Aq_B - 0.5q_B^2$$

   $$MR_B = \frac{dTR_B}{dq_B} = 120 - 0.5q_A - q_B$$

   $$MR_B = 120 - 0.5q_A - q_B = 34 = MC_B$$

   $$120 - 34 - 0.5q_A = 86 - 0.5q_A = q_B$$

8. **Substituting firm B's reaction function for q_B in firm A's reaction function enables you to solve for q_A.**

$$100 - 0.5q_B = 100 - 0.5(86 - 0.5q_A) = q_A$$
$$100 - 43 + 0.25q_A = q_A$$
$$57 = 0.75q_A \text{ or } q_A = 76$$

9. **Substituting $q_A = 76$ in firm B's reaction function enables you to solve for q_B.**

$$86 - 0.5q_A = 86 - 0.5(76) = 48 = q_B$$

Thus, in the profit maximizing Cournot duopolist, firm A, produces 76 units of output while firm B produces 48 units of output. Figure 11-2 illustrates this result.

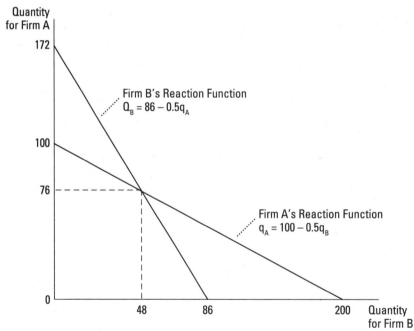

Figure 11-2:
A Cournot
duopoly.

In the Cournot duopoly model, both firms determine the profit-maximizing quantity simultaneously.

In the last example, firms A and B had different marginal costs. If the firms have the same marginal costs ($MC_A = MC_b$), each firm produces half the market output.

Leading your rivals with the Stackelberg model

Changing the assumptions of how firms react to one another changes the decision-making process. In the *Stackelberg model* of duopoly, one firm serves as the industry leader. As the industry leader, the firm is able to implement its decision before its rivals. Thus, if firm A makes its decision first, firm A is the industry leader and firm B reacts to or follows firm A's decision. However, in making its decision, firm A must anticipate how firm B reacts to that decision. An example of such leadership may be Microsoft's dominance in software markets. Although Microsoft can make decisions first, other smaller companies react to Microsoft's actions when making their own decisions. The actions of these followers, in turn, affect Microsoft.

The primary difference between the Cournot and Stackelberg duopoly models is that firms choose simultaneously in the Cournot model and sequentially in the Stackelberg model.

In this example, I use the same equations that I used in the Cournot duopoly example in the previous section. This consistency enables you to compare both the reaction functions and outcomes of the two situations.

The market demand curve now faced by the Stackelberg duopolies is:

$$P = 120 - 0.5Q_D$$

where Q_D is the market quantity demanded and P is the market price in dollars.

I continue assuming that firm A has a constant marginal cost of $20 and firm B has a constant marginal cost of $34. Derive the Stackelberg solution with the following steps:

1. **Firms A and B provide the entire market quantity demand, Q_D.**

   Thus,

   $$Q_D = q_A + q_B$$

2. **Substitute q_A and q_B for Q_D in the market demand curve to yield**

   $$P = 120 - 0.5(q_A + q_B) = 120 - 0.5q_A - 0.5q_B$$

3. **Because firm B reacts to firm A's output decision, I begin by deriving firm B's reaction function.**

Start by noting that total revenue equals price multiplied by quantity. For price, I substitute the equation from Step 2.

$$TR_B = P \times q_B = (120 - 0.5q_A - 0.5q_B) \times q_B = 120q_B - 0.5q_A q_B - 0.5q_B^2$$

4. **Firm B's marginal revenue equals the derivative of total revenue, *TR$_B$*, with respect to *q$_B$*.**

   Treat q_A as a constant because firm B can't change the quantity of output produced by firm A.

   $$MR_B = \frac{dTR_B}{dq_B} = 120 - 0.5q_A - q_B$$

5. **Firm B maximizes profit by equating its marginal revenue and marginal cost.**

   Remember that firm B's marginal cost equals $34.

   $$MR_B = 120 - 0.5q_A - q_B = 34 = MC_B$$

6. **Rearrange the equation in Step 5 to solve for *q$_B$* and to get firm B's reaction function.**

   $$120 - 34 - 0.5q_A = 86 - 0.5q_A = q_B$$

   For the next step, the demand curve faced by firm A is

   $$P = 120 - 0.5q_A - 0.5q_B$$

7. **At this point, substitute firm B's reaction function into firm A's demand curve.**

   This is the critical difference from the Cournot duopoly in the previous section. By substituting firm B's reaction function in its decision-making process, firm A is anticipating firm B's reaction to its output decision.

   $$P = 120 - 0.5q_A - 0.5q_B = 120 - 0.5q_A - 0.5(86 - 0.5q_A)$$
   $$= 120 - 0.5q_A - 43 + 0.25q_A = 77 - 0.25q_A$$

8. **Firm A's total revenue, *TR$_A$*, equals price times quantity.**

   $$TR_A = P \times q_A = (77 - 0.25q_A)q_A = 77q_A - 0.25q_A^2$$

9. **Firm A's marginal revenue is the derivative of total revenue taken with respect to *q$_A$*.**

$$MR_A = \frac{dTR_A}{dq_A} = 77 - 0.5q_A$$

10. Firm A determines the profit-maximizing quantity of output by setting marginal revenue equal to marginal cost and solving for q_A.

Remember that firm A's marginal cost is a constant $20.

$$MR_A = 77 - 0.5q_A = 20 = MC_A$$
$$77 - 20 = 57 = 0.5q_A \quad \text{or} \quad q_A = 114$$

11. Substitute q_A into firm B's reaction function from Step 6 to determine q_B.

$$q_B = 86 - 0.5q_A = 86 - 0.5(114) = 29$$

Thus, the profit-maximizing Stackelberg duopoly has firm A producing 114 units of output and firm B producing 29 units of output. Figure 11-3 illustrates the Stackelberg duopoly. Note that firm B has exactly the same reaction function as existed in the Cournot duopoly. On the other hand, firm A doesn't have a reaction function. Firm A sets it output first, and then firm B reacts to that output. Thus, the horizontal line for firm A at 114 units of output indicates it has set its output before firm B reacts.

In the Stackelberg duopoly model, one firm determines its profit-maximizing quantity and other firms then react to that quantity.

In the Cournot model, firm A simply notes that the market demand is satisfied by the output produced by it and firm B. The two firms make simultaneous decisions. In the Stackelberg model, firm A substitutes an equation to represent how firm B reacts to its production decision. The model reflects sequential decisions.

The simultaneous decision-making associated with the Cournot model leads to different outcomes from the outcomes associated with sequential decisions of the Stackelberg model. In the model examples, I use the same equations for market demand and each firm's marginal cost. In the Cournot model solution, firm A produces 76 units, and firm B produces 48 units. Thus, the total market output is 124 units. When you substitute these quantities into the market demand curve, the price is $62.00. In the Stackelberg model, firm A produces 114 units, and firm B produces 29 units, and the total market output is 143 units. Substituting these quantities into the market demand curve leads to a price of $48.50. Thus, the Stackelberg leadership model results in a higher market quantity and lower price for the good as compared to the Cournot model.

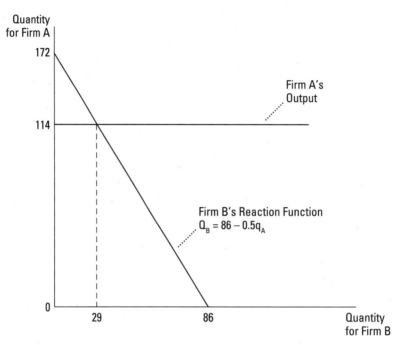

Figure 11-3:
A
Stackelberg
duopoly.

Competing for customers through the Bertrand model

The Cournot and Stackelberg duopoly theories focus on firms competing through the quantity of output they produce. The *Bertrand duopoly model* examines price competition among firms that produce differentiated but highly substitutable products. Each firm's quantity demanded is a function of not only the price it charges but also the price charged by its rival. Coca-Cola and Pepsi are examples of Bertrand duopolists.

TIP

With the Bertrand model, you focus on what price is selected to maximize your profits. In the Cournot and Stackelberg duopoly models (see the previous sections), the focus is on quantity.

EXAMPLE

The quantity demanded for firm A and firm B is a function of both the price the firm establishes and the price established by their rival because the goods are highly substitutable. Thus, the firms have the following demand curves relating quantity demanded to its price and its rival's price

Firm A: $q_A = 400 - 4P_A + 2P_B$
Firm B: $q_B = 240 - 3P_B + 1.5P_A$

To simplify the analysis, I assume that both firms have zero marginal cost for their products. Profit maximization then requires each firm to choose a price that maximizes its total revenue.

Derive the Bertrand reaction functions for each firm with the following steps:

1. **Firm A's total revenue equals price times quantity, so**

   $$TR_A = P_A \times q_A = P_A(400 - 4P_A + 2P_B) = 400P_A - 4P_A^2 + 2P_AP_B$$

2. **Taking the derivative of firm A's total revenue with respect to the price it charges yields**

   $$\frac{dTR_A}{dP_A} = 400 - 8P_A + 2P_B$$

3. **Setting the equation in Step 2 equal to zero and solving it for P_A generates firm A's reaction function.**

   Setting the derivative of total revenue equal to zero maximizes total revenue, which also maximizes profit given marginal cost equals zero.

   $$\frac{dTR_A}{dP_A} = 400 - 8P_A + 2P_B = 0 \ \text{ or } \ 400 + 2P_B = 8P_A$$
   $$P_A = 50 + 0.25P_B$$

4. **Repeat these steps for firm B to derive its reaction function.**

   $$TR_B = P_B \times q_B = P_B(240 - 3P_B + 1.5P_A) = 240P_B - 3P_B^2 + 1.5P_AP_B$$
   $$\frac{dTR_B}{dP_B} = 240 - 6P_B + 1.5P_A$$
   $$\frac{dTR_B}{dP_B} = 240 - 6P_B + 1.5P_A = 0 \ \text{ or } \ 240 + 1.5P_A = 6P_B$$
   $$P_B = 40 + 0.25P_A$$

5. **Substitute firm B's reaction function into firm A's reaction to determine P_A.**

   $$P_A = 50 + 0.25P_B = 50 + 0.25(40 + 0.25P_A) = 50 + 10 + 0.0625P_A$$
   $$P_A = 60 + 0.0625P_A \ \text{ or } \ 0.9375P_A = 60 \ \text{ or } \ P_A = 64$$

6. **Substitute P_A equals 64 in firm B's reaction function to determine P_B.**

   $$P_B = 40 + 0.25P_A = 40 + 0.25(64) = 56$$

The Bertrand duopoly model indicates that firm A maximizes profit by charging $64, and firm B maximizes profit by charging $56. Figure 11-4 illustrates the Bertrand duopoly model. Note that both the horizontal and vertical axes on the figure measure price and not quantity (as in the Cournot and Stackelberg models).

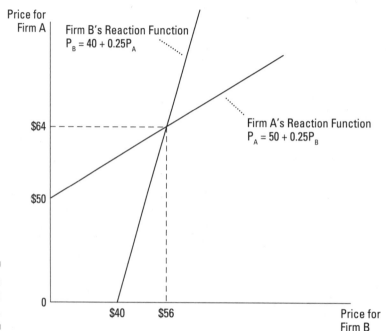

Figure 11-4:
A Bertrand
duopoly.

In the Bertrand model, firms compete with price. Therefore, reaction functions are expressed in terms of price, not quantities.

Leading the pack: Another view of price leadership

The Stackelberg model of oligopoly illustrates one firm's leadership in an oligopoly. In the Stackelberg model, the leader decides how much output to produce with other firms basing their decision on what the leader chooses. Another common form of leadership is for the leading firm to set price. Rival firms then use the same price for their products. However, as is always the case in oligopoly, the leading firm must take into account the behavior of its rivals.

The leading firm that initially sets price is called the *dominant firm.* The firms that use the price set by the dominant firm are typically smaller in size and called *following firms*. Markets for steel and agricultural implements have been observed to operate in this manner.

The theory of price leadership represents a combination of monopoly behavior on the dominant firm's part and perfectly competitive behavior on the part of following firms.

Figure 11-5 illustrates price leadership. The market has a downward-sloping demand curve labeled *D*. A crucial point: The dominant firm must take into account that its following firms satisfy part of that market demand. Because the following firms act as price takers, their marginal revenue curve is the price set by the dominant firm. To maximize profits, the following firms produce where price/marginal revenue equals marginal cost. Therefore, each following firm's supply curve corresponds to its marginal cost curve, and the aggregate supply curve for all following firms is the horizontal summation of the marginal cost curves. This horizontal summation of marginal cost is represented by the curve ΣMC_f.

In Figure 11-5, the dominant firm's demand curve, d_d, is derived from the market demand and the aggregate supply curve for the following firms. The dominant firm simply subtracts the quantity provided by the following firms from the quantity demanded in the market to determine its quantity demanded. In other words, the dominant firm's demand curve equals the market demand curve minus the sum of the following firm's marginal cost curves, ΣMC_f.

Given the linear relationships in Figure 11-5, the dominant firm's marginal revenue curve, MR_d, is twice as steep as its demand curve. The dominant firm maximizes profit by producing the quantity of output that corresponds to marginal revenue, MR_d, equals marginal cost, MC_d. This output level is q_d. The dominant firm determines price by going from the quantity q_d up to its demand curve, d_d. Thus, the dominant firm sets the price at P_d.

As already noted, following firms are price takers. The dominant firm's price P_d is the price that all following firms charge for every unit of the product they sell. For the following firms, the dominant firm's price becomes their marginal revenue, $P_d = MR_f$. The following firms then maximize profit by setting marginal revenue, MR_f, equal to marginal cost, MC_f. In aggregate, the following firms produce q_f of output.

For the market, consumers pay a price of P_d and consume the quantity Q. The quantity consumed Q equals q_d plus q_f.

The market demand for an oligopoly characterized by price leadership is

$$Q = 10,000 - 550P$$

where Q is the market quantity demanded and P is the good's price in dollars.

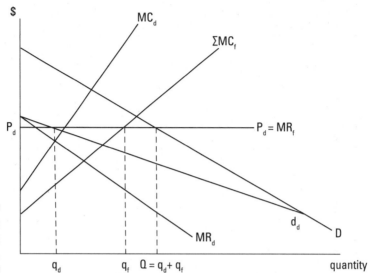

Figure 11-5:
Price
leadership.

The aggregate marginal cost for the following firms is represented by

$$\Sigma MC_f = 8 + 0.004q_f$$

where ΣMC_f is the horizontal summation of marginal cost for the following firms and q_f is the aggregate quantity produced by the following firms.

The dominant firm's marginal cost curve is

$$MC_d = 9 + 0.005q_d$$

where MC_d is the dominant firm's marginal cost in dollars and q_d is the quantity produced by the dominant firm.

In order to determine the good's market price and the quantity of the good produced by the dominant firm and the following firms, you take the following steps:

1. **Derive the dominant firm's demand curve.**

   Note that the market quantity demanded Q equals:

   $$Q = q_d + q_f \quad \text{or} \quad q_d = Q - q_f$$

2. **Rearrange the following firms' aggregate marginal cost curve to get**

   $MC_f = 8 + 0.004q_f$ or $0.004q_f = -8 + MC_f$

   or $q_f = -2,000 + 250MC_f$

3. **Substitute P for MC_f in the equation from Step 2.**

   This substitution is allowed because following firms produce where price equals marginal cost in order to maximize profit.

   $$q_f = -2,000 + 250P$$

4. **In the Step 1 equation, substitute the market demand equation for Q and the equation for q_f from Step 3.**

   This step generates the equation for the dominant firm's demand curve.

   $$q_f = -2,000 + 250P$$
   $$q_d = Q - q_f = (10,000 - 550P) - (-2,000 + 250P)$$
   $$q_d = 10,000 - 550P + 2,000 - 250P = 12,000 - 800P$$

5. **Rearrange the equation in Step 4 to solve for P as a function of q_d.**

   This form is converted to the total revenue equation in the next step.

   $$800P = 12,000 - q_d \quad \text{or} \quad P = 15 - 0.00125q_d$$

6. **Determine the dominant firm's total revenue equation.**

   Remember, total revenue equals price multiplied by quantity.

   $$TR_d = P \times q_d = (15 - 0.00125q_d) \times q_d = 15q_d - 0.00125q_d^2$$

7. **Determine the dominant firm's marginal revenue equation.**

   Take the derivative of total revenue with respect to q_d.

   $$MR_d = \frac{dTR_d}{dq_d} = 15 - 0.0025q_d$$

8. **Determine the dominant firm's profit-maximizing quantity of output.**

   Set the dominant firm's marginal revenue equal to the dominant firm's marginal cost and solve for q_d.

   $$MR_d = 15 - 0.0025q_d = 9 + 0.005q_d = MC_d$$
   $$6 = 0.0075q_d \quad \text{or} \quad \frac{6}{0.0075} = 800 = q_d$$

9. **Substitute q_d equals 800 into the dominant firm's demand curve in order to determine the price established by the dominant firm.**

   $$P = 15 - 0.00125q_d = 15 - 0.00125(800) = 14$$

   The dominant firm produces 800 units of output and charges a price of $14.

10. Determine the following firms aggregate quantity of output.

Following firms are price takers, so the dominant firm's price is the following firms' marginal revenue.

$$MR_f = P = 14 = 8 + 0.004q_f = MC_f$$

$$6 = 0.004q_f \text{ or } \frac{6}{0.004} = 1,500 = q_f$$

11. Determine the market quantity demanded.

Substitute 14 for price P in the market demand equation.

$$Q = 10,000 - 550P = 10,000 - 550(14) = 10,000 - 7,700 = 2,300$$

So the dominant firm produces 800 units of output at a price of $14. The following firms produce an aggregate of 1,500 units. The market quantity demanded given a price of $14 is 2,300 units — the same as q_d plus q_f.

In the price leadership model, only the dominant firm has monopoly power — only the dominant firm can set price.

Working together by using cartels and collusion

Recognizing that mutual interdependence can lead to undesirable outcomes, firms have an incentive to cooperate by colluding or forming cartels that limit competition. With *collusion,* rival firms cooperate for their mutual benefit. Although such behavior is generally illegal in the United States, in other parts of the world, collusion is permitted. Airbus, one of the two biggest civilian aircraft manufacturers in the world, arose from a consortium of European companies and, until recent years, collusion among Japanese firms manufacturing auto parts was widespread. A *cartel* is the result of an open, formal, and legal collusive agreement. Today, the Organization of Petroleum Exporting Countries (OPEC) is the most widely recognized cartel "success" story.

Through collusion, firms act together so their behavior mirrors a monopoly's behavior. In essence, the firms try to gain monopoly profits by eliminating competition among them. If the cartel's goal is to maximize the cartel's total profit, the cartel takes the actions represented in Figure 11-6.

The cartel's marginal cost is the horizontal summation of the individual firm marginal cost curves. In Figure 11-6, firms A and B have the marginal cost curves MC_A and MC_B. A marginal cost of $2 is associated with 6 units of output for firm A and 8 units of output for firm B. The horizontal summation of marginal cost means that, for the cartel, a marginal cost of $2 is associated with 14 units of output — 8 plus 6. The cartel's marginal cost curve is represented by ΣMC.

Exemptions to collusion in the United States

Collusion is prohibited in the United States through antitrust laws, including the Sherman Antitrust Act. However, some industries receive limited exemptions from the antitrust laws. Professional sports leagues receive exemptions and, as a result, owners of "competing" franchises have regular meetings. The professional sports antitrust exemption is justified because some collusion among teams is necessary to ensure fair competition. This results in owners jointly establishing rules, such as those associated with drafting players, locating franchises, and negotiating broadcasting rights. Each of these rules restrict business competition, while promoting fair athletic competition among the league's teams. U.S. airlines flying international routes are members of the International Air Transport Association (IATA). Historically, the IATA has established prices for international air travel. This price setting exemption from antitrust laws is justified to facilitate passenger travel involving intermediate stops and travel on different airlines. Coordination among airlines results in lower fares because multiple airlines can be used in one travel itinerary. In addition, the IATA coordinates scheduling, promotes safety standards, and assigns safety codes. Labor unions also receive exemptions from antitrust laws allowing for collective bargaining.

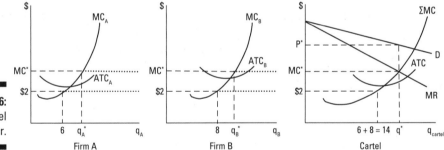

Figure 11-6:
Cartel
behavior.

In order for the cartel's marginal cost curve to equal the horizontal summation of the individual firm marginal cost curves, input prices can't change as the cartel organizes.

The cartel faces the market demand for the good and, from the market demand, derives marginal revenue. The graph on the far right of Figure 11-6 illustrates the market demand, labeled D, and marginal revenue, labeled MR.

The cartel maximizes its profit by producing the output level associated with marginal revenue equals marginal cost in the far right panel of Figure 11-6. This corresponds to the output level q^*. Based upon the profit-maximizing output level, the cartel goes up to the demand curve to determine the profit-maximizing price or monopoly price, P^*.

In order to maximize its total profit, the cartel must minimize production cost. In order to minimize production cost, the marginal cost of the last unit produced by each member of the cartel must equal the marginal cost associated with profit maximization — MC^* in Figure 11-6. Thus, firm A in Figure 11-6 produces q_A^* and firm B produces q_B^*.

Cartels tend to be unstable because members often have incentive to cheat on the arrangement. In Figure 11-6, firm A has an incentive to produce more than q_A^* because selling more output increases its profit. However, any change in output from q_A^* reduces the cartel's combined profit. Thus, if firm A's profit increases, it must be at another member's expense — firm B ends up with less profit. The different, conflicting interests of cartel participants lead to instability. And given that collusion is usually illegal, any agreements are legally unenforceable.

Assume that the following equations describe the cost functions for two firms forming a cartel.

Firm A's total cost and marginal cost equations are:

$$TC_A = 1,170 + 8q_A + 0.02q_A^2$$

$$MC_A = \frac{dTC_A}{dq_A} = 8 + 0.04q_A$$

where TC_A is firm A's total cost in dollars, MC_A is marginal cost in dollars, and q_A is the quantity firm A produces.

Firm B's total cost and marginal cost equations are:

$$TC_B = 980 + 2q_B + 0.04q_B^2$$

$$MC_B = \frac{dTC_B}{dq_B} = 2 + 0.08q_B$$

where TC_B is firm B's total cost in dollars, MC_B is marginal cost in dollars, and q_B is the quantity firm B produces.

The market demand for the good produced by firms A and B is:

$$P = 24 - 0.02Q$$

where P is the good's price in dollars and Q is good's market quantity demanded.

If firms A and B form a cartel, profit-maximization requires

$$MR = MC_A = MC_B$$

By solving this set of equations simultaneously, the cartel's profit-maximizing quantity of output and price are determined. In addition, the quantity of output each firm produces to minimize production cost is determined.

1. **Determine total revenue as a function of quantity.**

   Because firms A and B are acting together, the market demand curve becomes the cartel's demand curve. Determine total revenue as a function of quantity by multiplying price from the market demand curve times quantity.

   $$TR = P \times Q = (24 - 0.02Q) \times Q = 24Q - 0.02Q^2$$

2. **Determine marginal revenue.**

   To determine marginal revenue, take the derivative of total revenue with respect to Q.

   $$MR = \frac{dTR}{dq} = 24 - 0.04Q$$

3. **Set *MR = MC$_A$*.**

   $$MR = 24 - 0.04Q = 8 + 0.04q_A = MC_A$$

4. **Substitute $q_A + q_B$ for Q.**

   Because the total quantity of output the cartel sells, Q, is produced in some combination from firms A and B, the quantities produced by each firm added together must equal the quantity sold by the cartel.

   $$MR = 24 - 0.04(q_A + q_B) = 24 - 0.04q_A - 0.04q_B = 8 + 0.04q_A = MC_A$$

5. **Solve the equation in Step 4 for q_A.**

   $$24 - 0.04q_A - 0.04q_B = 8 + 0.04q_A$$
   $$24 - 0.04q_B = 8 + 0.08q_A$$
   $$16 - 0.04q_B = 0.08q_A$$
   $$200 - 0.5q_B = q_A$$

6. **Set *MC$_A$* equal to *MC$_B$*.**

   $$MC_A = 8 + 0.04q_A = 2 + 0.08q_B = MC_B$$

7. **Substitute $q_A = 200 - 0.5q_B$ in the equation in Step 6.**

   $$8 + 0.04q_A = 8 + 0.04(200 - 0.5q_B) = 2 + 0.08q_B$$

8. **Solve for q_B.**

$$8 + 0.04(200 - 0.5q_B) = 8 + 8 - 0.02q_B = 2 + 0.08q_B$$
$$16 - 0.02q_B = 2 + 0.08q_B \quad \text{or} \quad 14 = 0.1q_B \quad \text{or} \quad q_B = 140$$

9. **Substitute q_B = 140 in the equation from Step 5 to determine q_A.**

$$q_A = 200 - 0.5q_B = 200 - 0.5(140) = 130$$

10. **Solve for Q, the quantity the cartel produces.**

$$Q = q_A + q_B = 130 + 140 = 270$$

11. **Solve for P, the price the cartel establishes for the good.**

$$P = 24 - 0.02Q = 24 - 0.02(270) = 18.6$$

The cartel establishes a price of $18.60 for the good. Firm A produces 130 units and firm B produces 140 units.

Cartel participants jointly determine quantity and price based upon marginal revenue, derived from the market demand curve, equaling each participant's marginal cost.

Profiting from the Long Run

Economies of scale serve as a barrier to entry in oligopolistic markets. *Economies of scale* mean that existing firms produce a large quantity of the good at very low average total cost per unit. The existing firms tend to have substantial fixed costs, so producing a larger quantity of output reduces their fixed cost per unit and thus their average total cost per unit. On the other hand, a new firm entering the market isn't likely to have many customers at first. Therefore, the new firm produces a much smaller quantity of output and can't spread its fixed costs as far. The result is much higher average total cost per unit for a new firm.

Because their cost per unit is lower than the new firm's cost per unit, the existing firms charge lower prices than the new firm. Yet, even with the lower price, the existing firms earn positive economic profit because their cost per unit is so low. If the new firm tries to match this low price, it loses money because it has a much higher cost per unit. Thus, even with the attraction of positive profit, new firms can't effectively compete with existing firms who take advantage of economies of scale.

Positive economic profit means the firm earns more than a normal rate of return. When economic profit is positive, you're receiving more income — or a return that's higher than normal — as compared to your next best alternative.

Chapter 12

Game Theory: Fun Only if You Win

*F*inally, some fun. You get to play games, and you've probably heard the saying, "It's not whether you win or lose; it's how you play the game." A critical point for business that this quote misses is how you play the game determines whether you win or lose. And in business, whether you win — make profit — or lose — incur losses — means everything.

Strategic decision-making occurs when the game's outcomes depend on the choices made by different players. Because the outcomes are interdependent, players must consider how rivals respond to their decisions. Competition in these situations leads to mutual interdependence with conflict. The complexity of the resulting environment requires decision-making rules. Game theory provides a framework for making the decisions. Game theory's goal is to provide rules that enable you to correctly anticipate a rival's decision.

A great example of game theory is the board game Monopoly. Monopoly involves multiple decision-makers or players. The decisions each player makes influence the game's outcome. If I build a hotel on St. James Place and you land on it, you owe me $950. On the other hand, if you land on St. James Place when it has no house or hotel, your rent is only $14.

This chapter examines how decisions are made in game theory. I start by describing a game's possible structure. I then examine how decisions are made given the game's structure. A player chooses an action based on the competitor's decision and information the player possesses. I note that players never choose a dominated action because a better choice is always available through either a pure or mixed strategy. Next, I examine games that result in a lose-lose outcome because of the prisoner's dilemma. I examine games involving sequences of decisions to determine whether moving first is always desirable. The chapter concludes with some special situations applying game theory, including collusion and preemptive strategies. By understanding how to play a variety of games, game theory helps improve your ability to influence the strategic environment in a number of situations ranging from oligopolistic markets to auctions. Wherever outcomes are *interdependent* — that is, the outcome is jointly determined by the decisions made by two or more players — you should consider using game theory.

Winning Is Everything

A game is a competitive situation where two or more players pursue their own goals — such as profit maximization or cost minimization — with no single player able to dictate the game's outcome. Being competitive simply means that you play to win, and in business decision-making, winning means you make profit, and lots of it.

The mutual interdependence among firms in an oligopolistic market (see Chapter 11) resembles a game, and, thus, decision-makers are likely to find game theory useful in understanding these markets.

Players are the decision-makers. Players generally start with a given amount of resources. For example, in the board game of Monopoly, players start with two $500 bills, two $100 bills, two $50 bills, six $20 bills, five $10 bills, five $5 bills, and five $1 bills. In the business world, players may start with as little as their own labor and entrepreneurial abilities. Players must then decide how to use those resources.

Structuring the Game

A game is composed of rules, actions, and payoffs. The game's structure plays a crucial role in determining the ultimate outcome.

Making rules for the game

Rules of the game describe how the game is played. Rules of the game include whose turn it is, how resources can be employed, technological constraints, what government regulations permit, and so on. Like in Monopoly, the rule book can be quite lengthy and can include things like how to mortgage property and when to pay taxes.

Actions

Actions are the choices a player can make. In Monopoly, it may be the decision to buy or not to buy Boardwalk when you land on it. Players need to consider possible actions when making a decision — not only their own but also the possible actions of their rivals. If you don't buy Boardwalk, who might?

The actions chosen by all players ultimately determine the game's outcome. Thus, before starting the game, you need to recognize who all the players are, and the possible decisions they can make. Sound decisions require that you completely specify the actions you can take and what rivals do given each of your possible actions. Therefore, the game's structure must recognize how players respond to all possible circumstances at each stage in the game.

Determining the payoff

Payoffs represent the outcome or returns of the game. The payoff depends not only on the decisions you make, but also on the decisions your rivals make. Thus, payoffs are the result of a combination of actions indicating the players' strategic interdependence.

A payoff table summarizes the various combinations of outcomes for all players and all possible actions. Typically, players are assumed to be rational when they make decisions. Players subscribe to the philosophy "Don't harm thyself." This philosophy is a sound assumption to make in the profit-motivated business world.

Identifying whose turn it is in decision-making

The game theory framework requires knowing how players take turns while playing the game. In tic-tac-toe, the player who moves first has a much higher probability of winning because that player gets to move five times in the game while the player moving second gets only four possible moves. Similarly, in chess, numerous studies have shown that white, the color that always moves first, wins more than fifty percent of the games.

Similarly, how firms take turns in oligopoly influences the outcome. In Chapter 11's presentation of the Stackelberg model, the firm that is the leader and chooses first produces a lot more output than the firm that chooses second. Or if Coca-Cola comes out with a new advertising campaign, it might be able to steal customers from Pepsi. Similarly, the airline that cuts fares can increase the number of passengers it carries until rivals have an opportunity to respond.

Thus the order in which players select is crucial in determining the game's outcome. Check out the next section for details on how to make decisions in various game scenarios.

Making Decisions

The following sections outline how decisions are made in the following scenarios:

- ✔ **Simultaneous-move games:** Rock-paper-scissors is a simultaneous-move game. In the game, players make their decisions at the same time. A simultaneous-move game also exists if you make decisions without knowing what the other players have decided.

- ✔ **Sequential-move games:** Tic-tac-toe and chess are examples of sequential games — one player chooses first, and then the other player gets to respond. In sequential games, everybody except the player who moves first gets to observe their rivals' decisions before making their own decision.

- ✔ **One-shot games:** The game is played only once. The game isn't repeated among players. A duel is an example of a one-shot game that's also a sequential-move game. And as this example illustrates, it can be very important to play even one-shot games well.

- ✔ **Repeated games:** Players know the game is played over and over again. An infinitely-repeated game never ends. The baseball World Series is a repeated game with teams playing at least four and up to seven times. On the other hand, professional football's Super Bowl is another example of a one-shot game.

Simultaneous-move, one-shot games

In these games, players make decisions at the same time or, at the very least, they don't know their rival's decision prior to making their own. In addition, the game is played only once.

Assume that two players, you and me, are trying to determine whether or not to increase our sales by expanding our business to a second location in a neighboring town. Figure 12-1 illustrates the payoff table associated with our possible decision combinations.

My decisions are represented on the left side of the table. The top row represents my choice to expand, and the bottom row is my choice to not expand.

Your decisions appear across the top of the payoff table — the left column represents your choice to expand and the right column is your choice to not expand.

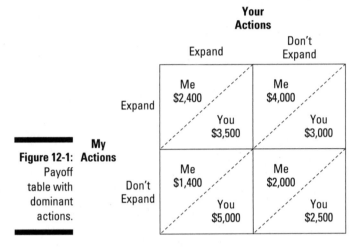

Your Actions

Figure 12-1: **My Actions** Payoff table with dominant actions.

Each cell in the payoff table presents the results of the actions you and I take. In this example, I assume the payoffs are the business's monthly profit. Thus, if I decide to expand and you decide to expand, the resulting payoffs are contained in the upper-left cell of the payoff table. The cell indicates that my monthly profit is $2,400 and your monthly profit is $3,500. If, instead, I decide to not expand while you decide to expand, my profit is $1,400, while your profit is $5,000.

Identifying dominant actions

A *dominant action* is an action whose payoff is always highest, regardless of the action chosen by your opponent. In Figure 12-1, your dominant action is to expand. To understand why, note the following:

- ✔ If I decide to expand, you read across the top row, and your possible payoffs are $3,500 if you also expand or $3,000 if you don't expand. You should expand because it leads to a better payoff.

- ✔ If I decide to not expand, you read across the bottom row, and your possible payoffs are $5,000 if you expand or $2,500 if you don't expand. Again, you should expand.

No matter what I choose, you always get a better payoff — higher profit — if you expand. To expand is a dominant action for you because its payoff is always better than not expanding.

A similar situation exists for me:

> ✔ If you decide to expand, I read down the left column, and my possible payoffs are $2,400 if I also expand or $1,400 if I don't expand. I should expand because it leads to a better payoff.
>
> ✔ If you decide to not expand, I read down the right column, and my possible payoffs are $4,000 if I expand or $2,000 if I don't expand. Again, I should expand.

To expand is a dominant action for me because no matter what you choose, I get a better payoff — higher profit — by deciding to expand instead of not expanding.

You should never choose an action that is dominated.

So, how does our game turn out? Because the dominant action for both of us is to expand, we both choose that action. I receive $2,400 in monthly profit, and you receive $3,500 in monthly profit. Our combined profit is $5,900. Interestingly, this payoff is not the best combined payoff for us. If I expand and you don't expand, our combined payoff would be $7,000 — $4,000 for me and $3,000 for you. This higher combined payoff provides an incentive for us to merge.

Considering the maxi-min rule and reaching the Nash equilibrium

The game in the previous section is fairly easy because we both have only two actions and one of them is a dominant action. Figure 12-2 illustrates a more complicated game because each player now has three possible actions — reduce fares, charge the same fares, or raise fares. This game is still a simultaneous-move, one-shot game, so each player gets to make a single decision without knowing what the other player decides. Figure 12-2 indicates the resulting annual profit in millions of dollars based upon the combination of actions each airline takes.

In Figure 12-2, neither airline has a dominant action. For Global Airline, none of the possible decisions regarding fares always has a higher payoff when compared to another fare decision. When comparing the columns for reduce fares and same fares, sometimes reduce fares has higher payoff — for example, when International charges the same fare, Global's reduce fare yields $38 and Global's same fare yields only $35. But sometimes, same fares has a higher payoff — for example, when International reduces fares, Global's same fare has $32 and reduce fare has only $18. Similarly, when comparing reduce fares to raise fares and same fares to raise fares, Global never has a situation where one action always has a higher payoff compared to the other action. The same situation exists for International Airline.

Global Airline

		Reduce Fares	Same Fares	Raise Fares
	Reduce Fares	International $27 / Global $18	International $35 / G Global $32	I International $44 / Global $14
International Airline	**Same Fares**	I International $36 / G Global $38	I International $42 / Global $35	International $25 / Global $17
	Raise Fares	International $29 / Global $32	International $34 / Global $37	International $33 / G Global $41

Figure 12-2: Payoff table for three-action game.

The maxi min rule

Because the situation in Figure 12-2 can't be simplified by dominant actions, rules are necessary to guide decision-making. One possible rule is called the *maxi min rule*. When using the maxi min decision rule, firms look at the worst possible outcome for each action, and then choose the action whose worst possible outcome is best — in other words, the firm maximizes the minimum gain. In oligopolistic markets, this rule can seem like a reasonable strategy for a firm to use, because its rivals are likely to pursue actions that result in the worst possible outcome for the firm.

If International Airline applies the maxi min rule in Figure 12-2, its goal is to choose the action that results in the best possible worst outcome, or to maximize the minimum payoff. To apply this rule, International takes the following steps.

1. **International determines its worst possible payoff if it reduces fares.**

   The worst possible payoff if International reduces fares is $27 that occurs if Global also reduces fares.

2. **International determines its worst possible payoff if it charges the same fare.**

The worst possible payoff in this situation is $25 that occurs if Global raises fares.

3. **International determines its worst possible payoff if it raises fares.**

   The worst outcome is $29 that occurs if Global reduces fares.

4. **International applies the maxi-min rule and raises fares.**

   International Airline raises fares because it results in the best possible worst outcome — $29 is better than either $27 or $25.

The maxi min rule is a very conservative strategy. It has a major problem because it looks only at the worst possible outcome. You don't even consider other possible outcomes. So, applying this rule means you would probably never invest in a business. Investing in a business means you might lose money. If you just hold onto your money, you won't lose it.

Another problem with the maxi min strategy is you ignore what your rival may choose. A better way to make decisions in game theory is to anticipate what your rival may do. For example, in playing the board game Monopoly, if your opponent already owns the orange properties of Tennessee Avenue and New York Avenue, when you land on St. James Place, you should buy it to prevent your opponent from getting a monopoly. You take into account that your opponent will certainly buy St. James if she lands on it.

What happens if International Airline anticipates Global's decision. In this case, if International reduces fares, Global charges the same fare, because that has the highest payoff — $32. If International charges the same fare, Global reduces fares to earn $38. If International raises fares, Global also raises fares to receive $41. These cells are marked with a "G" in Figure 12-2.

Alternatively, what happens if Global Airline anticipates International's decision. In this case, if Global reduces fares, International charges the same fare, because that has the highest payoff — $36. If Global charges the same fare, International charges the same fare to earn $42. If Global raises fares, International reduces fares to receive $44. These cells are marked with an "I" in Figure 12-2.

The Nash equilibrium

The game illustrated in Figure 12-2 ultimately results in International Airline deciding to charge the same fare and Global Airline deciding to reduce fares. This outcome is called a Nash equilibrium. A *Nash equilibrium* exists when no player can improve his or her payoff by unilaterally changing his or her action given the actions chosen by other players. In order to reach a Nash equilibrium, each player chooses the action that maximizes the payoff conditional on others doing the same.

So, in Figure 12-2, if International Airline changes its decision to either reduce or raise fares given that Global Airline has reduced fares, its profit is less than the $36 it receives from charging the same fare. Similarly, if Global Airline changes its decision to either charge the same fare or raise fares, its profit is less than the $38 it receives from reducing fares. International and Global airlines are in a Nash equilibrium because neither airline can improve its payoff given the decision made by the other player. The Nash equilibrium is indicated by the cell with *I* and *G*.

To find where a Nash equilibrium exists, simply note the firm's highest payoff cell given each decision its rival can make. Do the same thing with the rival. A cell that has the highest payoff for both firms is a Nash equilibrium.

Losing because of the prisoner's dilemma

A *prisoner's dilemma* refers to a game where players choose something less than the optimal combined actions.

Figure 12-3 presents the payoff table of monthly profits for two competing restaurants — Bob's Barbecue and Clara's Cafeteria. Both Bob and Clara are deciding whether or not to expand their menus, and the resulting payoff depends upon not only the decision each of them makes but also on the decision their rival makes. In determining the ultimate payoff, you should first identify whether or not either restaurant has a dominant action. To identify any dominant actions and determine the ultimate payoff, you take the following steps:

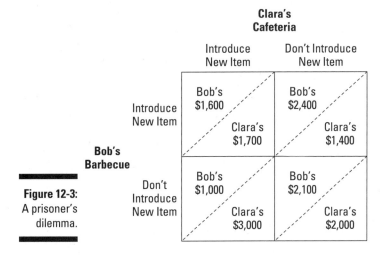

Figure 12-3: A prisoner's dilemma.

1. **Determine how Clara responds to Bob's decisions.**

   If Bob introduces a new menu item, Clara should also introduce a new menu item because her monthly profit is $1,700 instead of $1,400. If Bob doesn't introduce a new menu item, Clara should introduce a new menu item because her monthly profit is $3,000 instead of $2,000. Introducing a new menu item is a dominant action for Clara because its payoff is always higher than not introducing a new menu item.

2. **Determine how Bob responds to Clara's decisions.**

   If Clara introduces a new menu item, Bob should also introduce a new menu item because his monthly profit is $1,600 instead of $1,000. If Clara doesn't introduce a new menu item, Bob should introduce a new menu item because his monthly profit is $2,400 instead of $2,100. Introducing a new menu item is a dominant action for Bob because its payoff is always higher than not introducing a new menu item.

3. **Determine the ultimate payoff.**

   Because introducing a new menu item is the dominant action for both Bob and Clara, the ultimate payoff is in the upper left cell of the payoff table. Bob's Barbecue receives $1,600 profit and Clara's Cafeteria receives $1,700 profit.

This example leads to a prisoner's dilemma because Bob and Clara ultimately receive profits that are less than optimal. If both Bob and Clara decide not to introduce a new menu item, both receive more profit — $2,100 for Bob and $2,000 for Clara. But Bob and Clara don't do that, because in that situation, each could make more profit by introducing a new menu item. If Bob introduces a new menu item, his profit goes to $2,400, but Clara's profit goes down to $1,400. So, Clara is "forced" to also introduce a new menu item to get her profit from $1,400 to $1,700, but Bob's profit goes down to $1,600. Similarly, if Clara introduces a new menu item, her profit goes to $3,000, but Bob's profit goes down to $1,000. So, Bob is "forced" to also introduce a new menu item to get his profit from $1,000 to $1,600, but then Clara's profit goes down to $1,700. By acting out of self interest, both Bob and Clara end up with smaller profit, but ignoring what their rival does is even worse.

With a prisoner's dilemma, players chose the action that best serves their own interests. However, the result of this behavior is a combined payoff that's less than optimal.

Sequential-move, one-shot games

In many games, one player chooses before another, and it's difficult to know who has the advantage. As I note earlier in this chapter, in chess, if you move first, you have a greater probability of winning. On the other hand, in business situations, if you move first, your rival may be able to neutralize your decision by moving second. You need to develop a decision-making rule that helps you anticipate your rival's decision.

Decision-makers use backward induction in sequential games. *Backward induction* means that you develop your decision by looking at the future, or at how the game ends. Consider the decision tree in Figure 12-4. Two car dealers, Cathy's Cars and Otto's Autos, must decide whether to raise, lower, or charge the same price on their used cars. Because of her leadership position in the market, Cathy's Cars chooses her used car price first, and then Otto's Autos follows. When establishing her price, Cathy needs to consider how Otto responds by using backward induction. Using backward induction requires the following steps. Decision-makers start at the end of the game. The player making the last decision chooses the decision that has the greatest payoff. As a result, the player making a decision in the step before the last decision takes into account the likely decision in the last step when making her decision. Decision-makers continue working backward from the last decision, taking into account the likely decision made at each step in the sequence, until the first step — the initial decision step — is reached. Figure 12-4 illustrates the backward induction process.

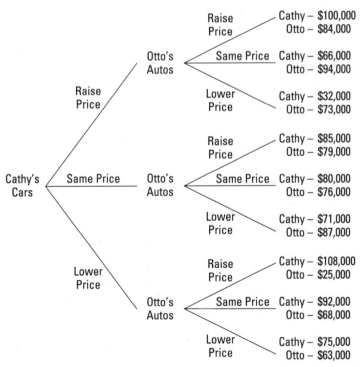

Figure 12-4: Backward induction.

Figure 12-4 summarizes the various outcomes that are possible in the situation. The far left starts with Cathy's possible choices — she can raise price, charge the same price, or lower price. In the middle, Otto's choices are portrayed for each possible choice Cathy can make. At the far right are the annual profits each dealer receives given their combined choices. For example, if Cathy lowers price, follow the lower branch from Cathy's Cars to Otto's Autos. If Otto charges the same price, follow the middle branch to the outcome — $92,000 profit for Cathy and $68,000 profit for Otto. Thus, when making her decision, Cathy needs to consider how Otto responds.

1. **If Cathy raises price, Otto charges the same price to earn $94,000.**

   Otto charges the same price because $94,000 is a higher profit for Otto than $84,000 if he raises price or $73,000 if he lowers price. As a result, Cathy's profit is $66,000.

2. **If Cathy charges the same price, Otto lowers price to earn $87,000.**

   Otto lowers price because $87,000 is a higher profit than $79,000 if Otto raises price or $76,000 if he charges the same price. Cathy's profit is $71,000 — the result of her charging the same price and Otto lowering price.

3. **If Cathy lowers price, Otto charges the same price to earn $68,000.**

   Otto charges the same price because $68,000 is a higher profit than $25,000 if Otto raises price or $63,000 if he lowers price. Cathy's profit is $92,000.

4. **Cathy's decision is to lower price.**

   When Cathy lowers her price, Otto charges the same price, resulting in $92,000 profit for Cathy and $68,000 profit for Otto. The $92,000 profit for Cathy is the best she can expect after Otto makes his choice. As indicated in Step 1, if Cathy raises price she ultimately receives $66,000 in profit and if she charges the same price, she receives $71,000 in profit as indicated in Step 2.

By using backward induction to anticipate Otto's response to her decision, Cathy is able to choose the best possible action.

Infinitely repeated games

One-shot games provide an excellent introduction to game theory; however, they can lead to mistaken conclusions when applied too rigidly to the business world. A crucial element missing in one-shot games is time. The business world is characterized by numerous decisions made over an extended period of time. A payoff is associated with each decision, and the players also have memory of past decisions. For all practical purposes, the business time horizon is infinite — the game is never-ending. The result is an *infinitely repeated game*.

In infinitely repeated games, you need to take into account not only how your rival plays this round, but also how this round of the game influences future rounds. Another factor you must consider in infinitely repeated games is the time value of money. A dollar received today is worth more than a dollar received one year from now, because the dollar received today can earn interest. Thus, future payoffs must be adjusted by using the present value calculation I describe in Chapter 1.

The typical strategy used in an infinitely repeated game is the trigger strategy. A *trigger strategy* is contingent on past play — a player takes the same action until another player takes an action that triggers a change in the first player's action. An example of a trigger strategy used in games involving a prisoner's dilemma is tit-for-tat. When you use a *tit-for-tat strategy,* you start by assuming players cooperate. In any subsequent round, you do whatever your rival did in the previous round. Thus, if your rival cheated on an understanding in the last round, you cheat this round. If your rival cooperated in the last round, you cooperate this round. A tit-for-tat strategy tends to lead to cooperation because it punishes cheaters in the next round. In addition, it forgives cheaters if they subsequently decide to cooperate. One requirement of the tit-for-tat strategy is that the players are stable. The players remember how the game was played in the previous period. New players can upset the necessary balance by not having the required memory of past behavior.

In this example, I talk about two railroads you may recognize from the board game Monopoly — the Pennsylvania Railroad and the B & O Railroad. Here, they're competing for traffic between the same cities. The railroads can either cheat on one another and charge low prices for freight, or they can cooperate and charge high prices. I show the resulting payoff table of annual profits in Figure 12-5.

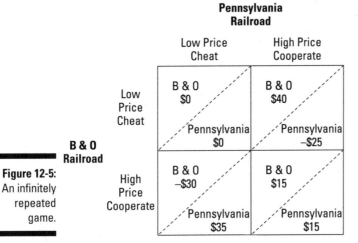

Figure 12-5:
An infinitely repeated game.

In this payoff table, both railroads have a dominant action — to charge a low price. As a result, they both earn $0. This result is yet another prisoner's dilemma.

If these railroads play the game a long time, they both recognize that cooperating by charging a high price allows both to earn $15 million each and every year. Cheating by charging a low price may lead to a large payoff one year, but the cost associated with having your rival cheat in the next year is very high. Consider what happens in a tit-for-tat strategy:

1. **If the B & O Railroad charges a high price, and the Pennsylvania Railroad cheats and charges a low price, B & O's losses are $30 million and Pennsylvania's profit is $35 million.**

2. **Following a tit-for-tat strategy, the B & O Railroad charges a low price the next year, and the Pennsylvania Railroad continues to charge a low price.**

   The railroads are locked into a situation of zero profit forever, because the B & O Railroad continues to charge the low price that the Pennsylvania Railroad charged the previous year. The railroads are in a prisoner's dilemma.

3. **Following a tit-for-tat strategy, the B & O charges a low price the next year and the Pennsylvania Railroad charges a high price.**

   The B & O Railroad earns $40 million in profit and Pennsylvania loses $25 million. But now the game can return to cooperation. The B & O forgives the Pennsylvania Railroad for cheating in the first round and in future rounds, each railroad earns $15 million.

In some sense, the Pennsylvania Railroad has to accept punishment for cheating in the first place. But accepting that punishment one year leads to a situation where both railroads return to $15 million annual profit. If the railroads continue to cheat by charging a low price, each will recognize that cooperation does not pay, and they will be forever locked into charging a low price and receiving zero profit.

In this infinite game, both railroads make more profit if they cooperate the entire time and never fall into a tit-for-tat strategy.

If you have an infinite time horizon, the present value of a constant stream of future net revenue equals

$$PV_{\text{Infinite Time}} = \frac{(1+i)\pi}{i}$$

where π is the net revenue earned each year and i is the interest rate.

In the previous example, if the B & O and Pennsylvania railroads cooperate, they each earn $15 million annual profit. If the B & O Railroad has an infinite time horizon, the present value of $15 million annual profit at a 5 percent interest rate is

$$PV_{\text{Infinite Time}} = \frac{(1+i)\pi}{i} = \frac{(1+0.05)15}{0.05} = \$315$$

or $315 million.

Playing Well

How you play the game determines whether you win or lose, so you want to play the game well. Playing any game well requires you to consider how your rival responds to your decisions. But as the next section on preempting rivals illustrates, you can also change your rival's behavior if you play well.

Preempting rivals

You've developed a highly-regarded bike shop in the local community. A larger neighboring community has a bike shop owned by a rival. Your rival's bike shop is larger and you fear that the rival may be considering entering your market. You need a strategy that enables you to preempt your rival. This is an obvious game theory situation where you must take into account your rival's actions.

Assume the possible scenarios are represented by the decision trees in Figure 12-6 with the payoff being annual profit. The upper panel describes the current situation. If your rival expands, you can either expand or not expand. Using backward induction, your rival takes the following steps:

1. **If your rival doesn't expand, the status quo continues.**

   The status quo is represented by the lower branch on the decision tree. If your rival doesn't expand, you won't do anything — there are no branches for your decision — and the profits are $100,000 for your rival and $80,000 for you.

2. **If your rival expands, you don't expand.**

   If your rival expands, you don't expand because if you expand your profits are $20,000 versus if you don't expand, your profits are $25,000.

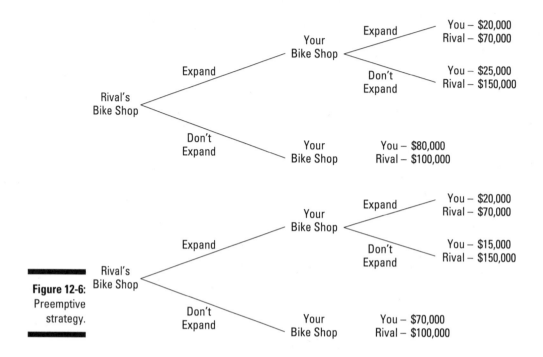

Figure 12-6: Preemptive strategy.

3. Your rival decides to expand by using backward induction.

Given you don't expand, your rival earns $150,000 by expanding into your community, while the rival earns only $100,000 if it doesn't expand. And the bad news for you is your profit is only $25,000. You aren't likely to enjoy this game, so how can you change it?

4. You engage in a preemptive strategy by renting a store location in your rival's community for $10,000 a year.

This is how much you would have to pay if you decide to expand into your rival's community. This changes the decision tree by lowering your profit by $10,000 in every situation you don't expand because of the added expense you incur. It doesn't change your expense if you do expand — you need the store. So in the decision tree in the lower panel, your profit for when both you and your rival expand doesn't change — it remains $20,000. Your profit for when your rival expands but you don't expand goes down by $10,000 from $25,000 to $15,000 because of the rent you pay on the unoccupied store front. Similarly, your profit if your rival decides not to expand goes down by $10,000 for the unoccupied store front, from $80,000 to $70,000.

5. Your rival uses backward induction.

If your rival doesn't expand, the status quo continues. The profits are $100,000 for your rival and now only $70,000 for you.

6. **If your rival expands, you also expand.**

   If you don't expand, your profit is $15,000. If you expand, your profit is $20,000.

7. **If both you and your rival expand, your rival earns $70,000 profit.**

   This combines both decisions to expand.

8. **Your rival decides not to expand.**

   By not expanding, your rival earns $100,000 profit as opposed to only $70,000 profit if your rival expands.

Your preemptive strategy changes your rival's behavior. Not taking the preemptive strategy results in you earning $25,000 profit. By spending $10,000 to rent a store front you never plan to use, you increase your profit to $70,000.

Working together through collusion

A logical question implied by the prisoner's dilemma is: Why don't both firms choose the combination of actions that yields the highest combined payoff? The answer is that they often do. Because oligopolistic markets are characterized by a small number of firms, they recognize their mutual interdependence. Such conditions favor collusion and the formation of cartels. However, as I note in Chapter 18, antitrust laws in the United States make most forms of collusion illegal.

Figure 12-7 again portrays the prisoner's dilemma experienced by Bob's Barbecue and Clara's Cafeteria (see the earlier section "Losing because of the prisoner's dilemma"). As a result of the prisoner's dilemma, Bob and Clara end up receiving $1,600 and $1,700 in monthly profit, respectively. However, if Bob and Clara collude, they both agree not to introduce a new item. In that case, Bob's profit is $2,100 and Clara's profit is $2,000. Both restaurants are better off.

This illustration also indicates why collusion often breaks down. Both Bob and Clara have an incentive to cheat on the collusive agreement. If Bob can secretly introduce an "off-menu" new item, he increases his profit from $2,100 to $2,400. Obviously, when Clara realizes Bob is cheating on their collusive agreement, Clara will also introduce a new menu item, resulting in the prisoner's dilemma outcome. A similar scenario develops if Clara gives in to her incentive to cheat. Nevertheless, methods such as the tit-for-tat strategy (see the "Infinitely repeated games" section earlier in this chapter) can discourage cheating on collusive agreements.

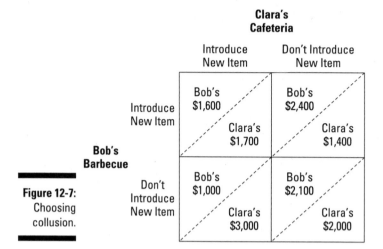

Figure 12-7:
Choosing collusion.

Testing commitment

You've heard a rumor that if you decide to expand your business into a rival's territory, the rival will respond by expanding into your territory. Before making your decision on whether or not to expand, you need to determine whether the threat is credible.

A *credible commitment* requires the commitment's benefit to exceed its cost. In that case, the commitment is credible because the firm has an incentive to follow through. In the situation of whether or not your rival expands into your territory after you expand into its, the commitment — threat — is credible if the benefit outweighs the cost. Figure 12-8 illustrates this situation.

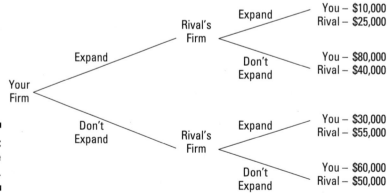

Figure 12-8:
Credible commitment.

Your rival says it will expand only if you expand first. You're concerned about your rival's threat to expand, because if both firms expand, your profit is only $10,000. You need to use backward induction to test whether or not your rival's commitment is credible. In Figure 12-8's decision tree, your decision appears at the far left, because you choose first. You have two possible choices — expand or don't expand. After you decide, your rival responds. To determine whether your rival's threat to expand is credible, you take the following steps:

1. **Because you're trying to decide whether to expand, focus on the upper branch of the decision tree that corresponds to expand.**

2. **If you expand, your rival can expand or not expand.**

   If your rival chooses to expand, his profit is $25,000. If your rival chooses not to expand, his profit is $40,000. As a result, your rival chooses not to expand for the higher profit.

3. **Your rival's commitment isn't credible.**

   If your rival chooses to expand after you expand, its profit is $15,000 less — only $25,000 instead of $40,000 — than if it didn't expand. Your rival is better off (makes a higher profit) by not expanding even if you choose to expand.

4. **You should expand, recognizing that your rival's commitment isn't credible.**

This example reinforces how fun game theory is. If you look again at Figure 12-8, you quickly see you just had $80,000 worth of fun because the way you play the game determines whether you win or lose.

Chapter 13

Monopolistic Competition: Competitors, Competitors Everywhere

*M*others often say, "Just worry about yourself." Well, that's a great attitude to have in monopolistic competition — just worry about yourself. Indeed, in monopolistic competition, that's all you can do. Monopolistically competitive markets have a large number of firms producing similar, but not identical, products. Thus, the products are differentiated, although their use is almost identical. Because there are so many firms, you can't pay attention to all of them, so you need to focus on your own actions. This situation is very different from oligopoly (see Chapter 11) where you have to pay attention to rivals.

One of monopolistic competition's most important characteristics is that firms produce slightly different products. Because of these product differences, each monopolistically competitive firm sets price. But any profit that results from the price you set can't last. The intense competition that exists in monopolistically competitive markets ultimately eliminates economic profit in the long run.

In this chapter, I explain how a large number of rivals affect your decision-making. I present how the profit-maximizing quantity and price are determined in the short run, and why the short-run decision ultimately causes profit to disappear in the long run. Finally, I present how you determine the ideal level of advertising expenditures.

Competing with Rivals All Around You in Monopolistic Competition

Although competitive behavior in oligopolies leads to mutual interdependence, monopolistically competitive markets are closer in similarity to perfectly competitive markets (see Chapter 9). Monopolistically competitive firms and perfectly competitive firms do, however, have one crucial difference. Although monopolistically competitive firms produce a standardized type of commodity, some differentiation exists among the goods produced by different firms. As a result, monopolistically competitive firms produce goods that are used in similar ways (standardized type of commodity), while some small difference, such as flavor, color, and/or branding, exists. On the other hand, perfectly competitive firms produce goods with no differentiation.

Product differentiation gives firms some degree of monopoly power so they can establish the good's price. On the other hand, perfect standardization, such as exists in prefect competition, results in the firm having no influence on price. Perfectly competitive firms are price takers.

Pizza is an example of a monopolistically competitive market. You know what a pizza is, and it is essentially the same type of product at any restaurant — it's a standardized type of product. But not all pizzas are identical; hence, you probably have a favorite. The differences that lead to you having a favorite pizza represent differentiation, and as a result, firms in monopolistically competitive markets are able to set the price they receive for their good. You're willing to pay a little more for your favorite pizza.

Characterizing Monopolistic Competition

The three major characteristics of monopolistically competitive markets are:

- ✔ **Large number of firms:** Because an individual firm is one out of a large number of firms, it provides a fairly small percentage of the good available in the market. Therefore, the individual firm has limited influence on the commodity's price. In addition, because of the large number of firms, monopolistically competitive firms don't regard themselves as being mutually interdependent and don't take into account how rivals respond to their actions. Finally, the large number of firms prevents collusive behavior in monopolistically competition.

- ✔ **Standardized type of commodity with interfirm differentiation:** Monopolistically competitive firms produce a standardized type of commodity with slight differentiation among firms. Several factors account for this *product differentiation*. For example, differences in product quality or the type of service performed can lead to differentiation. The firm's location is another source of the differentiation. Finally, differentiation may result from interfirm differences in promotion and packaging.

✔ **Easy entry and exit:** A monopolistically competitive market has no barriers to entry. New firms can easily establish themselves in the market, and similarly, existing firms can easily exit the market. Typically, easy entry and exit occurs because monopolistically competitive firms have relatively small fixed costs, so existing firms don't significantly benefit from lower per-unit production costs as compared to new firms.

Setting Price with Many Rivals

Interfirm differentiation allows the monopolistically competitive firm to set price. Therefore, the firm determines both the profit-maximizing quantity and the good's price. However, the degree of influence the firm has on price is limited because a large number of rival firms are producing similar products.

Recognizing the importance of product differentiation

The degree of influence a monopolistically competitive firm has on the good's price is dependent on the price elasticity of demand for the firm's good. The more elastic the demand, the less influence the firm has on price, because quantity demanded is very responsive to any price change. Two factors that influence the monopolistically competitive firm's price elasticity of demand are the number of firms, and the degree of product differentiation among firms.

A large number of firms results in consumers having a greater number of alternatives from which to choose. Therefore, consumers are more responsive to price changes. If your firm increases price, your customers are more likely to switch to one of your rivals. As a consequence, with a larger number of rival firms, the demand for your firm's good is more elastic and you have less influence over price.

A small degree of product differentiation also results in consumers being less concerned about which firm they purchase the good from. If firms produce nearly identical products (that is, the products have very little differentiation), consumers are very responsive to any price changes that occur. Because the products are so similar, consumers simply look for the lowest price. This minimizes your firm's ability to charge a higher price. If you charge a higher price, most of your customers simply switch to a product produced by a competitor that has a lower price. Your quantity demanded goes down a lot. As a consequence, the demand for your firm's product is more elastic — consumers are very responsive to any price change you make.

To have the greatest influence over price, you want to have fewer rivals and produce a good that's a lot different from what your rivals produce.

Making use of advertising and product differentiation

Monopolistically competitive firms engage in non-price competition, such as advertising and innovation.

With both advertising and innovation, you're trying to increase the degree of differentiation that exists between the good you produce and the goods produced by your rivals. In the case of advertising, you may stress that your pizza is made from the freshest ingredients.

Innovation is also a source of differentiation. You may introduce a new type of pizza — anchovy and spinach, anyone? — to attract new customers.

Maximizing short-run profit

Because a monopolistically competitive firm produces a differentiated good, short-run profit maximization requires the firm to determine both the profit-maximizing quantity and the good's price. Figure 13-1 illustrates short-run profit maximization for a monopolistically competitive firm.

Differentiation leads to a downward-sloping demand curve for the monopolistically competitive firm. This curve is labeled *d* in Figure 13-1. Because the demand curve is downward sloping, the monopolistically competitive firm must lower price in order to sell more of the good. This lower price is charged for all units of the good sold.

Marginal revenue represents the change in total revenue that occurs when one additional unit of output is produced and sold. Because the firm must charge a lower price for every unit sold in order to sell one additional unit of the good, marginal revenue is lower than the price of the last unit sold. The marginal-revenue curve, thus, lies below the demand curve, as illustrated by the curve labeled *MR* in Figure 13-1.

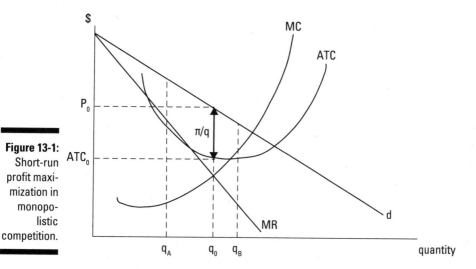

Figure 13-1:
Short-run
profit maxi-
mization in
monopo-
listic
competition.

Marginal cost is the change in total cost that occurs when one additional unit of output is produced. Because of diminishing returns, marginal cost, *MC*, is upward-sloping, as illustrated in Figure 13-1. In addition, marginal cost passes through the minimum point of the average-total-cost curve, *ATC*. I describe these relationships in more detail in Chapter 8.

The firm's total profit increases if an additional unit of output adds more to revenue than it adds to cost. As long as the marginal revenue of an additional unit exceeds marginal cost, as is the case at q_A, producing that unit increases the firm's total profit, and the firm should continue to produce more. On the other hand, if a unit of output adds more to cost than it adds to revenue, as with q_B, or if marginal cost is greater than marginal revenue, producing that unit decreases the firm's total profit. The firm needs to reduce production. The monopolistically competitive firm maximizes profit by producing the quantity of output associated with marginal revenue equals marginal cost. The profit-maximizing quantity of output is represented by q_0 in Figure 13-1.

After determining the profit-maximizing quantity of output, the firm establishes the good's price by going from that quantity, q_0 in Figure 13-1, to the demand curve and across to the vertical axis. The profit-maximizing price is P_0 in Figure 13-1.

The monopolistically competitive firm determines profit per unit by subtracting average total cost from price. In Figure 13-1, profit per unit is represented by π/q and equals price minus average total cost. Total profit, π, equals profit per unit multiplied by the profit-maximizing quantity, or

$$\pi = \left(\pi/q\right) \times q_0 = \left(P_0 - ATC_0\right) \times q_0$$

Relying on calculus in monopolistic competition

Profit is always maximized at the quantity where marginal revenue equals marginal cost. To determine marginal revenue, you take the derivative of total revenue with respect to quantity. To determine marginal cost, you take the derivative of total cost with respect to quantity.

Assume your monopolistically competitive firm's demand curve is

$$P = 40 - 0.0005q$$

where P is the good's price in dollars and q is the quantity produced by the monopolistically competitive firm.

Also assume your total cost equation is

$$TC = 168,000 + 10q + 0.0005q^2$$

where TC is total cost in dollars and q is the quantity of the good produced.

Given these equations, the profit-maximizing quantity of output, price, and profit are determined through the following steps:

1. **Determine total revenue.**

   Total revenue equals price multiplied by quantity.

   $$TR = P \times q = (40 - 0.0005q) \times q = 40q - 0.0005q^2$$

2. **Determine marginal revenue.**

   Marginal revenue is the derivative of total revenue taken with respect to quantity.

   $$MR = \frac{dTR}{dq} = 40 - 0.001q$$

3. **Determine marginal cost by taking the derivative of total cost with respect to quantity.**

   $$MC = \frac{dTC}{dq} = 10 + 0.001q$$

4. Set marginal revenue equal to marginal cost and solve for *q*.

$$MR = MC$$
$$40 - 0.001q = 10 + 0.001q$$
$$30 = 0.002q \text{ or } \frac{30}{0.002} = 15,000 = q$$

5. Substitute 15,000 for *q* in the demand equation to determine price.

$$P = 40 - 0.0005q = 40 - 0.0005(15,000) = 32.5$$

Thus, the profit maximizing quantity is 15,000 units and the price is $32.50 per unit.

The following steps enable you to determine the firm's economic profit per unit and total profit.

6. Determine the average total cost equation.

Average total cost equals total cost divided by the quantity of output *q*.

$$ATC = \frac{TC}{q} = \frac{168,000 + 10q + 0.0005q^2}{q} = \frac{168,000}{q} + 10 + 0.0005q$$

7. Substitute *q* equals 15,000 in order to determine average total cost at the profit-maximizing quantity of output.

$$ATC = \frac{168,000}{(15,000)} + 10 + 0.0005(15,000) = 28.7$$

Thus, average total cost is $28.70 at the profit-maximizing quantity of 15,000 units.

8. Calculate profit per unit.

$$\pi/q = P - ATC = 32.5 - 28.7 = 3.8$$

Profit per unit equals $3.80.

9. Determine total profit.

Total profit equals profit per unit multiplied by the profit-maximizing quantity of output.

$$\pi = (P - ATC) \times q = (32.5 - 28.7) \times 15,000 = 57,000$$

Total profit equals $57,000.

Adjusting to the Long-Run Tendency of Profit Elimination

Easy entry and exit indicate that firms have little or no difficulty in moving into and out of a monopolistically competitive market. If firms perceive an opportunity to earn economic profit in this market, they enter the market. The entry of new firms results in demand decreasing for other firms in the market as some customers switch to the new firm. Entry continues until the typical firm's demand decreases to the point where the firm earns zero economic profit. At that point, new firms no longer have incentive to enter.

Similarly, if initial economic losses (negative economic profit) exist, firms leave the market. This loss of firms results in an increase in demand for firms remaining in the market until zero economic profit is reached. Demand increases for remaining firms as customers for the firms that left switch to surviving firms.

The long-run equilibrium in monopolistically competitive markets is associated with firms receiving a normal rate of return. A firm receives a normal rate of return when its price equals average total cost.

Figure 13-2 illustrates the movement to the long-run equilibrium from an initial situation with positive economic profit. Initially, the firm's demand and marginal revenue curves correspond to d^* and MR^*. Given these curves and the illustrated cost curves, the profit-maximizing quantity and price are q^* and p^*. The firm is earning positive profit because price is greater than average total cost at q^*.

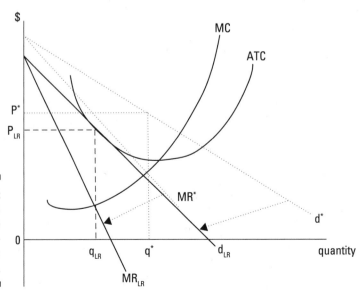

Figure 13-2:
Long-run equilibrium in monopolistic competition.

Because the firm is earning positive economic profit, new firms enter the market. The entry of new firms causes the original firm's demand to decrease to d_{LR} as some of the firm's customers switch to the new firms. The decrease in demand causes marginal revenue to decrease to MR_{LR}. The resulting new profit-maximizing quantity is q_{LR} and price is p_{LR}. At this point, price equals average total cost, as represented by the demand curve being just tangent to the average total cost curve. Because price equals average total cost, firms earn zero economic profit, and new firms no longer have incentive to enter the market.

The determination of economic profit includes all costs associated with the good's production, including the opportunity cost of resources contributed by the firm's owner. Zero economic profit indicates that the firm's owner is receiving exactly as much as the owner would receive in the next best alternative. In other words, the owner is receiving a normal rate of return.

As is illustrated in Figure 13-2, although price equals average total cost in monopolistic competition's long-run equilibrium, average total cost isn't at its minimum. Because average total cost isn't minimized, monopolistically competitive firms are characterized by *excess capacity*. This excess capacity simply means the firm can produce greater output at lower per unit cost. However, selling this larger amount of output would require the firm to lower price on all units resulting in negative profit. (Note that at the quantity of output associated with minimum average total cost, price off the demand curve is below minimum average total cost.)

Determining the Ideal Amount of Advertising

One factor contributing to product differentiation in monopolistically competitive markets is advertising. Determining the appropriate or profit-maximizing level of advertising is crucial to the firm's success.

Advertising's affect on consumer taste and preferences enables it to influence consumer demand for a product. For the monopolistically competitive firm, an increase in advertising increases demand for its product, while a decrease in advertising decreases the firm's demand. However, in addition to shifting demand, you must recognize that changes in advertising expenditures affect your cost.

Advertising increases your profit as long as the marginal revenue obtained through the sale of additional units is greater than the marginal cost of producing those units plus the cost of the additional advertising expenditures.

Mathematically, the additional profit that's made through the production and sale of one additional unit of output is price minus marginal cost, $P - MC$. The change in gross profit that occurs with an additional dollar spent on advertising equals the change in the quantity sold that occurs, Δq, multiplied by $P - MC$. This amount is gross profit, because it doesn't include the cost of advertising. The monopolistically competitive firm's net profit increases as long as each additional dollar spent on advertising generates more than an additional dollar's worth of gross profit. In other words, net profit increases as long as

$$\Delta q \times (P - MC) > 1$$

In order to maximize the net profits associated with advertising, the firm should continue increasing advertising expenditures until

$$\Delta q \times (P - MC) = 1$$

At this point, an additional dollar's worth of advertising adds one dollar to gross profit, resulting in no gain in the firm's net profit.

Here I manipulate the previous equation to derive a very important relationship. If you want to skip the manipulation, that's fine. Go straight to the result, and take my word for it, the relationship really works.

If you take the previous equation and divide both sides by $(P - MC)$, you get

$$\Delta q = \frac{1}{(P - MC)}$$

Now, multiplying both sides of the equation by P yields

$$\Delta q \times P = \frac{P}{(P - MC)}$$

At the point of profit maximization, marginal revenue equals marginal cost. Substituting MR for MC in the equation leads to

$$\Delta q \times P = \frac{P}{(P - MR)}$$

Chapter 4 shows that the right side of this equation equals the negative price elasticity of demand, η, for the firm's product. The left side of the equation represents the marginal revenue of an additional dollar's worth of advertising. Therefore, the optimal level of advertising expenditures corresponds to

$$MR_{advertising} = \eta$$

Wow, there's the price elasticity of demand again. Maybe mothers should stop saying, "Just worry about yourself," and instead say, "Just remember your price elasticity of demand."

You believe the price elasticity of demand for your product is –2.0. Your advertising department is requesting an additional $50,000 of advertising, arguing that the additional advertising will increase sales by $80,000. In order to determine whether or not to support the advertising department's request, you take the following steps:

1. **Determine the marginal revenue of an additional dollar's worth of advertising.**

   Divide the additional revenue by the additional amount spent on advertising to determine the marginal revenue of an additional dollar's worth of advertising.

   $$MR_{advertising} = \frac{\text{additional revenue}}{\text{additional advertising}} = \frac{80,000}{50,000} = 1.60$$

2. **Determine the negative price elasticity of demand.**

   $$-\eta = -(-2.0) = 2.0$$

3. **Make your decision.**

   Because the marginal revenue associated with an additional dollar's worth of advertising is less than $-\eta$ (1.60 < 2.0) you should not advertise. In order to justify advertising, the marginal revenue of an additional dollar's worth of advertising has to be greater than 2.0.

Chapter 14

Increasing Revenue with Advanced Pricing Strategies

*Y*ou've probably seen the game show *The Price Is Right.* In the show, contestants are shown a product and asked to guess its price. The contestant who guesses closest to the actual retail price without going over is declared the winner.

The question of the right price is crucial in business decision-making. The price marked on a product isn't necessarily the right price. As a consumer, I tend to think that most prices are wrong — they're way too high. For a business losing money, the price probably seems way too low. Before deciding whether or not a price is right, you need to know what your goal is.

Throughout this book, I emphasize various methods to determine price. In this chapter, I introduce more advance pricing techniques. I start by looking at how to determine price by using the price elasticity of demand, and then move to two of the simplest strategies — cost-plus pricing and breakeven analysis. Next comes a more advanced strategy — price discrimination. Price discrimination enables you to charge different prices for the same good. I wonder how that would work on the television show *The Price Is Right.* Another advanced pricing strategy is to bundle goods. Rather than sell goods individually to the customer, you allow the customer to buy them together as a bundle — think Happy Meal. The chapter concludes with short-run pricing strategies that temporarily reduce profit in order to earn even greater profit in the future.

Simplifying Price Determination by Using the Price Elasticity of Demand

Long-term success and profitability depend upon producing a good to the point where the additional revenue of an extra unit of output equals the additional cost of producing that unit; in other words, producing where marginal revenue equals marginal cost. Previous chapters derive marginal revenue from the firm's demand. However, an easier method of deriving marginal revenue is to use the price elasticity of demand.

Chapter 4 notes the following relationship between marginal revenue and the price elasticity of demand:

$$MR = P\left(1 + \frac{1}{\eta}\right)$$

where *MR* is marginal revenue, *P* is the good's price, and η is the price elasticity of demand.

Maximizing profit requires marginal revenue equals marginal cost, so

$$MR = P\left(1 + \frac{1}{\eta}\right) = MC$$

Rearranging the previous equation yields

$$P = \frac{MC}{\left(1 + \frac{1}{\eta}\right)} = MC \times \frac{1}{\left(1 + \frac{1}{\eta}\right)} = MC \times \left(\frac{\eta}{\eta + 1}\right)$$

Thus, the profit-maximizing price equals

$$P = MC \times \left(\frac{\eta}{\eta + 1}\right)$$

Remember that the price elasticity of demand is a negative number because an inverse relationship exists between price and quantity demanded.

Your company produces a good at a constant marginal cost of $6.00. The price elasticity of demand for the good is –4.0. In order to determine the profit-maximizing price, you follow these steps:

1. **Substitute $6.00 for *MC* and –4.0 for η.**

$$P = MC\left(\frac{\eta}{\eta+1}\right) = 6.00\left(\frac{-4}{-4+1}\right)$$

2. **Calculate the value in the parentheses.**

$$P = 6.00\left(\frac{-4}{-3}\right) = 6.00\left(\frac{4}{3}\right)$$

3. **Multiply values to yield a price of $8.00.**

Pricing Based upon Cost: Cost-Plus Pricing and Breakeven Analysis

Two pricing policies you commonly encounter in business are cost-plus pricing and breakeven pricing. These policies are very simple pricing strategies based upon production costs. Simple doesn't mean better or worse. The advantage of simple in these cases is that calculating price is easy. The disadvantage of these simple strategies is that they ignore demand. Thus, it's important to understand under what circumstances these simple methods of price determination help you reach your goal of maximum profit.

Cost-plus pricing

Cost-plus pricing means that you determine price by starting with the good's cost and then adding a fixed percentage or amount to that cost. One of the primary reasons cost-plus pricing is so popular is its simplicity. Often information on marginal revenue and marginal cost is difficult to obtain with precision, making it impossible to exactly determine the point of profit maximization. By using cost-plus pricing, you can simply include a desired rate of return in the mark-up. Another advantage of cost-plus pricing is its desirability from the standpoint of public relations. This pricing technique provides an obvious rationale for price increases when cost increases occur.

Cost-plus pricing typically involves two steps. First, the firm determines the per unit cost or average total cost of producing the good. Because average total cost varies as the quantity of output produced changes, the firm's determination of per unit cost requires the specification of an output level. After the firm establishes the per unit cost, the firm adds a mark-up to the per unit cost. The mark-up is typically in the form of a percentage, and it represents costs that can't be easily allocated to a specific product produced by the firm plus a return on the firm's investment.

The following equation illustrates how to determine price with cost-plus pricing:

$$P = ATC \times (1 + \text{mark-up})$$

where P is the good's price, ATC is the average total cost or cost per unit, and the mark-up is the percentage added to average total cost.

One criticism of cost-plus pricing is that it focuses on average rather than marginal costs. Because profit maximization requires marginal cost equals marginal revenue, cost-plus pricing may not result in profit maximization. Another criticism of cost-plus pricing is that it ignores demand conditions. By ignoring demand, the firm can establish a cost-plus price that's above the market's equilibrium price, resulting in a surplus. As a consequence, the firm doesn't sell all the units it produces.

It's logical to wonder whether cost-plus pricing ever maximizes profit. In order for profit-maximization to occur, cost-plus pricing must result in the firm producing the output level where marginal revenue equals marginal cost. In the short-run, the difference between marginal cost and average total cost may be sizeable. However, studies have shown that long-run average total cost is typically constant for many firms. Constant long-run average total cost implies constant marginal cost; therefore, marginal cost equals average total cost in this situation. The use of average total cost in the place of marginal cost for pricing results in minimal differences, or

$$P = MC \times (1 + \text{mark-up})$$

Still, because this simple approach ignores demand, it's unlikely to result in maximum profit. However, when you use marginal cost in the previous equation, it looks very similar to the profit-maximizing equation in the previous section of this chapter.

$$P = MC \times \left(\frac{\eta}{\eta + 1} \right)$$

Thus, if one plus your mark-up equals the second part of the earlier equation, or

$$1 + \text{mark-up} = \left(\frac{\eta}{\eta + 1} \right)$$

cost-plus pricing maximizes your profit.

Manipulating the earlier equation allows you to determine the mark-up

$$\text{mark-up} = \frac{-1}{\eta + 1}$$

Your company determines that the price elasticity of demand for its product is –4. In order to determine the profit-maximizing mark-up, you take the following steps:

1. **Substitute –4 for the price elasticity of demand in the mark-up equation.**

$$\text{mark-up} = \frac{-1}{\eta + 1} = \frac{-1}{-4 + 1}$$

2. **Calculate the value of the denominator.**

$$\text{mark-up} = \frac{-1}{-3}$$

3. **Divide the numerator by the denominator.**

The resulting value is 0.33, or the markup should be 33%.

Breakeven analysis

A firm using *breakeven analysis* determines the smallest output level that leads to zero economic profit. Recall that zero economic profit doesn't mean that the firm's owners receive nothing — it means that the firm's owners are receiving a normal rate of return. In other words, the firm's owners are receiving exactly as much as they would in their next best alternative.

In breakeven pricing, your total revenue equals total cost — hence, zero profit. Because the focus is on the point where you earn zero profit, it's unlikely that breakeven analysis maximizes your profit.

However, breakeven analysis is a useful managerial tool. Managers use breakeven analysis to determine how a price change affects profit. If you lower price, how many more units do you have to sell in order to achieve zero profit — or to break even? If your firm has a large fixed cost, breakeven analysis enables you to determine the quantity of output you must sell in order to avoid losses. In either of these situations, as a manager, you can then determine whether or not sales of that amount are feasible.

Your company has total fixed cost of $300,000, and its average variable cost (variable cost per unit of output) is $2.00. In addition, you sell the good at a price of $5.00 per unit. The following steps are used to determine the breakeven point:

1. **Set total revenue equal to total cost.**

   Remember that total revenue equals price multiplied by the quantity sold, and total cost equals total fixed cost plus total variable cost.

   $$TR = TC$$
   $$P \times q = TFC + TVC$$

2. **Substitute AVC×q for TVC.**

   Recall that total variable cost equals average variable cost multiplied by the number of units produced q.

   $$P \times q = TFC + AVC \times q$$

3. **Subtract AVC×q from both sides of the equation in Step 2 and simplify.**

   $$P \times q - AVC \times q = TFC$$
   $$(P - AVC) \times q = TFC$$

4. **Divide both sides of the equation by (P – AVC).**

   This step enables you to solve for the breakeven quantity, q.

   $$q = \frac{TFC}{P - AVC}$$

5. **Substitute the values for TFC, P, and AVC and solve for q.**

   $$q = \frac{TFC}{P - AVC} = \frac{300,000}{5 - 2} = \frac{300,000}{3} = 100,000$$

   Your breakeven quantity is 100,000 units.

Discriminating among Customers

Price discrimination refers to a situation where the same good is sold to different groups of consumers for different prices. For example, the couple sitting next to you at the movie paid a lower price to get in because they're senior citizens. Or, perhaps you get a student discount at a local restaurant that non-students don't get.

Price discrimination exists in a variety of situations. Therefore, economists define different degrees of price discrimination to reflect the various situations associated with this pricing policy. However, no significance is attached to whether or not price discrimination is of the first degree or third degree — one isn't more important than the other. (See the upcoming section "Identifying Who Wants to Pay More: Types of Price Discrimination" for details on the different degrees of price discrimination.)

Recognizing the conditions necessary for price discrimination

Price discrimination requires the following conditions

✔ You can segment the market into customers who have different price elasticities of demand.

✔ The firm possesses some degree of monopoly power and can set price.

✔ Finally, customers can't resell the good. If customers are able to resell the good, those who pay a lower price can buy the good and sell it for a higher price, but not as high as the firm charges, to customers willing to pay the high price. This process is called *arbitrage,* and it limits the firm's ability to benefit from price discrimination.

Assessing price discrimination's impact

Firms that engage in price discrimination generally

✔ **Produce a greater quantity of output.** Because the firm is able to charge different prices to different groups of consumers, it can attract more buyers who are willing to pay a low price without sacrificing revenue from buyers willing to pay a higher price. By selling to both groups at different prices the firm increases the quantity of the good it sells.

✔ **Increase their profit.** By charging different prices, the firm is able to capture more *consumer surplus* — the difference between the price a consumer is willing to pay and the price the consumer actually pays. This additional consumer surplus adds to the firm's producer surplus.

Identifying Who Wants to Pay More: Types of Price Discrimination

As a business owner, you want customers to pay higher prices. Obviously those same customers want to pay lower prices. But as a demand curve illustrates, the prices some customers are willing and able to pay are much higher than the prices others are willing and able to pay. You can increase your profit if you're able to separate customers who are willing to pay higher prices from those willing to pay lower prices.

You should charge customers who have a less elastic demand a higher price, because a less elastic demand means the customer is less responsive to price changes. Customers whose demand is more elastic are more responsive to price changes. These customers should be charged a lower price in order to get them to buy a lot more.

Wishing for first-degree price discrimination

First-degree price discrimination, sometimes referred to as *perfect price discrimination,* exists when a firm charges a different price for each unit of the good sold — every customer pays a different price for the good. This degree is the ultimate extreme in price discrimination — hence, its designation as "perfect."

When first-degree price discrimination exists, the firm's marginal revenue curve corresponds to its demand curve. Because a different price — the maximum price each customer is willing and able to pay — is set for each unit of the good, each unit adds its price to total revenue. So, marginal revenue, the change in total revenue, equals the price determined from the demand curve.

Figure 14-1 illustrates a monopoly that's using first-degree price discrimination. In the graph, marginal cost, *MC,* and average total cost, *ATC,* have the usual shapes with marginal cost passing through the minimum point on the average-total-cost curve. The firm faces a downward-sloping market demand curve that's the same as the firm's demand curve, $D = d$, given that it's a monopoly. Because the firm charges every consumer the maximum price he or she is willing to pay, marginal revenue corresponds to the firm's demand curve, $d = MR$.

Profit maximization occurs at the output level corresponding to marginal revenue equals marginal cost, q_0 in Figure 14-1. Each unit of output has a unique price, so P_{last} is the price only for the last unit sold. Every other unit has a higher price. The resulting profit for the firm equals the revenue it receives for each unit minus the average total cost per unit, ATC_0. Because the price for each unit is the maximum price as determined from the demand curve, the shaded area labeled π in Figure 14-1 represents the firm's total profit.

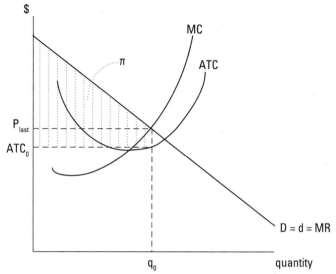

Figure 14-1:
First-degree
price dis-
crimination.

First-degree price discrimination is virtually impossible to implement. First, the firm must know exactly the maximum price each consumer will pay for each unit of the good purchased, which isn't likely. In addition, the firm must negotiate separately with each individual consumer, and be able to prevent resale between consumers. The cost of these negotiations is likely to far outweigh the benefits to the firm of first-degree price discrimination. Nevertheless, the closer your firm gets to first-degree price discrimination, the greater the benefits.

Using second-degree price discrimination

Charging different prices for different ranges or blocks of output results in *second-degree price discrimination* or *declining block pricing*. Typically, consumers pay one price for the first, small block of output, and lower prices for additional ranges or blocks of output. Electric companies frequently use this type of price discrimination. For example, an electric company charges 9 cents per kilowatt hour for the first 300 kilowatt hours of electricity used in a month, 5 cents per kilowatt hour for the block 301 to 1,000 kilowatt hours, and 4 cents for each kilowatt hour over 1,000. A consumer using 1,200 kilowatt hours pays $70.00 = \$0.09 \times 300 + \$0.05 \times 700 + \$0.04 \times 200$.

A firm engaging in second-degree price discrimination faces a marginal revenue curve that appears as a series of steps. The marginal revenue curve is a horizontal line corresponding to the price for that block of output. Figure 14-2 illustrates second-degree price discrimination.

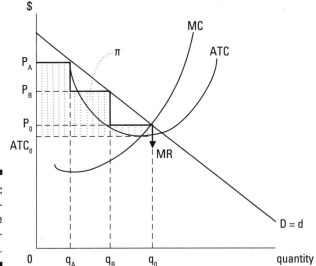

Figure 14-2:
Second-
degree
price dis-
crimination.

The marginal-cost, *MC*, and average-total-cost, *ATC*, curves in Figure 14-2 have the typical shape. The firm in Figure 14-2 represents a monopoly so the downward-sloping market demand corresponds to the firm's demand curve, $D = d$.

To derive the marginal-revenue curve, note for the block of output from 0 to q_A, you charge P_A for each unit of output. Thus, each unit adds P_A to your total revenue and P_A is your marginal revenue. For the block of output from q_A to q_B, you charge the lower P_B and your marginal revenue "steps down" to correspond to P_B. For the block of output from q_B to q_0, you again lower price, this time to P_0 and marginal revenue takes another step down to P_0. To sell more units of output beyond q_0, you have to further lower price, so marginal revenue continues to take steps down. Marginal revenue, *MR*, in Figure 14-2 reflects this series of steps.

The profit-maximizing firm always produces the output level corresponding to marginal revenue equals marginal cost. This is the output level q_0 in Figure 14-2. The firm doesn't charge a single price. Instead, the firm charges the price P_A for the block of output from 0 to q_A, P_B for the block of output from q_A to q_B, and P_0 for the remaining output.

The amount of profit the firm receives for each unit is the difference between price and average total cost, so the shaded area labeled with the symbol π in Figure 14-2 represents the firm's total profit. Note that the profit area in second-degree price discrimination is smaller than the profit area illustrated in Figure 14-1 for first-degree price discrimination.

Applying third-degree price discrimination

Third-degree price discrimination exists when you partition the market into two or more different groups of consumers based upon different price elasticities of demand. The differences in elasticity enable you to charge customers in each group purchasing the good different prices. Groups possess different price elasticities of demand for any number of reasons. Differences in income, tastes, or availability of substitutes can account for variation in elasticities. Examples of third-degree price discrimination include different prices for senior citizens, variation in airline ticket prices depending upon when the ticket is purchased, and student discounts.

After you determine that you can separate potential consumers into two or more groups with different price elasticities of demand, you must determine the quantity of output to sell to each group and the good's price for each group. Assuming your goal is profit maximization (and why wouldn't it be?), you allocate output in order to satisfy two criteria. First, you sell the quantity of output that results in the marginal revenue of the last unit sold to each group equal for all groups. Second, the marginal revenue of the last unit sold to any group must equal the marginal cost of the last unit your firm produces. If marginal revenue isn't equal for all groups, you can increase profit by reallocating units of the good to the group that has the higher marginal revenue. If marginal revenue is greater than marginal cost, you're able to increase profit by producing more units of output.

Figure 14-3 illustrates third-degree price discrimination. The curves labeled d_A and MR_A represent the demand and marginal revenue for the group A consumers. Because this demand curve is relatively steep, it's less elastic. Similarly, the curves labeled d_B and MR_B represent the demand and marginal revenue for group B consumers. Group B's flatter demand curve indicates a more elastic demand.

The marginal cost of the last unit you produce is constant and labeled MC^*. The profit-maximizing quantity for each group corresponds to the output where the group's marginal revenue equals marginal cost. To determine price, you go from the profit-maximizing output level up to the group's demand curve and across to the vertical axis. For group A, the profit-maximizing quantity is q_{A0} and the price is P_A. For group B, the profit-maximizing quantity is q_{B0} and the price is P_B.

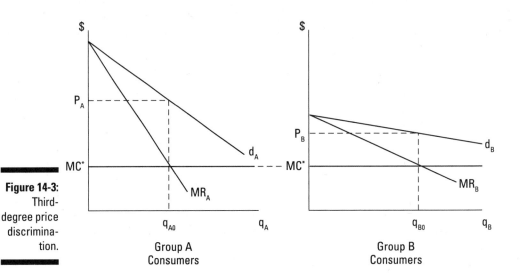

Figure 14-3:
Third-
degree price
discrimina-
tion.

Group A
Consumers

Group B
Consumers

Determining third-degree price discrimination with calculus (if you're interested)

In order to determine the profit-maximizing price and quantity for each group of customers by using third-degree price discrimination, you must satisfy the condition

$$MR_A = MR_B = \ldots = MC$$

where MR_A is group A's marginal revenue for the last unit it buys, MR_B is group B's marginal revenue for the last unit it buys, and MC is marginal cost for the last unit you produce.

Assume that the following equations describe the demand for your firm's product for two different groups of customers. Group A's demand is

$$P_A = 100 - 0.2q_A$$

where P_A is the price in dollars charged to group A customers, and q_A is the quantity sold to group A customers. Group B's demand is

$$P_B = 80 - 0.1q_B$$

where P_B is the price in dollars charged to group B customers, and q_B is the quantity sold to group B customers.

Your firm's total cost and marginal cost equations are

$$TC = 14,000 + 5q + 0.05q^2$$

$$MC = \frac{dTC}{dq} = 5 + 0.1q$$

where TC is your total cost in dollars, MC is marginal cost in dollars, and q is the total quantity of the good your firm produces.

Using this information and the following steps, you can determine the price to charge each group of consumers, how much to sell each group of consumers, and how much to produce:

1. **Determine the marginal revenue for group A customers.**

   First, multiply the demand equation by q_A to determine total revenue, and then take the derivative of total revenue with respect to q_A to determine marginal revenue.

   $$TR_A = P_A \times q_A = (100 - 0.2q_A) \times q_A = 100q_A - 0.2q_A^2$$

   $$MR_A = \frac{dTR_A}{dq_A} = 100 - 0.4q_A$$

2. **Determine the marginal revenue for group B customers.**

   First, determine total revenue by multiplying P_B by q_B, and then take the derivative of total revenue with respect to q_B to determine marginal revenue.

   $$TR_B = P_B \times q_B = (80 - 0.1q_B) \times q_B = 80q_B - 0.1q_B^2$$

   $$MR_B = \frac{dTR_B}{dq_B} = 80 - 0.2q_B$$

3. **Set $MR_A = MC$.**

   $$MR_A = 100 - 0.4q_A = 5 + 0.1q = MC$$

4. **Substitute $q_A + q_B$ for q.**

   The total quantity of output you produce and sell, q, is sold to customers in either group A or group B.

   $$MR_A = 100 - 0.4q_A = 5 + 0.1(q_A + q_B) = 5 + 0.1q_A + 0.1q_B = MC$$

5. **Solve the equation in Step 4 for q_B.**

$$100 - 0.4q_A = 5 + 0.1q_A + 0.1q_B$$
$$95 - 0.4q_A = 0.1q_A + 0.1q_B$$
$$95 - 0.4q_A - 0.1q_A = 95 - 0.5q_A = 0.1q_B$$
$$950 - 5q_A = q_B$$

6. **Set MR_A equal to MR_B.**

$$MR_A = 100 - 0.4q_A = 80 - 0.2q_B = MR_B$$

7. **Substitute $q_B = 950 - 5q_A$ in the equation in Step 6.**

$$100 - 0.4q_A = 80 - 0.2q_B = 80 - 0.2(950 - 5q_A)$$
$$100 - 0.4q_A = 80 - 190 + q_A = -110 + q_A$$

8. **Solve for q_A.**

$$100 - 0.4q_A = -110 + q_A \quad \text{or} \quad 210 = 1.4q_A$$
$$\frac{210}{1.4} = 150 = q_A$$

9. **Substitute $q_A = 150$ in group A's demand equation to determine the price, P_A, to charge customers in group A.**

$$P_A = 100 - 0.2q_A = 100 - 0.2(150) = 70$$

10. **Substitute $q_A = 150$ in the equation from Step 5 to determine q_B.**

$$q_B = 950 - 5q_A = 950 - 5(150) = 200$$

11. **Substitute $q_B = 200$ in group B's demand equation to determine the price, P_B, to charge customers in group B.**

$$P_B = 80 - 0.1q_B = 80 - 0.1(200) = 60$$

12. **Determine the total quantity of output that your firm produces.**

$$q = q_A + q_B = 150 + 200 = 350$$

Your firm produces 350 units of the good. It sells 150 units to customers in group A at a price of $70 per unit and 200 units to customers in group B at a price of $60 per unit.

Pricing coupons

Coupons are a very effective way to price discriminate. Customers who are very responsive to price changes — that is, customers with a very elastic demand — are likely to take time to find coupons that effectively lower the good's price. On the other hand, customers less responsive to price changes because of their less elastic demand aren't as likely to take the time to find coupons.

When you use coupons, you start by establishing a single price for the good. The price is then lower for customers possessing a coupon. So, customers not using a coupon pay the price P, while customers using the coupon pay the price $P - C$, where C represents the coupon's value.

In essence, coupons are another way to implement third-degree price discrimination. The rule for maximizing profit with third-degree price discrimination is

$$\text{MR}_A = \text{MR}_B = \text{MC}$$

The first section in this chapter notes that marginal revenue is a function of the price elasticity of demand, or

$$\text{MR} = P\left(1 + \frac{1}{\eta}\right)$$

Assume that customers in group A have the less elastic demand; therefore, they pay the good's full price P. Customers in group B have the more elastic demand and use a coupon. These customers essentially pay the price $P - C$ for the good. Combining the last two equations with this information yields

$$P\left(1 + \frac{1}{\eta_A}\right) = (P - C)\left(1 + \frac{1}{\eta_B}\right) = \text{MC}$$

where P is the good's price, C is the coupon's value, η_A is the price elasticity of demand for group A customers who have a less elastic demand, η_B is the price elasticity of demand for group B customers who have a more elastic demand, and MC is marginal cost.

You own a restaurant at a vacation destination. Your customers fall into two major groups — vacation travelers who must eat out and have a less elastic demand and local residents who can stay home and eat and thus have a more elastic demand for restaurant meals. Assume that the price elasticity of demand for vacation travelers is –1.5 and the price elasticity of demand for local residents is –3. In addition, the marginal cost of providing a meal, including labor, ingredients, and so on, is $6.00.

Use the following steps to determine the price to charge for a meal and the coupon's value:

1. **The following equation maximizes profit.**

   In the equation, P is the price of a restaurant meal in dollars, C is the coupon's value in dollars, η_V is the price elasticity of demand for vacation travelers, η_L is the price elasticity of demand for local residents, and MC is marginal cost in dollars.

   $$P\left(1+\frac{1}{\eta_V}\right)=(P-C)\left(1+\frac{1}{\eta_L}\right)=MC$$

2. **Determine the price for a restaurant meal.**

   Use the vacation traveler portion of the equation in Step 1 and marginal cost.

   $$P\left(1+\frac{1}{\eta_V}\right)=P\left(1+\frac{1}{-1.5}\right)=6.00=MC$$

   $$P\left(1-\frac{2}{3}\right)=\frac{1}{3}P=6.00 \text{ or } P=18.00$$

3. **Determine the coupon's value.**

   Use the price determined in Step 2 and the local resident portion of the equation in Step 1.

   $$(P-C)\left(1+\frac{1}{\eta_L}\right)=(18-C)\left(1+\frac{1}{-3}\right)=6.00=MC$$

   $$(18-C)\left(1-\frac{1}{3}\right)=\frac{2}{3}(18-C)=12-\frac{2}{3}C=6.00$$

   $$12-6.00=6=\frac{2}{3}C \text{ or } C=9$$

Your restaurant should establish a price of $18.00 for a meal. It should provide $9.00 coupons to local residents. One method of providing coupons to local residents that would generally exclude vacation travelers is to use advertising mailers delivered to local addresses or publish coupons in local newspapers.

Perfecting price discrimination

A pharmacy I go to has a nifty little card that gives me discounts when I use it to make purchases. The store scans the card with every purchase, collecting information on what products I buy. This information is used to determine my price elasticity of demand for products I purchase. It's also used to determine what products are complements or substitutes for the things I buy. Perhaps the most important use is to move toward perfect price discrimination. When my receipt prints out, it usually includes one or more coupons giving me price discounts on various items. Because the coupons appear on my receipt, coupons are tailored to individual customers for both the items and coupon amount, moving closer to perfect price discrimination.

Making a Bundle through Bundling

Bundling refers to a situation where you package two or more goods together and sell them as a single unit. Firms use bundling to increase profit — make a bundle. A fast food restaurant may bundle a sandwich, French fries, and soft drink, selling all three bundled together for a single price.

You're most likely to increase profit by bundling goods that have large differences in the prices customers are willing to pay. Economists use the term *reservation price* to indicate the price where the consumer is indifferent between purchasing the good or continuing to search for a lower price. In essence, the reservation price is the maximum price the consumer is willing to pay.

Effective bundling requires you to package goods that are negatively correlated across consumers. Therefore, for some consumers, good A has a high reservation price, and good B has a low reservation price. For other consumers, good A has a low reservation price, and good B has a high reservation price. This reverse relationship or negative correlation across consumers enables you to bundle goods A and B and have both sets of consumers purchase the bundle consisting of goods A and B. The result is all customers buy both goods instead of having only the consumers with high reservation prices buying the good.

Using pure bundling

Pure bundling exists when consumers can only purchase the goods together. It isn't possible to purchase the goods separately. This pricing strategy is found in many restaurants where the entrée comes automatically with a side dish — the entrée and side dish can't be purchased separately. Satellite and cable television also use pure bundling — you can't pick and choose the channels you want; you must choose among the packages offered by the service.

Figure 14-4 illustrates pure bundling for two computer software programs — a word-processing program, Software W, and a spreadsheet program, Software X. In order to simplify the analysis, 1,200 customers are uniformly distributed over the range of possible reservation prices for both software programs. The reservation prices for Software W appear on the vertical axis and range from $0 to $40.00. The reservation prices for Software X appear on the horizontal axis and range from $0 to $30.00.

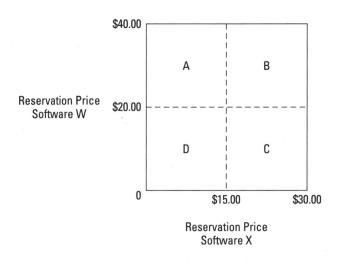

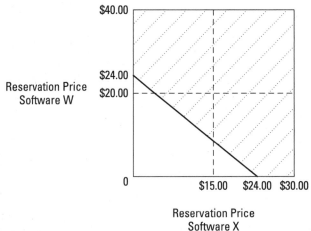

Figure 14-4:
Pure
bundling.

Assume that you initially price each software program separately. You charge $20.00 for Software W and $15.00 for Software X. These prices divide the upper panel in Figure 14-4 into four quadrants of equal size. Going back to the assumption that you have 1,200 customers, each quadrant represents one-quarter of the customers or 300 customers. Given this situation, 300 customers purchase only Software W at $20.00 because their reservation price is $20.00 or higher. These customers are in block A of the figure.

Customers purchase a good only if its price is less than the customer's reservation price. Customers with a reservation price higher than $20.00 — for example, $25.00, or even the highest reservation price of $40.00 — will purchase Software W. Customers with reservation prices less than $20.00 — for example, $18.00 — won't purchase Software W because it isn't worth $20.00 to them.

Another 300 customers purchase only Software X because their reservation price is higher than Software X's $15.00 price. These customers are in block C of the figure. A third group of customers is in block B. These customers buy both Software W and Software X because their reservation price for Software W is higher than $20.00 and their reservation price for Software X is higher than $15.00. Finally, the customers in block D don't buy anything, because their reservation price for Software W is less than $20.00 and their reservation price for Software X is less than $15.00.

Your total revenue in this case equals $21,000. To determine your total revenue, you take the following steps:

1. **Calculate the revenue for customers who purchase only Software W.**

   Multiply 300 customers by the $20.00 price.

   $$\text{Revenue}_{\text{Software W}} = 300 \times 20 = 6,000$$

2. **Calculate the revenue for customers who purchase only Software X.**

   Multiply 300 customers by the $15.00 price.

   $$\text{Revenue}_{\text{Software X}} = 300 \times 15 = 4,500$$

3. **Calculate the revenue for customers who purchase both Software W and Software X.**

   Multiply 300 customers by $35.00, the combined prices of Software W, $20.00, and Software X, $15.00.

   $$\text{Revenue}_{\text{Software W and X}} = 300 \times 35 = 10,500$$

4. Add the revenue you receive from all three groups of customers.

Total Revenue $= 6,000 + 4,500 + 10,500 = 21,000$

By pricing each software program separately, you earn $21,000 in revenue.

Instead of selling each software program separately, you can sell them as a pure bundle — customers must buy software programs W and X together. In this situation, you charge a single price for both programs — for example, you set a price of $24.00 for a package containing both Software W and Software X. The lower panel in Figure 14-4 describes this situation.

Customers consider whether or not to purchase the pure bundle by adding together their reservation prices for Software W and Software X. So, if the customer's reservation price for Software W is $22.00 and the customer's reservation price for Software X is $16.00, the customer purchases the pure bundle because the combined reservation price of $38.00 is higher than the actual price of $24.00. However, note that given these reservation prices, this customer purchases the two software programs even if they're priced separately at $20.00 and $15.00.

On the other hand, another customer has a reservation price of $18.00 for Software W and $10.00 for Software X. If the software programs are priced separately at $20.00 and $15.00, this customer purchases neither program. The customer's reservation price is less than the actual price for each program. However, if the software programs are sold as a bundle for $24.00, the customer purchases the bundle because the customer's combined reservation price of $28.00 — $18.00 plus $10.00 — is higher than the actual price of $24.00. Thus, you're able to sell the pure bundle to customers who purchase nothing if the programs are priced separately. This enables you to increase your revenue. In the lower panel of Figure 14-4, the diagonal line separates the customers who don't purchase the pure bundle, the lower left corner, from customers who do purchase the bundle, the upper right shaded area.

Determining your total revenue with pure bundling is a little tricky. In the example, you have 1,200 customers. If you calculate the area of the rectangle that represents the uniform distribution of customers across their reservation prices, the area equals 1,200 — the length of the vertical axis, 40, multiplied by the length of the horizontal axis, 30. Thus, the area of the rectangle has a one-to-one correspondence with the number of customers. The area of the lower left triangle represents customers who didn't buy the pure bundle. This area equals $\frac{1}{2} \times 24 \times 24 = 288$, or 288 customers who didn't buy the bundle. Thus, 912 customers did buy the bundle (1,200 – 288). Each of those 912 customers pays $24.00 so your total revenue is $21,888 (912 × 24). You increase your revenue by $888 ($21,888 – $21,000) with pure bundling as compared to selling each program separately.

Allowing mixed bundling

Mixed bundling allows customers to purchase the goods either together as a bundle or separately. One of the crucial differences between mixed bundling and pure bundling is that some customers purchase only a single item. These customers have a reservation price greater than the actual price for one item. However, they don't buy the bundle because the difference between the bundle price and the price of the first item is less than their reservation price for the second item.

For example, say you're willing to pay $30.00 for Software W and only $2.00 for Software X. In addition, the price of Software W separately is $20.00, the price of Software X separately is $15.00, and the price of the bundle is $24.00. Obviously, you're willing to buy Software W separately — its $20.00 price is less than your reservation price of $30.00. Similarly, you're not willing to buy Software X separately because its $15.00 price is greater than your reservation price of $2.00.

In a surprising result, you're not willing to buy the bundle. To move from buying Software W for $20.00 to buying the bundle requires you to pay $24.00. This is $4.00 more than you have to pay to purchase Software W alone. Because your reservation price for Software X is only $2.00, it's not worth spending the extra $4.00 to buy the bundle. The point labeled *U* in Figure 14-5 represents this situation.

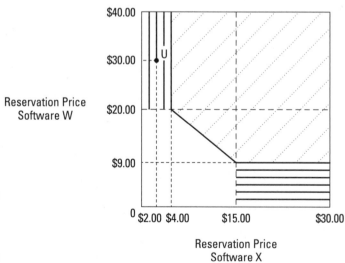

Figure 14-5:
Mixed
bundling.

In order for you to purchase the bundle, the difference between the separate price for the first item and the bundle price must be less than your reservation price for the second item. Now assume that your reservation price for Software W remains $30.00, but your reservation price for Software X is $7.00. In this situation you'll buy the bundle because you're willing to pay $30.00 for Software W. That's higher than Software W's actual price. You can then add Software X for another $4.00 because the price of the bundle is $24.00. So, instead of purchasing Software W alone for $20.00, you can purchase the bundle including both Software W and Software X for $24.00. Because Software X is worth $7.00 to you, adding Software X to the bundle is worth it to you. You get something you're willing to pay $7.00 for and it costs you only an extra $4.00.

In Figure 14-5, the vertical shaded area represents customers who buy only Software W. Note for this shaded area, customers' reservation prices for Software W are higher than Software W's $20.00 price. However, their reservation prices for Software X are less than $4.00. Because adding Software X to the bundle costs $4.00, they're not willing to buy the bundle.

The horizontal shaded area represents customers who buy only Software X. In this horizontal shaded area, customers' reservation prices for Software X are higher than its $15.00 price. If these customers add Software W to the bundle, it increases the price by $9.00 to $24.00. For this group of customers, their reservation prices for Software W are less than $9.00; so, they're not willing to add Software W to their purchase of Software X.

Customers in the diagonal shaded area buy the bundle of Software W and Software X. For these customers, the reservation price of adding the second software package to the bundle is greater than the price difference. Finally, the area that isn't shaded represents customers who don't buy any software package.

Customers only add another good to the bundle if the actual price difference between the bundle and buying an item separately is less than the additional item's reservation price.

Determining your total revenue with mixed bundling is very tricky. Again, assume you have 1,200 uniformly distributed customers that correspond to the area of the rectangle. Of those customers, 80 purchase just Software W at a price of $20, 135 purchase just Software X at a price of $15, and 745.5 purchase the bundle at a price of $24. The remaining 239.5 don't purchase any software program because the price of each individual program is higher than their reservation price for that program, and the bundle's price is higher than the customer's reservation prices for the two programs added together. Thus, your total revenue equals $21,517 — that is, $(80 \times 20) + (135 \times 15) + (745.5 \times 24)$. Your revenue increases by $517 with mixed bundling as compared to selling each program separately.

So You Want War: Pricing for Business Battles

I know a bicycle rider who once passed another bicycle rider on a hill. When passed, the second bicycle rider said, "I didn't know it was a race." To which the first rider responded, "It's always a race."

In a very real sense, businesses are always at war fighting battles with one another. Businesses compete for resources and customers. The wages one business pays for labor affect what other businesses have to pay, and the price one business charges its customers affects the price other businesses charge.

This section describes three weapons that help you fight these battles.

Penetration pricing: Here I come

Firms use penetration pricing to quickly establish a large market share. In order to attract customers, the firm establishes a very low price. This is a useful strategy for a new firm entering a market.

Effective penetration pricing requires a very elastic demand for the good. Because customers are very responsive to price changes, establishing a low price leads to a large increase in quantity demanded. Later, if you're successful in establishing customer loyalty, you can raise the price.

In addition to attracting new customers, an effective penetration price leads to lower per unit costs if economies of scale are present. By quickly attracting customers, you can establish a large market share leading to economies of scale that become a barrier to entry for other firms thinking about entering the market.

Penetration pricing is also used to sell complementary products. For example, a low penetration price on a game console can lead to more sales of compatible games that have high mark-ups.

You need to take into account several factors before using penetration pricing. First, consider whether your firm is able to produce enough output to satisfy customers. If you run out of product to sell, customers are likely to be dissatisfied with you. Second, price can't be associated with quality. If customers associate a low price with poor quality, they won't buy the product. Finally, if rivals meet the lower price you charge, the advantages of penetration pricing are negated.

Limit pricing: Keep out

Firms use *limit pricing* to prevent other firms from entering the market. Limit pricing occurs when the firm establishes a price below the profit-maximizing level. The lower price leads to a higher quantity demanded, leaving very little residual demand for a new firm to satisfy.

Figure 14-6 illustrates limit pricing. Initially, the market is a monopoly, so the market-demand curve, D, corresponds to the firm's demand curve, d. As I note in Chapter 10, the marginal-revenue curve associated with a linear demand curve starts at the same point on the vertical axis and is twice as steep as the demand curve. The monopoly's marginal-revenue curve in Figure 14-6 is labeled MR.

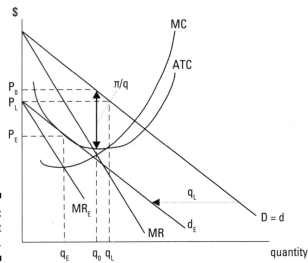

Figure 14-6:
Limit
pricing.

Given typical average total cost and marginal cost curves, the profit-maximizing monopolist produces the quantity q_0, based on marginal revenue equals marginal cost, and charges the price P_0. The monopolist's economic profit per unit is the difference between price and average total cost as represented by the double-headed arrow labeled π/q.

The positive economic profit the monopolist earns attracts new firms. If these firms enter the market, the existing firm's profit decreases or perhaps even disappears. So, to discourage entry, the monopolist charges a lower price, P_L. At this price, the monopolist must produce q_L to satisfy consumer demand.

Firms considering whether or not to enter the market now see an entirely different situation. The potential demand for an entering firm equals the market demand minus the quantity, q_L, provided by the current firm. The entrant's residual demand curve is represented by d_E and the associated marginal revenue curve is MR_E. The entering firm would then produce where its marginal revenue equals marginal cost. (For the moment, assume the entering firm has exactly the same costs as the current monopoly.) The entering firm's profit-maximizing quantity and price are q_E and P_E. But at this output level, price equals average total cost, so the entering firm earns zero profit. Thus, the new firm has no incentive to enter the market, and the original firm has succeeded in keeping rivals out.

Predatory pricing: Get out

Predatory pricing is used to drive existing rival firms out of a market. With predatory pricing, a firm establishes a price that's below its marginal cost. After the rival leaves the market, the remaining firm, or predator, raises price in order to increase its profit. The predator in essence is trading a temporary short-run loss for higher future profit.

Predatory pricing depends upon the correct assessment of the relative health of the predator and prey. The predator is assuming that it's healthier than the prey and can withstand the temporary losses better than the prey. If the predator is wrong in this assessment, predatory pricing can backfire and leave the predator vulnerable.

Predator and prey: Which is which?

In *The Life and Legend of Jay Gould* (published by The Johns Hopkins University Press), author Maury Klein tells the story of a price war between the owner of the New York Central Railroad, Commodore Cornelius Vanderbilt, and the Erie Railroad's owners, Jay Gould and Jim Fisk. The price war concerned eastbound livestock traffic between Buffalo and New York City and the normal freight rate $125 a carload. Vanderbilt initiated a price war by lowering the New York Central's rate to $100 carload. Gould and Fisk responded by lowering the Erie Railroad's rate to $75. Vanderbilt then reduced the New York Central's rate to $50, and Gould and Fisk dropped to $25. In a final effort to ruin the Erie Railroad's livestock trade, Vanderbilt set his rate at $1 per carload, and as a result, the New York Central cars were full while the Erie's cars ran empty. However, as Vanderbilt enjoyed his victory, Gould and Fisk bought every steer in Buffalo and shipped them to New York via the Central. As a result, Gould and Fisk enjoyed great profit, while Vanderbilt and the New York Central carried their cattle at tremendous cost.

Successful predators establish a reputation as tough, perhaps even ruthless, rivals. This reputation is likely to deter future entry so that you can realize additional benefits.

Sometimes, the right price is as simple as the price associated with a mutually beneficial exchange. Both the customer and the firm are willing to buy and sell at that price. But as a business manager, you want to find the price that maximizes profit — that is, your right price.

Part IV

Anticipating Surprises: Risk and Uncertainty

In this part . . .

Business decisions are made in an uncertain environment. Because of uncertainty, you can't know future outcomes and profit for sure, so you require techniques for decision-making with unknown or uncertain payoffs. This is especially important when budgeting for capital investments. I also consider how members of a business organization may have different goals and examine the actions managers and owners can take to "get everyone on the same page." Finally, I consider the government policy's impact on business.

Chapter 15

Risk Analysis: Walking Through the Fog

You may remember Mattel's Magic 8 Ball. It's a black globe that answers questions about the future. You hold it, ask a question, turn it over, and in a window the answer to your question appears. The answer I always seem to get is "Reply hazy, try again." Such is the future — hazy. Or consider Yogi Berra's contribution to planning, "If you don't know where you're going, you might wind up someplace else."

To this point, I've examined decision-making in a certain or known environment. However, frequently the consequences or payoffs resulting from a decision or action are uncertain, depending upon factors outside your control. Therefore, it's essential to develop criteria that are used to evaluate different actions.

In an uncertain environment, decision-making criteria don't guarantee you the highest payoff, because the payoff is influenced by factors outside of your control. These criteria, however, allow you to systematically evaluate alternative actions with variable and uncertain payoffs.

This chapter develops decision-making rules for environments where outcomes aren't known in advance with certainty. The chapter starts with two simple decision-making criteria — the maxi-min and the mini-max regret rules. A more sophisticated criterion — expected monetary value — bases decisions on the likelihood of any outcome occurring. By using probability and expected value, you can also determine the value of additional information — for example, the value of hiring a consultant. Differences in risk preferences are incorporated in decision-making by using the expected utility criterion. The chapter concludes with strategies for determining prices through auctions.

Differentiating between Risk and Uncertainty

Risk and uncertainty refer to situations where outcomes aren't known in advance. You don't know which outcome will occur. Although many individuals use the terms *risk* and *uncertainty* interchangeably, economist Frank Knight (1885–1972) thinks these concepts are different. Knight believes a situation is *risky* when objective probabilities can be assigned to the situation's possible outcomes. Therefore, as a decision-maker, you possess information concerning the likelihood of each possible outcome. (Using probabilities to measure risk is examined in the next section.)

On the other hand, Knight regards a situation to be *uncertain* when objective probabilities can't be assigned to the possible outcomes. As a consequence, you have no objective information concerning the likelihood of a given outcome.

Assessing risk requires knowledge of the probability of various outcomes occurring. Uncertainty means the future can't be objectively known.

Determining the Odds with Probability

In a risky environment, you want to play the odds when making a decision. Remember that risk exists when objective probabilities can be assigned to the possible outcomes. *Probability* is simply the likelihood or chance that an event occurs. Probabilities are expressed as numbers between 0, meaning impossible, and 1.0, meaning certain. A probability of 0.50 represents a 50–50 chance or 50-percent chance that the event occurs. That's the probability that "heads" comes up when you flip a coin.

Probabilities are further subdivided into objective, subjective, and expected probability.

> ✔ An *objective probability* is a probability determined by unbiased evidence, such as observed long-run relative frequencies of occurrence. For example, by collecting information, insurance companies determine objective probabilities to represent the likelihood of a home being robbed.

✔ A *subjective probability* is determined by an individual based upon the individual's knowledge, information, and expertise.

✔ An *expected probability* is a theoretical probability based upon assumptions. For example, the 50-percent probability that a flipped coin comes up "heads" assumes you have a fair, two-sided coin.

The sum of the probabilities for all possible outcomes must equal 1.

Considering Factors In and Out of Your Control

If only you could control everything, decision-making would be easy. But you can't, so it's important to differentiate between the things you can and can't control. The terms *actions* and *states of nature* make a distinction between factors that are within or outside your control.

✔ **Actions** **represent alternatives that you can choose.** These are the things you control. In the decision-making process, you evaluate the desirability of alternative actions. Examples of actions include your firm's pricing and advertising policies.

✔ **States of nature** **also affect your outcome.** However, states of nature are things outside your control. Examples of states of nature are the advertising and pricing policies of rival firms, or whether or not the economy goes into a recession.

Payoff refers to the consequence or result of the simultaneous occurrence of a particular action and a specific state of nature. A payoff matrix includes all possible payoffs for several actions and several states of nature. Figure 15-1 illustrates a possible payoff matrix. The top of the matrix lists the three possible actions for Global Airlines: reduce fares, charge the same fares, and raise fares. These actions represent the alternatives that Global's managers can choose.

The four possible states of nature are on the side of the payoff matrix. These states of nature represent what happens to the price of oil. Because Global's managers can't determine what happens to the price of oil, they're uncertain about which state of nature will occur.

Assume that the payoffs in the payoff matrix represent Global Airline's annual profit in millions of dollars for various scenarios. For example, if Global decides to reduce fares and oil prices increase by 10 percent, Global's annual profit is $43 million. Similarly, if Global raises fares and oil prices don't change, Global's annual profit is $48 million.

Oil Prices	Global Airline: Reduce Fares	Global Airline: Same Fares	Global Airline: Raise Fares
10% Decrease	$50	$52	$42
No Change	$56	$51	$48
10% Increase	$43	$49	$47
20% Increase	$35	$41	$44

Figure 15-1: Payoff matrix.

Simplifying Decision-Making Criteria

After you identify your possible actions and how the various states of nature affect the outcome of those actions, you need to decide what to do. A variety of criteria enable you to choose among alternative actions after you develop the payoff matrix; each criterion has different advantages and disadvantages.

Determining the biggest guaranteed win with the maxi-min rule

You've probably been told to make the best of a bad situation. That in essence is the maxi-min criterion. With the maxi-min criterion, your decision is based upon the minimum or worst payoff associated with each action. For each action, you note the minimum payoff.

REMEMBER

You make the best of a bad situation by choosing the action whose minimum payoff is best or largest.

Because it doesn't know what's going to happen to the price of oil, Global Airlines uses the maxi-min criterion to determine what fare to set. To apply the maxi-min criterion, Global takes the following steps:

1. **Determine the worst payoff for reducing fares.** For reduced fares, the possible payoffs are $50, $56, $43, and $35. The worst payoff is $35.

2. **Determine the worst payoff for charging the same fares.** For charging the same fares, the possible payoffs are $52, $51, $49, and $41. The worst payoff is $41.

3. **Determine the worst payoff for raising fares.** For raised fares, the possible payoffs are $42, $48, $47, and $44. The worst payoff is $42.

4. **Chose the action with the best worst payoff.** Global Airlines should raise fares because its worst payoff is $42 million, as compared to reduced fares' worst payoff of $35 million and same fares' worst payoff of $41 million.

Global Airlines raises fares because its worst payoff is $42 million. However, $42 million isn't necessarily the profit it makes. The actual profit ultimately depends upon which state of nature actually occurs. So the actual profit depends on what actually happens to the price of oil.

The advantage of the maxi-min criterion is its simplicity. However, this criterion's disadvantages include its emphasis on only the worst possible outcome of an action. Therefore, variation in payoffs and the better payoffs are ignored. In addition, this criterion ignores an outcome's probability of occurring. It ignores risk.

The maxi-min criterion is used when you're very conservative, and as a result you have a strong aversion to risk. This standard can be a good rule to use with a new business, when the firm's continued existence necessitates that you avoid losses.

Making the best worst-case by using the mini-max regret rule

Don't live with regrets. This phrase isn't just a life philosophy, it's a way to make business decisions. The mini-max regret criterion bases decisions on the maximum regret associated with each action. *Regret* measures the difference between each action's payoff for a given state of nature and the best possible payoff for that state of nature.

You choose the action that has the smallest maximum regret.

Given the information in Figure 15-1, Global Airlines uses the mini-max regret criterion to determine what fare to set given it doesn't know what's going to happen to the price of oil. To apply the mini-max regret criterion, Global takes the following steps:

1. **Determine the regret for a 10-percent decrease in the price of oil.**

   For a 10-percent decrease in the price of oil, the best payoff is $52 million with same fares. The regret for reducing fares is $2 million, $52 – $50, and the regret for raising fares is $10 million, $52 – $42. The maximum regret is $10 million.

2. **Determine the regret for no change in the price of oil.**

   For no change in the price of oil, the best payoff is $56 million with reduced fares. The regret for keeping the same fares is $5 million, $56 – $51, and the regret for raising fares is $8 million, $56 – $48. The maximum regret is $8 million.

3. **Determine the regret for a 10-percent increase in the price of oil.**

   For a 10-percent increase in the price of oil, the best payoff is $49 million with the same fares. The regret for reducing fares is $6 million, $49 – $43, and the regret for raising fares is $2 million, $49 – $47. The maximum regret is $6 million.

4. **Determine the regret for a 20-percent increase in the price of oil.**

   For a 20-percent increase in the price of oil, the best payoff is $44 million with raising fares. The regret for reducing fares is $9 million, $44 – $35, and the regret for keeping the same fares is $3 million, $44 – $41. The maximum regret is $9 million.

5. **Choose the action with the minimum or smallest maximum regret.**

   Figure 15-2 summarizes the regrets for each action. The maximum regret associated with reducing fares is $9 million. The maximum regret in the same-fares column is $5 million, and the maximum regret you see with raising fares is $10 million. Global Airlines should charge the same fares because its maximum regret of $5 million is smaller than the maximum regret associated with any other action.

The primary advantage of the mini-max regret decision criterion is its relative simplicity. This criterion's disadvantages include its emphasis on the worst possible outcome, and it ignores risk as represented by an outcome's probability of occurring.

Global
Airline

	Reduce Fares	Same Fares	Raise Fares
10% Decrease	$2	$0	$10
No Change	$0	$5	$8
10% Increase	$6	$0	$2
20% Increase	$9	$3	$0

Oil Prices *(row label, left of the table)*

Figure 15-2:
Regret
matrix.

Calculating the expected value

Hope for the best but expect the worst. That's in essence what the maxi-min and mini-max regret criteria are all about. Both of those decision-making criteria focus upon the worst possible outcome, and if you're like Eeyore, the extremely pessimistic donkey in the Winnie-the-Pooh books, they're probably the criteria you should use.

But I like at least some of my perspective to be based on a "hope for the best" attitude. I don't want to ignore the worst-case scenario, but I don't want it to be the exclusive basis for my decision.

The expected monetary value decision-making criterion overcomes the pessimistic approach by incorporating all possible outcomes in the decision-making process. Each state of nature is assigned a probability of occurrence. This probability can be determined from historical data, subjective criteria, or theory. In determining probabilities, however, the sum of the probabilities for all states of nature must equal 1. In other words, you have to specify all possible situations.

After you determine probabilities, calculate the expected monetary value (*EMV*) of a specific action, a_j, through the following formula:

$$\text{EMV}\left(a_j\right) = \sum_{i=1}^{n} P\left(\Theta_i\right)\pi_{ij}$$

This formula indicates that action a_j's expected monetary value equals the summation for all states of nature $i = 1$ through $i = n$ of the probability of θ_i occurring, $P(\theta_i)$, multiplied by the payoff associated with action a_j and state of nature θ_i, π_{ij}.

After you calculate the expected monetary value, you choose the action with the best expected payoff.

To use the expected monetary value criterion, Global Airlines must determine the probability associated with each state of nature — what happens to oil prices. Currently, Global believes the probability that the price of oil decreases 10 percent is 0.05, the probability that oil prices stay the same is 0.35, the probability that oil prices increase 10 percent is 0.45, and the probability that oil prices increase 20 percent is 0.15. Note that adding the probabilities for all possible states of nature equals 1.0 (0.05+0.35+0.45+0.15). Thus, Global has considered all possibilities.

To determine the expected monetary value for each action, you take the following steps:

1. **Calculate the expected monetary value for reducing fares.**

   Let reducing fares represent action a_j. For each state of nature, multiply the probability of that state of nature by the payoff associated with that state of nature and action a_j, reduce fares. Add the resulting values to determine the expected monetary value.

   $$\text{EMV}(a_j) = \text{EMV}(\text{reduce fares}) = \sum_{i=1}^{n} P(\Theta_i)\pi_{ij}$$
   $$= P(-10\%) \times 50 + P(0\%) \times 56 + P(+10\%) \times 43 + P(+20\%) \times 35$$
   $$= (0.05 \times 50) + (0.35 \times 56) + (0.45 \times 43) + (0.15 \times 35) = 46.7$$

2. **Calculate the expected monetary value for keeping the same fares.**

   Let the same fares represent action a_j. For each state of nature, multiply the probability of that state of nature by the payoff associated with that state of nature and action a_j, same fares. Add the resulting values to determine the expected monetary value.

   $$\text{EMV}(a_j) = \text{EMV}(\text{same fares}) = \sum_{i=1}^{n} P(\Theta_i)\pi_{ij}$$
   $$= (0.05 \times 52) + (0.35 \times 51) + (0.45 \times 49) + (0.15 \times 41) = 48.65$$

3. **Calculate the expected monetary value for raising fares.**

   Let raising fares represent action a_j. For each state of nature, multiply the probability of that state of nature by the payoff associated with that state of nature and action a_j, raise fares. Add the resulting values to determine the expected monetary value.

$$\text{EMV}\left(a_j\right) = \text{EMV}\left(\text{raise fares}\right) = \sum_{i=1}^{n} P\left(\Theta_i\right)\pi_{ij}$$

$$= \left(0.05 \times 42\right) + \left(0.35 \times 48\right) + \left(0.45 \times 47\right) + \left(0.15 \times 44\right) = 46.65$$

4. **Choose the action with the highest expected monetary value.**

   Global Airlines should charge the same fares because its expected monetary value is $48.65 million. That's higher than the expected monetary value of reducing fares — $46.7 million — and the expected monetary value of raising fares — $46.65 million.

The major advantages associated with the expected monetary value criterion are its inclusion of all possible outcomes and the probability of an outcome occurring. However, although this criterion includes all possible outcomes, it doesn't take into account an individual's risk preferences. I introduce risk preferences later in this chapter.

Changing the Odds by Using New Information to Revise Probabilities

A common lament is "If only I'd known this earlier." This lament emphasizes the importance of information. Risk analysis exists because the future can't be known with certainty. Nevertheless, more information enables you to better anticipate what the future holds. Because of this situation, more information has value to you. The crucial question is whether the value of this additional information is worth its cost.

This section deals extensively with statistical techniques that enable you to manipulate probabilities. If you're unfamiliar with concepts like conditional probabilities, you should review those concepts and probability theory in general before tackling this section. I call this technical stuff because the warning icon doesn't use a mushroom cloud; thus, it seems insufficient for this caution.

Starting with prior probabilities

Prior probabilities are the probabilities of various states of nature associated with the problem's initial specification. A prior probability is symbolically represented as $P(\theta_i)$, or the probability of state of nature θ_i occurring. These probabilities are determined prior to the acquisition of additional information. The probabilities in the illustration of the expected monetary value criterion in the previous section are prior probabilities.

Incorporating likelihoods

Prior probabilities can be revised based on new information. Frequently, this new information is the result of a sample. An old saying regarding Broadway plays is, "Did it play in Peoria?" Peoria refers to Peoria, Illinois, and the quote recognizes Peoria's traditional role as a test market because many individuals believe Peoria represents "Main Street" America. So a business may test-market a new product in Peoria and, based upon the results, decide whether or not to launch the product nationally. Or, in the case of a Broadway play, a producer may do trial performances in Peoria before moving to Broadway.

In order to revise a prior probability, you need to know the probability of obtaining a specific sample outcome S given the various states of nature, θ_i. This probability is called a *likelihood,* and symbolically it's represented as $P(S|\theta_i)$, or the probability of obtaining sample result S given state of nature θ_i. The vertical line within the parentheses indicates given. Likelihoods are usually based on previous experience.

Determining marginal probabilities

Likelihoods are the probability of a certain sample result given a specific state of nature occurs. A *marginal probability* is the probability of getting a certain sample result irrespective of the state of nature. Thus, the probability of getting sample result S is $P(S)$.

The formula used to determine a marginal probability is

$$P(S) = \sum_{i=1}^{n} P(S|\Theta_i) \times P(\Theta_i)$$

where $P(S)$ is the probability of getting sample result S, $P(S|\theta_i)$ is the likelihood or probability of getting sample result S given state of nature θ_i has already occurred, and $P(\theta_i)$ is the probability of state of nature θ_i occurring.

Revising probabilities

After sampling provides additional information, you can revise prior probabilities. For example, an oil company can use the results of an extensive geological survey to revise the probability that they'll hit a given size oil reserve when they drill. Or a business can use an economic forecast to revise the probability that the economy will enter a recession.

Symbolically, the posterior probability is represented as $P(\theta_i|S)$, or the probability of state of nature θ_i occurring given sample result S. Again, the vertical line within the parentheses indicates given.

In order to revise a prior probability, you need to know the likelihoods — the probability of obtaining some sample outcome S given the various states of nature, θ_i, or the $P(S|\theta_i)$.

Assuming both prior probabilities and likelihoods are known, you can calculate the posterior probability given sample result S. The formula for calculating the posterior probability is

$$P(\Theta_k|S) = \frac{P(S|\Theta_k) \times P(\Theta_k)}{\sum_{i=1}^{n} P(S|\Theta_i) \times P(\Theta_i)}$$

where $P(\theta_k|S)$ is the posterior probability of state of nature θ_k occurring given sample result S, $P(S|\theta_i)$ is the likelihood, and $P(\theta_i)$ is the prior probability.

The denominator in this formula is simply the marginal probability of a given sample result. Thus the formula can be rewritten as

$$P(\Theta_k|S) = \frac{P(S|\Theta_k) \times P(\Theta_k)}{P(S)}$$

where $P(S)$ is the probability of getting sample result S.

Recalculating expected values

Although new information enables you to revise probabilities, obtaining that information is costly. You need to balance the cost of obtaining the information with its expected value. You want to obtain additional information only when its expected value exceeds the cost of obtaining it. The following example illustrates the process you use to determine the value of additional information.

Global Airlines profit depends upon the fares it charges (an action) and what happens to oil prices (states of nature). Based upon past experience, Global currently believes the probability that the price of oil decreases by 10 percent is 0.05, the probability that oil prices stay the same is 0.35, the probability that oil prices increase by 10 percent is 0.45, and the probability that oil prices increase by 20 percent is 0.15. These are prior probabilities because no new information is incorporated. Given these prior probabilities, as illustrated earlier in this chapter, Global Airlines decides to charge the same fares because its expected monetary value of $48.65 million is higher than the expected monetary value of reducing fares — $46.7 million — and the expected monetary value of raising fares — $46.65 million. However, if Global Airlines obtains additional information, such as an expert's forecast on oil prices, it may find an alternative action more desirable.

Global is considering hiring a consultant to advise it on oil market conditions. Before hiring the consultant, Global Airlines must determine how the consultant's forecast affects its decision. Obviously, if Global's best course of action is the same regardless of the consultant's forecast, hiring the expert is pointless.

To determine whether or not to hire the consultant, Global first notes the information the consultant provides. In this situation, the consultant will make a positive (P_o) or negative (N_e) prediction regarding the price of oil. The consultant's past track record shows the following:

- ✔ When the price of oil decreased by 10 percent, the probability the consultant made a positive (P_o) prediction was 0.3, $P(P_o|-10\%) = 0.3$, and the probability the consultant made a negative (N_e) prediction was 0.7, $P(N_e|-10\%) = 0.7$.

- ✔ When the price of oil remained the same, the probability of a positive (P_o) prediction was 0.5, $P(P_o|0\%) = 0.5$, and a negative (N_e) prediction was 0.5, $P(N_e|0\%) = 0.5$.

- ✔ When the price of oil increased by 10 percent, the probability of a positive (P_o) prediction was 0.2, $P(P_o|+10\%) = 0.2$, and a negative (N_e) prediction was 0.8, $P(N_e|+10\%) = 0.8$.

- ✔ When the price of oil increased by 20 percent, the probability of a positive (P_o) prediction was 0.1, $P(P_o|+20\%) = 0.1$, and a negative (N_e) prediction was 0.9, $P(N_e|+20\%) = 0.9$.

These points are likelihoods.

Based upon the prior probabilities and likelihoods, Global Airlines can determine the value of the consultant's report.

1. Calculate the probability of a positive (P_o) report.

Because you've not yet decided whether or not to hire the consultant, you don't know what report you may get. Therefore, to determine the expected value of the consultant's report, you need to determine the marginal probability of a positive report.

$$P(P) = \sum_{i=1}^{n} P(P_o|\Theta_i) \times P(\Theta_i)$$
$$= P(P_o|-10\%) \times P(-10\%) + P(P_o|0\%) \times P(0\%) +$$
$$P(P_o|+10\%) \times P(+10\%) + P(P_o|+20\%) \times P(+20\%)$$
$$= (0.3 \times 0.05) + (0.5 \times 0.35) + (0.2 \times 0.45) + (0.1 \times 0.15) = 0.295$$

2. Calculate the probability of a negative (N_e) report.

Determine the marginal probability of a negative report.

$$P(N_e) = \sum_{i=1}^{n} P(N_e|\Theta_i) \times P(\Theta_i)$$
$$= P(N_e|-10\%) \times P(-10\%) + P(N_e|0\%) \times P(0\%) +$$
$$P(N_e|+10\%) \times P(+10\%) + P(N_e|+20\%) \times P(+20\%)$$
$$= (0.7 \times 0.05) + (0.5 \times 0.35) + (0.8 \times 0.45) + (0.9 \times 0.15) = 0.705$$

3. Calculate the posterior probability for oil prices decreasing by 10 percent given a positive (P_o) report.

$$P(-10\%|P_o) = \frac{P(P_o|-10\%) \times P(-10\%)}{P(P_o)} = \frac{0.3 \times 0.05}{0.295} = 0.0508$$

4. Calculate the remaining posterior probabilities given a positive (P_o) report.

Posterior probabilities need to be calculated for oil prices that remain the same, oil prices that increase by 10 percent, and oil prices that increase by 20 percent given a positive report.

$$P(0\%|P_o) = \frac{P(P_o|0\%) \times P(0\%)}{P(P_o)} = \frac{0.5 \times 0.35}{0.295} = 0.5932$$

$$P(+10\%|P_o) = \frac{P(P_o|+10\%) \times P(+10\%)}{P(P_o)} = \frac{0.2 \times 0.45}{0.295} = 0.3051$$

$$P(+20\%|P_o) = \frac{P(P_o|+20\%) \times P(+20\%)}{P(P_o)} = \frac{0.1 \times 0.15}{0.295} = 0.0508$$

5. Calculate the posterior probabilities for oil price changes given a negative (N_e) report.

Given a negative report, you need to calculate the probabilities that oil prices decrease by 10 percent, oil prices remain the same, oil prices increase by 10 percent, and oil prices increase by 20 percent.

$$P\left(-10\%|N_e\right) = \frac{P\left(N_e|-10\%\right) \times P\left(-10\%\right)}{P\left(N_e\right)} = \frac{0.7 \times 0.05}{0.705} = 0.0496$$

$$P\left(0\%|N_e\right) = \frac{P\left(N_e|0\%\right) \times P\left(0\%\right)}{P\left(N_e\right)} = \frac{0.5 \times 0.35}{0.705} = 0.2482$$

$$P\left(+10\%|N_e\right) = \frac{P\left(N_e|+10\%\right) \times P\left(+10\%\right)}{P\left(N_e\right)} = \frac{0.8 \times 0.45}{0.705} = 0.5106$$

$$P\left(+20\%|N_e\right) = \frac{P\left(N_e|+20\%\right) \times P\left(+20\%\right)}{P\left(N_e\right)} = \frac{0.9 \times 0.15}{0.705} = 0.1915$$

6. **Calculate the expected monetary value for reducing fares given a positive (P_o) consultant report.**

   Based upon the posterior probabilities, you can recalculate the expected monetary value of each action. In this calculation, the payoffs associated with each combination of action and state of nature are multiplied by the posterior probability in the place of the prior probability. Reducing fares represents action a_j. For each state of nature, multiply the posterior probability of that state of nature given a positive consultant's report by the payoff associated with that state of nature and action a_j. Add the resulting values to determine the expected monetary value.

$$EMV\left(a_j\right) = EMV\left(\text{reduce}\right) = \sum_{i=1}^{n} P\left(\Theta_i|P_o\right)\pi_{i,\text{reduce}}$$
$$= \left(0.0508 \times 50\right) + \left(0.5932 \times 56\right) + \left(0.3051 \times 43\right) + \left(0.0508 \times 35\right)$$
$$= 50.6565$$

7. **Calculate the expected monetary value for charging the same fares and increasing fares given a positive (P_o) consultant's report.**

   For each action, multiply the posterior probability of each state of nature given a positive consultant's report by the payoff associated with that state of nature and the appropriate action — same fares or raised fares.

$$EMV\left(\text{same}\right) = \sum_{i=1}^{n} P\left(\Theta_i|P_o\right)\pi_{i,\text{same}}$$
$$= \left(0.0508 \times 52\right) + \left(0.5932 \times 51\right) + \left(0.3051 \times 49\right) + \left(0.0508 \times 41\right)$$
$$= 49.9275$$

$$EMV\left(\text{raise}\right) = \sum_{i=1}^{n} P\left(\Theta_i|P_o\right)\pi_{i,\text{raise}}$$
$$= \left(0.0508 \times 42\right) + \left(0.5932 \times 48\right) + \left(0.3051 \times 47\right) + \left(0.0508 \times 44\right)$$
$$= 47.1821$$

8. **Choose the action with the highest expected monetary value given a positive consultant's report.**

Global Airlines should reduce fares because its expected monetary value is $50.6565 million. That's higher than the expected monetary value of keeping the same fares — $49.9275 million — and the expected monetary value of raising fares — $47.1821 million.

9. **Calculate the expected monetary value for reducing fares, keeping the same fares, and increasing fares given a negative (N_e) consultant's report.**

Expected monetary values based upon posterior probabilities must also be calculated for the other possible forecasts — you need to know what decision you'll make if the consultant's report is negative instead of positive. Remember to use the posterior probabilities associated with a negative consultant's report.

$$\text{EMV}(\text{reduce}) = \sum_{i=1}^{n} P(\Theta_i | N_e) \pi_{i,\text{reduce}}$$

$$= (0.0496 \times 50) + (0.2482 \times 56) + (0.5106 \times 43) + (0.1915 \times 35)$$

$$= 45.0375$$

$$\text{EMV}(\text{same}) = \sum_{i=1}^{n} P(\Theta_i | N_e) \pi_{i,\text{same}}$$

$$= (0.0496 \times 52) + (0.2482 \times 51) + (0.5106 \times 49) + (0.1915 \times 41)$$

$$= 48.1083$$

$$\text{EMV}(\text{raise}) = \sum_{i=1}^{n} P(\Theta_i | N_e) \pi_{i,\text{increase}}$$

$$= (0.0496 \times 42) + (0.2482 \times 48) + (0.5106 \times 47) + (0.1915 \times 44)$$

$$= 46.421$$

10. **Choose the action with the highest expected monetary value given a negative consultant's report.**

Global Airlines should charge the same fares because its expected monetary value is $48.1083 million. That's higher than the expected monetary value of reducing fares — $45.0375 million — and the expected monetary value of raising fares — $46.421 million.

11. **Determine the value of the consultant's report.**

The consultant's report affects your decision. If it's positive, you'll reduce fares, and if it's negative, you'll charge the same fares. Multiply the expected payoff of your decision by the probability of getting a consultant's report that leads to that decision.

$$\text{EMV}(\text{consultant}) = \text{EMV}_{\text{reduce fares}} \times P(P_o) + \text{EMV}_{\text{same fares}} \times P(N_e)$$

$$= (50.6565 \times 0.295) + (48.1083 \times 0.705) = 48.8601$$

12. **Determine the value of the consultant's report.**

The expected value of the consultant's report is determined by comparing the *EMV* for the consultant with the *EMV* for the best action determined based on prior probabilities. Based upon prior probabilities used in the previous example, Global Airlines charged the same fares with an expected monetary value of $48.65 million. If Global Airlines hires the consultant and acts on the consultant's report, the expected monetary value increases to $48.8601. The difference between the expected monetary value given the consultant's report and the expected monetary value based on prior probabilities is the maximum amount Global Airlines is willing to pay the consultant. This difference is $0.2101 million or $210,100 — $48.8601 minus $48.65.

Taking Chances with Risk Preferences

Individuals have different risk preferences. Some people buy lottery tickets all the time, while others never buy them. Some people invest millions in the newest innovation, while others stay with the tried and true. Different risk preferences result from differences in individual satisfaction or dissatisfaction arising from risk.

As I note in Chapter 5, utility is a subjective measure of satisfaction that's unique to an individual. A utility function is an index or scale that measures the relative utility of various outcomes. Economists use *utils* to measure the amount of an individual's satisfaction. The concept of utility enables individual risk preferences to be incorporated in decision-making criteria.

Constructing a utility function

Because utility is subjective, one individual's utility function can't be compared to another individual's utility function. You must construct a utility function by determining the individual's utility associated with each possible outcome.

To construct a utility function, you need to compare two alternatives. One alternative is called the standard lottery. The standard lottery has two possible outcomes, such as a payoff of $A occurring with probability P and a payoff of $B occurring with probability $1 - P$. The second alternative is called the certainty equivalent. This alternative has a certain payoff of $C.

You're *indifferent* when the expected utility from the certainty equivalent (first alternative) equals the expected utility from the standard lottery (second alternative). Mathematically, an individual is indifferent if

$$U(\$C) = P \times U(\$A) + (1 - P) \times U(\$B)$$

where $U(\$)$ represents the utility associated with that payoff and P and $(1-P)$ represent probabilities.

In order to construct a utility function, you take the following steps:

1. **Assign utility values to two outcomes.**

   For example, receiving $0 may have a utility value of 0, while receiving $100 has a utility value of 200.

2. **Define the monetary certainty equivalent.**

   Assume the two outcomes specified in Step 1 represent a standard lottery, where each outcome has a 50 percent chance of occurring. After you specify the standard lottery, you must determine what amount of money received with certainty would make you indifferent to the standard lottery. For example, you may decide that you'd be indifferent between receiving $45 for certain and taking the gamble represented by the standard lottery.

3. **Determine the utility of the certainty equivalent.**

$$U(\$45) = P \times U(\$0) + (1-P) \times U(\$100)$$
$$= 0.5 \times 0 + 0.5 \times 200 = 100$$

   Thus, you get 100 utils of satisfaction from $45.

4. **Repeat these calculations for other standard lottery and certainty equivalent combinations to lead to other utilities.**

   For example, the new standard lottery has two possible outcomes: receive $0 or $45. Each outcome has a 50 percent chance of occurring. You decide that you'd be indifferent between receiving $25 for certain and taking the gamble represented by the standard lottery.

$$U(\$25) = P \times U(\$0) + (1-P) \times U(\$45)$$
$$= 0.5 \times 0 + 0.5 \times 100 = 50$$

   You get 50 utils of satisfaction from $25.

Risking attitude

Attitudes toward risk vary among individuals. Some individuals gladly take on additional risk, while other individuals willingly pay a substantial premium, such as with health insurance, to reduce their risk of loss. Individual attitudes toward risk are grouped into the following three categories:

✔ You're *risk adverse* if you have two alternatives with the same expected monetary value, and you choose the alternative with less variation in outcomes.

    ✔ You're **risk neutral** if you have two alternatives with different varia-
tions in outcomes and the same expected monetary value and you're
indifferent between those alternatives. Risk neutral individuals aren't
influenced positively or negatively by risk. Risk neutral individuals will
always choose the alternative with the highest expected value.

    ✔ You're a **risk taker** or **risk lover** if two alternatives have the same
expected monetary value and you choose the one with the highest variability. Lottery players are risk takers.

Figure 15-3 illustrates the relationship between the expected payoff and utility for individuals with different risk preferences. Note that the additional satisfaction risk adverse individuals get from higher payoffs is decreasing while
the additional satisfaction risk takers get from higher payoffs is increasing.

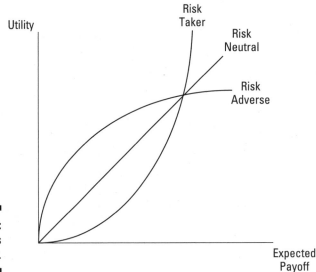

Figure 15-3:
Attitudes
toward risk.

Using the expected utility criterion

After you determine the utilities, you maximize a decision's expected utility.
Expected utility equals the sum of each possible outcome's utility multiplied
by the probability of the outcome occurring.

$$E\left(\text{utility } a_j\right) = \sum_{i=1}^{n} U\left(\pi_{i,j}\right) \times P\left(\Theta_i\right)$$

where the expected utility of action a_j, E(utility a_j), equals the summation for all states of nature of the utility associated with the payoff corresponding to action a_j and state of nature θ_i, $U(\pi_{ij})$, multiplied by the probability of state of nature θ_i occurring, $P(\theta_i)$.

After calculating the expected utility, the decision-maker chooses the action with the highest expected utility.

You want to determine whether to expand your business or maintain its current size. The resulting payoff depends on the action you take and whether or not the economy goes into a recession. Figure 15-4 illustrates the resulting payoff matrix with annual profit in millions of dollars. In addition, the payoff matrix includes the utility you associate with each payoff. To use the expected utility criterion, you first determine the probability associated with each state of nature — what happens to the economy. You currently believe the probability that the economy experiences no change is 0.6 and the probability that the economy goes into recession is 0.4.

Possible Actions

		Don't Expand	Expand
State of Economy	No Change	$2 150	$3 175
	Recession	$1 100	-$1 -150

Figure 15-4: Payoff matrix for business expansion.

To determine which action to take based upon the expected utility criterion, you take the following steps:

1. Calculate the expected utility for not expanding.

For each state of nature, multiply the probability of that state of nature by the payoff's utility given that state of nature and not expanding. Add the resulting values to determine the expected utility.

$$E\left(U_{\text{don't expand}}\right) = \sum_{i=1}^{n} U\left(\pi_{i,\text{don't expand}}\right) \times P(\Theta_i)$$
$$= 150 \times 0.6 + 100 \times 0.4 = 130$$

2. **Calculate the expected utility for expanding.**

$$E\left(U_{expand}\right) = \sum_{i=1}^{n} U\left(\pi_{i,expand}\right) \times P(\Theta_i)$$
$$= 175 \times 0.6 + (-150) \times 0.4 = 45$$

3. **Choose the action with the highest expected utility.**

You shouldn't expand. The expected utility of not expanding is 130, which is higher than the expected utility of expanding, which is only 45.

Major advantages of the expected utility criterion include its incorporation of all possible outcomes and the probability of an outcome occurring. In addition, the reliance on utility enables you to incorporate risk preferences in the decision-making process. The primary disadvantage associated with this criterion is its reliance on a subjective measure. Risk preferences and utility functions vary from individual to individual; therefore, it's impossible to make comparisons between different people. This concern is crucial when more than one person is involved in the decision.

Using Auctions

There's nothing like an eBay auction. First, you can find almost anything on eBay — from accordions to z-scale model trains. And there's nothing like bidding. You hover over the computer as the seconds tick off, waiting to get in that last bid. But be careful — get too excited and you may pay more than the item is worth to you.

Auctions are situations where potential buyers compete for the right to own a good, or anything of value. As in any situation, the seller in an auction wants the highest possible price, while the buyer wants the lowest possible price. What makes an auction different is the competition among buyers, which can lead to a higher price for the seller.

Bidding last wins: The English auction

An English auction is the auction you're probably most familiar with. In an *English auction,* the auction starts at a low price set by the seller. Potential buyers, or bidders, incrementally raise the price until no one is willing to bid the price higher. At that point, the item is sold to the last individual to bid.

In an English auction, you know what other bidders are willing to pay at any given point. Your decision on whether or not to bid is simply determined by whether or not you're willing to pay a higher amount.

Five hundred acres of farmland are being auctioned. There are three individuals willing to bid on the land — Oliver Wendell Douglas, John Kent, and Owen Lars. Douglas is willing to pay $4,000 per acre, Kent is willing to pay $4,200 per acre, and Lars is willing to pay $5,000 per acre. To determine who ultimately purchases the land in an English auction and how much the individual pays, you take the following steps:

1. **All three individuals will bid as long as the price is $4,000 or less.**

   All three individuals are willing to pay less than $4,000 for the land.

2. **Only Kent and Lars bid at prices between $4,000 and $4,200.**

   Douglas drops out of the auction because he's not willing to pay more than $4,000.

3. **Lars purchases the land at the first bid over $4,200.**

   After the price per acre exceeds $4,200, Kent drops out of the auction, leaving Lars as the only bidder. Thus, the minimum amount Lars must spend to purchase the land is $4,200.01.

The winner of the English auction generally has to bid just a little more than the individual who places the second highest value on the item.

Bidding first wins: The Dutch auction

In a Dutch auction, the first bid wins. The bidding starts with the seller asking an extremely high price — a price nobody is willing to pay. The price is then gradually lowered until one buyer indicates a willingness to purchase the item. At that point, the auction is over and the item sold.

In a Dutch auction, no information regarding other bidders' preferences is available to potential buyers. Because the first bid is the winning bid, potential buyers can't determine the item's potential value to anyone else. As a result, to avoid losing the opportunity to purchase the item, buyers tend to bid the maximum amount they're willing to pay.

As with the English auction in the last example, assume that 500 acres of farmland are being auctioned. Again, three individuals are willing to bid on the land — Oliver Wendell Douglas, John Kent, and Owen Lars. Douglas is willing to pay $4,000 per acre, Kent is willing to pay $4,200 per acre, and Lars is willing to pay $5,000 per acre. To determine who ultimately purchases the land in a Dutch auction and how much the individual pays, you take the following steps:

1. **The auction starts at an extremely high price; perhaps $10,000 per acre.**

   The auctioneer sets the price so high that nobody is willing to purchase the land.

2. **The auctioneer progressively lowers price.**

    As long as the price remains higher than the price anyone is willing to pay, no one bids. However, potential buyers don't know anything about other bidders' preferences. Therefore, potential buyers start getting nervous about losing the opportunity to buy the land as the auction price is lowered toward the price they're willing to pay.

3. **The price is lowered to \$5,000 and Lars purchases the land by making the first and only bid.**

    Because Lars knows nothing about the other bidders' preferences, he bids as soon as the land hits the price he's willing to pay. Because the first bid is both the only bid and the winning bid, at this point the auction is over.

Dutch auction winners tend to bid the maximum amount they're willing to pay.

In comparing the English auction to the Dutch auction, you should note that the winning bidder remains the same — Lars in the examples. However, in the English auction, Lars winning bid was only \$4,200.01, while in the Dutch auction his winning bid was \$5,000.

Sealing the deal: The sealed-bid auction

In a *first-price, sealed-bid auction,* potential buyers submit written bids without knowing what anyone else is bidding. The auctioneer collects the bids and sells the item to the highest bidder.

In both an English auction and a sealed-bid auction, the item is sold to the highest bidder. However, in a sealed-bid auction, potential buyers don't know anything about the amount others are willing to bid. There is no bidding back-and-forth. As a result, bidders tend to bid the maximum amount they're willing to pay with the result being similar to a Dutch auction.

Whenever risk is present, even the risk of not buying an item you want at an auction, you can't be sure of the outcome. This risk can be very stressful. So, if you want to further reduce stress, you can always follow humorist Frank McKinney Hubbard's advice, "The safe way to double your money is to fold it over once and put it in your pocket."

Chapter 16

Using Capital Budgeting to Prepare for the Future

....

....

*P*urchasing machinery and equipment and building factories require spending today in order to receive future revenue. Thus, capital budgeting is one of the most important and yet uncertain decision-making areas because it's critically influenced by time.

Capital budgeting decisions require a substantial amount of forecasting — I hope you have your crystal ball or Magic 8 ball handy. Biased or poorly developed forecasts adversely affect the quality of investment decisions. Therefore, techniques for evaluating capital investment projects have limited value in the absence of unbiased, well-developed forecasts.

In this chapter, I show you the critical components for evaluating alternative investment projects and selecting from them. That process includes understanding critical aspects of estimating future cash flows and procedures for determining the cost of capital. Understanding these critical components provides the foundation for comparing and evaluating alternative investment projects.

Investing in Capital

Economists define *capital* as the machinery, equipment, and factories you use in the production process. *Investment* refers to the purchasing of capital.

To an economist, buying stock on the New York Stock Exchange isn't investment because you're not buying an actual machine or building a factory.

Investment requires long-term decisions. You spend/invest money and incur a cost today in order to realize future revenue. Although they're always long-term, investment decisions address different purposes and have different affects on the firm. Investment purposes include the following:

- ✔ **Replacement investment decisions** are expenditures to replace existing machinery and equipment. A restaurant deciding to replace kitchen equipment and a firm replacing assembly line machinery are examples of replacement investment decisions.

- ✔ **Modernization investment decisions** reduce production costs. A modernization decision emphasizes more efficient operation — it may involve the renovation of a factory or the installation of automated machinery.

- ✔ **Expansion investment decisions** increase the firm's productive capacity or introduce new products or markets. A firm's decisions to build an additional factory or expand sales to a new region are examples of expansion decisions.

- ✔ **Operating investment decisions** involve changes in inventories. Economists regard inventory as an investment because inventory represents goods produced but not immediately sold. A car dealer may increase the number of cars it keeps to interest new customers.

- ✔ **Seed investment decisions** represent investment expenditures whose returns aren't immediately realized. Typical seed investment decisions include expenditures into research and development, training, market research, and advertising.

- ✔ **Pollution-control or safety investment decisions** include investments necessary for compliance with regulations established by government agencies such as the Environmental Protection Agency (EPA) and the Occupational Safety and Health Administration (OSHA). In addition, investments related to worker safety may be required by labor agreements or insurance policies.

Each type of investment decision represents an immediate cash outlay for some future revenue or benefit.

Selecting among Alternative Investments

You face a variety of investment opportunities at any given point of time; therefore, it's important to develop criteria that enable you to choose among these projects. Determining which projects to undertake during a given period determines your firm's current capital expenditures. In addition, the projects selected influence your firm's future operations and profit.

In determining whether or not to invest in a project, you still maximize profits. To accomplish this goal, you undertake all investment projects that have marginal revenue exceeding marginal cost (MR>MC). In capital budgeting, the investment's rate of return represents marginal revenue, while the firm's cost of capital represents marginal cost.

Figure 16-1 illustrates the capital budgeting process. The investment return curve, *IR*, represents the anticipated return on various investment projects. The curve is disjointed, reflecting the different sizes and returns for various projects. For example, project A requires a $10 million investment and yields an expected 18-percent rate of return. Project B requires a $30 million investment — increasing the total capital investment to $40 million — and yields an expected 15-percent return. The downward tendency of the curve indicates that you undertake investment projects with highest expected return first.

The investment return curve in Figure 16-1 is disjointed, reflecting the fixed investment required for each project. Thus, project A requires a $10 million investment — a partial investment can't be made.

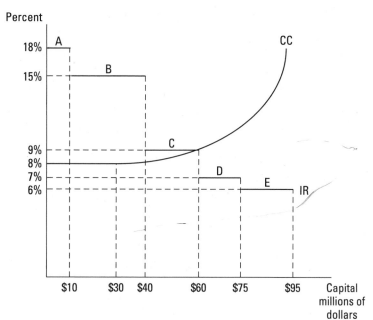

Figure 16-1:
Investment
selection
process.

The cost of capital curve, *CC*, indicates the marginal cost of obtaining each additional investment dollar. In Figure 16-1, this curve is horizontal until $30 million, representing a constant cost of capital at 8 percent. After $30 million, the curve slopes upward, indicating rising cost associated with the firm's increasing debt load.

The firm's optimal investment level corresponds to the intersection of the investment return curve and the cost of capital curve. In Figure 16-1, this corresponds to a total investment of $60 million.

In Figure 16-1, you spend $60 million on investment projects A, B, and C. The first $30 million invested costs 8 percent, and the marginal cost of the last dollar invested is 9 percent. You won't invest in projects D and E because their expected return (IR) is less than the cost of the money invested (CC).

The actual capital budgeting process is more complicated than Figure 16-1 implies. First, proposals for potential investment projects have to be generated. Then you must estimate future cash flows and the cost of capital for those projects. With this information, you can evaluate the alternative investment proposals and determine which, if any, to pursue. Finally, after their implementation, projects are subject to ongoing review.

Estimating Cash Flows in an Uncertain Environment

Estimates of future cash flows — both cash receipts and expenditures — are a crucial element in any investment decision. Four important elements enter into the determination of future cash flows.

- ✔ Cash flows must be determined on an incremental basis. Only include cash flows that are directly affected by whether or not the project is accepted.

- ✔ All affected cash flows must be included in the calculation. An investment project's impact on other activities of the firm must be included. For example, if a restaurant is evaluating a new menu item, it must consider the impact the item's introduction has on the sales of current menu items.

- ✔ Cash flows are determined on an after-tax basis. Estimated cash flows are dependent upon the firm's marginal tax rate.

- ✔ Because depreciation isn't associated with a cash flow, it shouldn't be directly included. However, any impact depreciation has on taxes is incorporated in cash-flow estimates.

As these elements indicate, the determination of cash flows is heavily dependent upon your accounting data.

Future cash-flow estimates may reflect forecaster's biases, especially if the forecaster is very enthusiastic or unenthusiastic about the particular project. It's important to carefully examine the assumptions underlying cash flow forecasts.

Budgeting for Capital

Firms raise investment funds through both internal and external sources. Methods for raising funds internally include using retained earnings or funds the owner contributes, while external financing includes borrowing money or issuing more stock. Regardless of how funds are raised, the firm incurs costs.

Determining the Cost of Capital

The cost of capital associated with external funds is easily recognized as the interest you have to pay on the borrowed funds. Internal funds represent using equity — either the firm's or the firm's owner's financial resources — to finance the project. However, internal funds also cost you — even if you contribute those funds.

The opportunity cost of funds you invest in the firm is the interest you could have earned if you had invested those funds elsewhere. This cost is very real, and your investment project has to generate enough cash to offset this lost opportunity.

Using internal funds: I'll pay for it myself

Because the cost of using internally generated funds or equity is the lost opportunity for you to invest these funds in the next best alternative, you must use a method that estimates the return the next best alternative generates. Typically, one of three methods — risk-premium, dividend-valuation, or capital-asset pricing — is used to determine the cost of internal or equity capital.

Risk-premium method

The risk premium method assumes that you incur some additional risk in the investment. This method's cost estimation uses a risk-free rate of return, r_f, plus an additional risk premium, r_p, or

$$k_e = r_f + r_p$$

where k_e is the cost of equity capital. It's common to use the U.S. Treasury Bill rate as the risk-free rate of return (r_f). The risk premium (r_p) that's added to the risk-free rate of return has two components. First, it includes the difference between the interest rate on company bonds as compared to the U.S. Treasury Bill rate. Second, it includes an additional premium reflecting the added risk of owning the specific company's stock instead of its bonds. The risk premium has historically averaged four percent; however, this amount varies substantially among companies and over different length time periods.

Dividend-valuation method

The dividend valuation method uses shareholder attitudes to determine the cost of equity capital. Shareholder wealth is a function of dividends and changing stock prices. Therefore, a shareholder's rate of return is a function of the ratio of the dividend, D, divided by the stock price per share, P, plus the expected or historic earnings growth, g. Using this shareholder return as the cost of equity capital results in

$$k_e = \frac{D}{P} + g$$

Your firm's stock currently sells at $24.00 a share and the current annual dividend is $0.96. Your firm's historic growth rate is 5 percent. Given this information, use the following steps to calculate the cost of equity capital by using the dividend-valuation method:

1. **Determine the ratio of D/P.**

   This ratio determines the rate of return your invested funds earn through dividends.

   $$\frac{D}{P} = \frac{0.96}{24.00} = 0.04 \quad \text{or} \quad 4\%$$

2. **Add the historic growth rate to the D/P ratio.**

   This determines the cost of equity capital by including the anticipated growth in the stock's price.

   $$k_e = \frac{D}{P} + g = 0.04 + 0.05 = 0.09 \quad \text{or} \quad 9\%$$

Capital-asset-pricing method

The third method for estimating the cost of equity capital is the capital-asset-pricing method. This method incorporates a risk premium for variability in a company's return. The risk premium is higher for stocks whose returns are more variable, and lower for stocks with stable returns. The formula used to determine the cost of equity capital using the capital-asset-pricing method is

$$k_e = r_f + \beta(k_m - r_f)$$

where r_f is the risk-free return, k_m is an average stock's return, and β measures the variability in the specific firm's common stock return relative to the variability in the average stock's return. If β equals 1, the firm has average variability or risk. β values greater than 1 indicate higher than average variability or risk while values less than 1 indicate below average risk. The term $\beta(k_m - r_f)$ gives the risk premium for holding the firm's common stock.

The return on U.S. Treasury bills is 2 percent and the average return on stock is 7 percent. Variability in your firm's stock return relative to variability in the average stock's return is 1.8. Given this information, the cost of equity capital using the capital-asset-pricing method is calculated through the following steps:

1. **Determine the risk premium.**

   The risk premium is determined by subtracting the risk-free rate of return from the average stock's return and multiplying by β.

   $$\beta(k_m - r_f) = 1.8(0.07 - 0.02) = 1.8(0.05) = 0.09$$

2. **Add the risk premium to the risk-free rate of return.**

   This addition determines the cost of equity capital by including the risk premium.

   $$k_e = r_f + \beta(k_m - r_f) = 0.02 + 0.09 = 0.11 \quad \text{or} \quad 11\%$$

Relying on external funds: Help!

The cost of using external funds, or the cost of debt capital, is the interest rate you must pay lenders. However, because interest expenses are tax deductible, the after-tax cost of debt, k_d, is the interest rate, r, multiplied by 1 minus the firm's marginal tax rate, t, or

$$k_d = r(1 - t)$$

You've decided to finance a capital investment by issuing bonds that have a 6 percent annual interest rate. In addition, your company's marginal tax rate is 35 percent. The cost of using debt to finance the project equals

$$k_d = r(1 - t) = 0.06(1 - 0.35) = 0.039 \quad \text{or} \quad 3.9\%$$

Calculating the composite cost of capital

Firms commonly raise funds for capital investment from both internal and external sources. The composite cost of capital, k_c, is a weighted average of the cost of equity capital and the cost of debt capital. Therefore,

$$k_c = (w_e \times k_e) + (w_d \times k_d)$$

where w_e and w_d are the weights or proportions of equity and debt capital you use to finance the project.

You decide to fund a capital investment through a combination of equity and debt capital. You plan to fund 25 percent of your capital investment through equity and 75 percent through debt. To determine the composite cost of capital, start by separately calculating the cost of equity capital and the cost of debt capital. Assume your firm's β coefficient is 2.1 and the average stock return is 6 percent. The return on U.S. Treasury bills is 1 percent, which is the risk-free rate of return. Your firm can borrow funds at 9-percent interest and its marginal tax rate is 34 percent.

1. **Determine the cost of equity capital.**

   In this example, I'm using the capital-asset-pricing method.

   $$k_e = r_f + \beta(k_m - r_f) = 0.01 + 2.1(0.06 - 0.01) = 0.115$$

2. **Determine the cost of debt by using the marginal tax rate.**

   $$k_d = r(1 - t) = 0.09(1 - 0.34) = 0.0594$$

3. **Determine the composite cost of capital.**

   Remember to weight each component by the percentage of funds raised through that method — equity or debt.

   $$k_c = (w_e \times k_e) + (w_d \times k_d) = (0.25 \times 0.115) + (0.75 \times 0.0594) = 0.0733$$

   Thus, the composite cost of capital is 7.33 percent.

Cashing in on opportunity

In his biography *Andrew Carnegie and the Rise of Big Business* (Pearson), author Harold C. Livesay notes that improvements in technology make existing capital investments obsolete. In addition, improvements in technology often require even greater capital investments. This was the case for Andrew Carnegie and the steel industry at the end of the nineteenth century. Because the steel industry experienced tremendous technology improvements that required large capital investments, Carnegie had to use his profits to purchase new equipment rather than give dividends to stockholders.

This situation clearly indicates an opportunity cost of investing equity capital — Carnegie didn't issue very many dividends to partners and owners of the firm. But one advantage of this policy that's less apparent is a benefit that results from avoiding external funds. By avoiding external funds, Carnegie was able maintain greater control of future costs and production by not having a future cash outlay associated with payments on external debt. This lack of external debt is especially important if national economic conditions, such as a recession, adversely affect your firm's cash flow.

Avoiding pitfalls in capital budgeting

George Burns is credited with saying, "Look to the future, because that is where you'll spend the rest of your life." This quote is the essence of capital budgeting. But trying to guess the future makes it easy to make some common mistakes.

One common mistake is to overestimate your cost of capital. Business managers are often conservative, so they want to screen out all but the most promising projects. The consequence of this very conservative strategy is that profitable investment projects aren't undertaken.

Another common error is for firms to assume profit levels won't change even if capital investment isn't undertaken. Because rival firms are investing, the lack of investment ultimately leads to profits eroding. Estimated cash flows should reflect this incremental difference. If they don't, new project profitability is underestimated.

Firms must also be careful not to exclude qualitative factors. Investment may enable you to decrease production time, enabling you to fill customer orders in a more timely fashion. Although this impact is difficult to quantify, there's no doubt that it positively affects your firm's sales and profitability.

Finally, firms typically are too cautious with ambitious projects. Smaller investments are frequently undertaken with minimal management approval, while larger projects may require several levels of management approval. As a consequence, managers have an incentive to propose smaller rather than larger projects.

Evaluating Investment Proposals

After determining cash flows and the cost of capital, managers can begin to evaluate various investment alternatives. The most commonly employed technique for evaluating investment alternatives is the net present value technique. Variations of this technique include the profitability index and the internal rate of return.

Determining today's net present value

The net present value (*NPV*) technique is based on the concept that you prefer receiving cash today rather than in the future. One obvious reason for this preference is the fact that cash received today can earn interest through the purchase of government securities or other types of bonds. Therefore, any future cash you receive needs to be discounted by an appropriate interest rate.

If all the capital investment project's expenditures occur during the current year, the project's net present value (*NPV*) equals

$$NPV = \sum_{t=1}^{n} \frac{CF_t}{(1+r)^t} - I$$

where CF_t represents the net after-tax cash flow in year t, r is the cost of capital, and I is the capital investment project's cash outlay assumed to occur in the current year, or year 0. I summarize the determination of r in the previous section.

If the capital investment project has any salvage value at the end of its use, the salvage value is included in the last year's cash flow.

Any investment project with a positive net present value is profitable for the firm and should be undertaken.

You're evaluating a capital investment project that generates cash flows the next four years. Net cash flow estimates are $18,000 the first year, $45,000 the second year, $50,000 the third year, and $12,000 the fourth and final year. The capital project's initial investment is $105,000 and there is no salvage value at the end. Finally, the cost of capital is 8 percent. In order to determine whether or not to undertake the project, you take the following steps:

1. **Determine the present value for the first year's cash flow.**

   Divide the first year's net cash flow by $(1 + r)^1$.

   $$NPV_1 = \frac{CF_1}{(1+r)^1} = \frac{18,000}{(1+0.08)^1} = 16,667$$

2. **Determine the present values for the second, third, and fourth years' cash flow.**

   Note how the exponent changes in the denominator of the calculation.

   $$NPV_2 = \frac{CF_2}{(1+r)^2} = \frac{45,000}{(1+0.08)^2} = 38,580$$

   $$NPV_3 = \frac{CF_3}{(1+r)^3} = \frac{50,000}{(1+0.08)^3} = 39,692$$

   $$NPV_4 = \frac{CF_4}{(1+r)^4} = \frac{12,000}{(1+0.08)^4} = 8,820$$

3. **Add the four years' present values.**

$$\sum_{t=1}^{n} \frac{CF_t}{(1+r)^t} = 16,667 + 38,580 + 39,692 + 8,820 = 103,759$$

4. **Determine the capital investment project's net present value.**

   Subtract the initial investment required from the sum of the four years' present values.

$$NPV = \sum_{t=1}^{n} \frac{CF_t}{(1+r)^t} - I = 103,759 - 105,000 = -1,241$$

5. **Don't make the capital investment.**

   Because the project's net present value is negative, you shouldn't invest in the project.

You must consider the time value of money when investing in a capital project. In this example, the sum of the undiscounted net cash flows is $125,000, which is greater than the $105,000 required investment. But remember that money received in the future isn't worth as much as money received today. Or, as an alternative to the project, you could buy a government bond today and earn 8-percent interest or $8,400 (0.08 × 105,000) annually.

Indexing profitability

The profitability index is a variation of the net present value technique. The *profitability index (PI)* is calculated as follows

$$PI = \frac{\sum_{t=1}^{n} \frac{CF_t}{(1+r)^t}}{I}$$

where *PI* represents the profitability index, CF_t represents the net after-tax cash flow in year t, r is the cost of capital, and I is the capital investment project's cash outlay assumed to occur in the current year, or year 0.

Any project with a profitability index greater than 1 (PI>1) should be undertaken because the present value of its future cash flow exceeds the current investment — the numerator is larger than the denominator.

An important advantage of the profitability index is realized when circumstances prevent you from undertaking all profitable investments. In these situations, you use the profitability index to rank projects, undertaking projects with the highest profitability index first.

You're evaluating a capital investment project that generates cash flows the next three years. Net cash flows are estimated to be $1 million the first year, $4 million the second year, and $3 million the third and final year. The capital project's initial investment is $6 million and there is no salvage value at the end. Finally, the cost of capital is 10 percent. In order to determine whether or not to undertake the project, you take the following steps:

1. Determine the present value for the firm's future net cash flow.

$$PV_{\text{net cash flow}} = \sum_{t=1}^{n} \frac{CF_t}{(1+r)^t} = \frac{1,000,000}{(1+0.1)^1} + \frac{4,000,000}{(1+0.1)^2} + \frac{3,000,000}{(1+0.1)^3}$$

$$= 909,091 + 3,305,785 + 2,253,944 = 6,468,820$$

2. Divide the project's present value of future cash flows by the project's cost.

$$PI = \frac{\sum_{t=1}^{n} \frac{CF_t}{(1+r)^t}}{I} = \frac{6,468,820}{6,000,000} = 1.078$$

3. Because the profitability index is greater than 1, you should undertake the project.

An index value greater than 1 indicates the present value of future cash flows exceeds the project's initial cost.

One problem with the profitability index is that it tends to be biased in favor of smaller projects. For example, a project that requires a $50,000 investment and has a present value of net cash flow equal to $60,000 has a profitability index of 1.20. On the other hand, a project requiring a $5,000,000 investment that has a present value of net cash flow equal to $5,500,000 has a profitability index of only 1.10. Clearly, the $500,000 additional profit from the second project is better than the $10,000 additional profit from the first project even though the second project has a lower profitability index.

Calculating the internal rate of return

Calculating the internal rate of return is another alternative application of the net present value technique. The *internal rate of return* is the interest rate that equates the project's present value of future net cash flows with the project's initial investment outlay. Mathematically,

$$\sum_{t=1}^{n} \frac{CF_t}{(1+r^*)^t} = I \quad \text{or} \quad \sum_{t=1}^{n} \frac{CF_t}{(1+r^*)^t} - I = 0$$

The equation is solved for r^*, which represents the internal rate of return.

If the project's internal rate of return exceeds the cost of capital, the firm should undertake the project. This is similar to the situation described earlier in Figure 16-1.

The solution for the internal rate of return when done by hand is typically a laborious trial-and-error process. However, computers can be used to quickly solve this type of problem.

Chapter 17

Principal–Agent Issues and Adverse Selection: Can Everyone Agree?

In This Chapter

▶ Working together as principals and agents

▶ Eliminating information inequality

▶ Reducing adverse selection's poor choices

▶ Minimizing moral hazard

---

*I*t's a well-known childhood taunt: "I know something you don't know." Whenever children use this taunt, you know that they've pulled out the heavy artillery in a battle of wits. And as I was once told, don't engage in a battle of wits unless you come fully armed.

That childhood taunt has special significance in managerial economics. Because individuals tend to be motivated by self interest, yet must interact with one another in mutually beneficial exchange, it's very important that they have the same information. But frequently everyone participating in an exchange doesn't have the same information. These situations have asymmetric information, and if I know something you don't know, I can skew the exchange to my benefit. I say the used car I'm trying to sell you is great; how do you know whether or not it's great? If one individual possesses better information than another, there is an increased probability that the exchange won't be mutually beneficial. And if the used car I sell you is a lemon, you're going to be mad. When this situation exists for a large number of market participants, mutually beneficial exchanges are less likely to take place. This is reflected in the perception that "used car" salesmen are less trustworthy when compared to other occupations. Therefore, it is crucial for successful markets and businesses to develop mechanisms that offset the information inequality or asymmetric information.

In this chapter, I focus on the problems created by differences in individual goals and asymmetric information and how to overcome these problems. You discover how incentives help convince individuals with different goals to work toward a common objective. In situations where somebody doubts the accuracy of your statements — "I only drove this ten-year-old car to church on the months with five Sundays" — I show you how to make a persuasive, true argument. (I'm not teaching you how to lie. I'm teaching you how to convincingly tell the truth.) In situations where you have less information and doubt another's claims, I explain how you can get the individual to reveal the information he or she possesses. And finally, you discover the hazard of your actions inadvertently changing individual behavior and how to prevent those changes. Indeed, this is a very informative chapter on information.

Principal–Agent Problem #1: When Managers and Owners Disagree

Incentives matter. If you disagree, have you ever been bribed to eat your vegetables with the offer of dessert? If you have and you ate your vegetables, you know incentives matter.

Businesses are comprised of many individuals who possess different goals. *Principals* are the ultimate recipient of a situation's outcome. In the case of a business, the firm's principals are its owners and the ultimate outcome they receive is profit. *Agents* serve as the principal's representatives and make decisions on the principal's behalf. In a business, agents include the managers and workers.

The *principal–agent problem* exists when the agent's objectives differ from the principal's objectives.

Recognizing that incentives matter isn't enough for owners and managers. Different employees of the firm with different jobs ultimately have to work for the same thing — maximum profit. Therefore, it's important to establish incentives that result in a coordinated, cooperative effort to maximize profit. Incentives must make objectives complementary or identical and eliminate the principal–agent problem. The challenge is to accomplish this task given individuals have different interests and preferences.

The principal–agent problem is especially evident when the agent's effort isn't observable or measurable.

Contributing to the principal–agent problem is the lack of information. It's difficult to know how much effort an employee makes unless you sit and watch the employee all the time — but that in and of itself is very unproductive. In general, two major issues contribute to the principal–agent problem:

> ✔ Principals frequently don't directly observe the agent's actions.
>
> ✔ The agent's actions aren't the sole determinant of the ultimate outcome.

When a company loses a million dollars, was it because of poor managers, or did good managers keep the company from losing two million dollars? Simply looking at the firm's profit doesn't provide enough information to tell whether the management is good or bad just like looking at a coach's record in a given season doesn't indicate whether the individual is a good or bad coach. Winning half the games with less talented players may indicate great coaching while winning half the games with extremely talented players may indicate bad coaching.

Shareholders in a large corporation, the principals, want to maximize their wealth — the return on their investment. Agents, in this case the firm's managers, may pursue some combination of other goals, including less effort, higher income, greater job security, lower risk of failure, and better reputation. It's a difficult challenge to coordinate these various objectives and make them consistent with maximizing the firm's return on investment.

As principals try to get all employees to work toward maximizing the company's return on investment or profit, they must determine whether to use sticks or carrots. Sticks focus on supervision and negative consequences such as an employee being fired. The advantage of using sticks is they're inexpensive to implement. On the other hand, sticks only motivate individuals to a point. That point is the minimum effort necessary to avoid the stick.

On the other hand, carrots focus on rewards. Employees are rewarded for good effort, such as with a profit-sharing plan. The advantage of carrots is employees have an incentive or reward, such as a bonus, for continued hard work past the minimum effort necessary to keep their job. The disadvantage is carrots are expensive.

Behaving badly with a flat salary

As an absentee owner, you realize your firm's profit increases as your manager's efforts increase. You decide to pay your manager a flat salary. Regardless of the manager's effort, the salary doesn't change. On the other hand, extra effort is bad for the manager — it's hard work. Instead of working hard, the manager would rather talk with employees, surf the web, or play solitaire on the company's computers. These activities give pleasure or utility, while managerial effort is hard and thus gives disutility. The resulting "compensation" for the manager equals the utility that comes from the flat salary minus the disutility associated with extra effort.

Figure 17-1 describes the relationship between managerial effort — measured on the horizontal axis — and the principal's goal (profit) and manager's goal (utility) — measured on the vertical axis. The solid lines represent the situation from the perspective of the company's owners, or principals. As managerial effort increases, net revenue increases at a decreasing rate. That is, the curve is rising but becoming flatter. Given the manager receives a flat or constant salary, net revenue minus the manager's salary also increases at a decreasing rate. So the company's owners continue to get more and more profit — net revenue minus the manager's salary — as the manager's efforts increase. Maximum profit requires the manager's best effort.

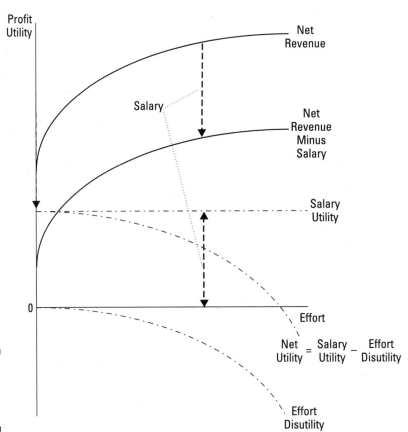

Figure 17-1:
Optimal
effort with a
flat salary.

The manager faces a different situation as described by the dash-dot lines in Figure 17-1. The pleasure or utility the manager receives from salary is constant because salary doesn't change. No matter how much effort the manager makes, the salary stays the same. The manager receives no additional reward for greater effort. However, effort is hard — so more effort leads to disutility. The manager would rather be surfing the web as opposed to expending a lot of energy working. Thus, effort results in disutility — instead of pleasure it generates "pain."

The manager's net utility equals the utility gained from salary minus the disutility of effort. In the case of a flat salary, the manager maximizes net utility by expending zero effort. This result isn't surprising. Effort results only in pain; it doesn't generate any more income or utility for the manager. Not surprisingly, the manager wants to expend as little effort as possible.

You should note that changing the flat salary doesn't change this result. A higher flat salary simply shifts the dash-dot curves upward, but the maximum utility is still associated with zero effort.

Flat salaries tend to lead to the minimum level of managerial effort.

Behaving better with profit sharing

Managers increase effort if they have an incentive to do so. One method absentee owners use to increase effort is through profit sharing. *Profit sharing* indicates that managers receive some share or percent of profit. Thus, as profit increases due to increases in managerial efforts, managerial compensation increases.

Figure 17-2 illustrates the impact of a profit-sharing arrangement for both the firm — solid lines — and manager — dash-dot lines. The firm's net revenue again increases at a decreasing rate. However, net revenue minus managerial compensation now changes. Initially, net revenue minus compensation increases at a decreasing rate; however, it now reaches a maximum and then begins to decrease. This decrease is the result of the continued increase in managerial compensation. The vertical difference between the net revenue curve and the net revenue minus managerial compensation curve gets larger as the manager receives more compensation for greater effort.

For the manager, compensation increases as effort increases. However, the utility the manager receives from that additional compensation increases at a decreasing rate due to the law of diminishing marginal utility from Chapter 5. At the same time, greater effort continues to generate disutility. As a result, the manager's net utility — the utility from compensation minus the disutility of effort — initially increases, eventually reaches a maximum, and then begins to decrease. The manager's situation is represented by the dash-dot lines in Figure 17-2.

The manager chooses the level of effort that maximizes net utility. In Figure 17-2, this corresponds to the effort level E_0. Note how this is different from the flat salary. With the flat salary, the manager wants to expend as little effort as possible. With compensation tied to effort, the manager now works harder in order to get more utility or satisfaction.

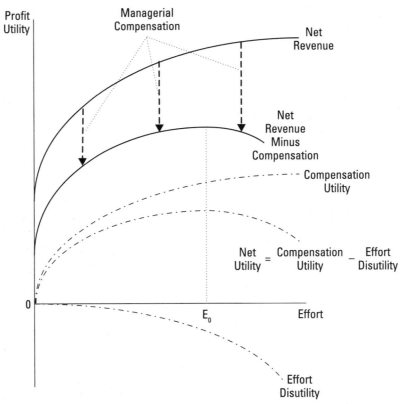

Figure 17-2: Optimal effort with incentive salary.

 The owner needs to develop a profit-sharing plan that results in managers maximizing their net utility at the same level of effort that maximizes net revenue minus the manager's salary — the owner's profit. Determining this balance point is a critical task for the owner.

Behaving better with stock options

Stock options are another method to increase managerial effort. A *stock option* provides its holder a future opportunity to buy the company's stock at a predetermined price — the *call price.* Frequently, the option's call price is its current price, although there is no single method for determining the call price. Typically, a stock option can be exercised only during a specified period of time and at some point the option expires.

If the company's stock value increases, the holder of the stock option makes a very quick financial gain through the difference between the call price and the higher future price. If the company's stock price falls below the call price, the holder of the call is under no obligation to buy the stock and the option isn't exercised. Any holder of a stock option has an incentive to work harder to increase the company's stock price.

Your company offers its manager a 1,000-share stock option that can be exercised six months from now at the current price of $20.00 per share, the call price. If six months from now the stock price is $25.00 a share, the manager can make a quick $5,000. Here's how:

1. **The manager exercises the option and buys 1,000 shares at $20.00 per share.**

   The total cost is $20,000.

2. **The manager sells the 1,000 shares at the market price of $25.00 per share.**

   The revenue from the sale is $25,000.

3. **The difference between the revenue and cost is the manager's financial gain, or $5,000.**

If instead the company's stock price decreased to $15.00, the manager wouldn't exercise the option. Thus, the manager with a stock option has no risk of loss.

Stock options can carry a variety of restrictions. *Vesting requirements* limit the manager's ability to sell the shares or options. Typical vesting requirements include requiring the manager to continue to work for the company for a specified number of years; some specific event to occur, such as an initial public offering (IPO); or certain performance targets to be reached, such as sales or profit goals. These vesting requirements help ensure that the owner's and manager's interests are the same.

In addition to increasing managerial effort, stock options can be used by start-up companies to reward employees, while keeping wages and salaries low. Thus, a new firm's employees have a strong incentive to work hard to make the company successful.

One advantage of stock options over profit-sharing is managers focus more on the long-run value of the stock. Profit-sharing may lead to a shorter-term focus because it's based on current outcomes.

Keeping managers in line

Profit sharing and stock options involve using carrots to increase managerial effort. As an alternative, you can use a stick in the form of a negative consequence for poor performance. The advantage of this method to the firm's owner is that it's very cheap to administer. If the owner is present, the owner can monitor the manager's effort. Thus, the risk of termination insures some minimal level of effort — at least enough effort for the manager to avoid losing his or her job.

Mergers and takeovers can be another stick that increases managerial effort. Poor effort by a manager can make a company an attractive merger or take-over opportunity. The acquiring company recognizes that greater profit can be made with the right managers. Thus, the new company may try to increase profit by replacing the previous manager.

Non-monetary rewards can also be used to increase managerial effort. Managerial effort is linked to reputation. Being recognized as an outstanding manager increases job mobility by making the manager an attractive employee for other firms, and job offers from rival firms may lead to more compensation from the new firm or the manager's current firm. In this scenario, managers essentially recognize effort as an investment that leads to higher compensation or returns in the future. Perks, such as the so-called corner office, are also used to increase effort.

Principal–Agent Problem #2: When Managers and Workers Disagree

Just as goals for owners and managers may not coincide, the goals of managers and workers may not coincide. Again, owners and managers must choose between using carrots or sticks.

Determining worker compensation

Carrots can also be used with workers. Compensation arrangements increase worker effort if the worker's compensation is directly tied to the firm's success. Profit sharing is one example of a compensation arrangement (see the earlier section "Behaving better with profit sharing" for details). Another common form of linking worker compensation to the firm's success is revenue sharing. In revenue sharing, workers get some amount of additional compensation based upon how much they sell. Examples of revenue sharing are car salespeople receiving a commission after selling a car, waiters and waitresses receiving a tip as a percentage of their sales, and insurance agents receiving a commission.

A deal nobody could beat

Great care must be taken in setting incentives. Ask whether the owner's and worker's goals really coincide. Years ago I worked for a pizza restaurant. The restaurant's manager received a base salary plus 3 percent of all sales revenue. Although pizza prices were set by the corporate headquarters, managers had the discretion of lowering prices on group sales. So, if a group came in wanting 20 pizzas, the manager could offer a special price.

Because the manager received 3 percent of the sale, he had a tremendous incentive to make sure he made the sale. So, he offered a flat price for all 20 pizzas that no other restaurant was willing to match, because the price was so low it lost money. Lost money for the owner, but made 3 percent for the manager.

Another method for increasing worker effort is to use piece rates. In this situation, worker compensation is based upon how much output they produce — workers get paid a specified amount for each piece produced. One caution with piece rates is quality control must be maintained. Producing a lot of poor quality pieces won't help the company.

Keeping workers in line

And sticks can also be used to ensure some minimal level of effort among workers. Unannounced random spot checks to monitor effort are inexpensive to implement but must include a penalty and be frequent enough to have real risk.

Time clocks generally aren't a good method to monitor worker effort. Time clocks simply measure presence, not effort — think of Dagwood Bumstead in the comic strip Blondie.

Recognizing Asymmetric Information and The Market for Lemons

Usually the participants in an exchange don't have the same information. *Asymmetric information* refers to a situation where some participants have better information than other participants. In such circumstances, rational individuals with less information ultimately choose not to participate.

Asymmetric information isn't the same as imperfect information. *Imperfect information* simply means that participants don't have all relevant information. No farmer can guess what the weather will be next summer, so all farmers have imperfect information. However, the market for agricultural commodities can still operate efficiently because nobody has an advantage. With asymmetric information, at least two individuals are involved. In these situations, the individual with better information can take advantage of the individual with less information. In these situations, markets don't operate efficiently.

An excellent example of asymmetric information is the market for used cars. The seller of the car knows exactly what kind of shape it's in. If the car has been well taken care of, the current owner wants the maximum price.

On the other hand, you're in the market for a used car. You don't know much about cars, so you ask the owner, "Have you taken good care of the car?" Assume the owner hasn't taken good care. When asked your question, he's still likely to respond "yes," with the idea that he wants to make as much money as possible. Thus, from your perspective as a buyer you get the same answer — yes — from a person who has taken good care of a car and from a person who has taken poor care of a car. The "yes" answer doesn't differentiate.

If the answer doesn't differentiate, you're rational to doubt its accuracy; thus, you discount the "yes" answer. Instead of paying the value of a car well taken care of, you offer something less. The person who has taken good care of the car refuses your offer. Only the person who has taken poor care of the car is likely to accept your offer — he's selling you a lemon. Anybody who accepts your offer does so knowing he's getting a good deal, but a good deal for him is likely to be a bad deal for you. This is an exchange you don't want to make, so you stop offering to buy used cars because the current owner has more information than you do.

Obviously, there is a market for used cars, but note how this develops. One way to get around the lemons problem is to ask the owner for the car's maintenance records. Accurate, up-to-date records provide you information to support the owner's claim and overcome the asymmetric information. The lack of this information defaults you into thinking the car is a lemon, so owners have an incentive to keep accurate records.

Another alternative is for used-car dealers to offer warranties. A warranty reduces the risk of asymmetric information by reducing the cost of unexpected repairs. But note the burden on the seller. If the buyer takes poor care of the car, the repair may be due to the buyer's carelessness. Thus, warranties tend to have exclusions.

The general solution to asymmetric information is for the party with less information to try to collect more. This information has value. Thus, organizations have been established to provide information. Examples of such organizations include the Good Housekeeping Seal of Approval for household goods, Underwriters Laboratory — UL for electrical appliances, and CARFAX for used cars.

Asymmetric information also exists in the hiring process. Applicants know whether they're good or bad workers, but employers don't. If the employer asks, "Are you a good worker?" every applicant responds, "Yes." So the employer needs to somehow separate good workers from bad workers. One method companies use to separate good from bad workers is college grades. Statistically, individuals with high grade point averages are more likely to be good workers; therefore, employers look at course transcripts to find information on grades. This is an example of *statistical discrimination* where the employer uses group information to make inferences about individual characteristics. Similar statistical discrimination may occur based upon the individual's major — for example, a bank preferring to hire an applicant with a finance major over an applicant with a philosophy major.

Increasing Insurance Costs with Adverse Selection

One effect of asymmetric information is adverse selection. *Adverse selection* arises when an individual has hidden characteristics before the transaction takes place. With hidden characteristics, one party knows things about himself that the other party doesn't know. This leads to a *self-selection bias* where individuals act in their own self interest and use private information to determine their optimal action, usually at another party's disadvantage or cost.

Adverse selection is readily apparent in the market for insurance. The insurance company doesn't know who is a good driver or who is a bad driver. On the other hand, drivers know whether they're good or bad. Thus, there is asymmetric information with drivers knowing more about their driving habits and risks than the insurance company.

However, the insurance company does know that on average all drivers have a certain number and value of claims. So, you may wonder whether the insurance company can just set the insurance premium equal to the average claim value, plus a little bit more for profit. And, because of adverse selection, the somewhat surprising answer is "no."

If you assume that drivers aren't legally required to buy car insurance, what happens if insurance companies set the insurance premium equal to the average claim value? Bad drivers are likely to pay the average premium because the bad drivers know they have a high likelihood of being in an accident. The bad drivers have a great need for insurance. Thus, the insurance company pays a lot of claims. On the other hand, good drivers believe they have a fairly low likelihood of being in an accident. Given the insurance premium partially reflects the high cost of covering bad drivers, the good drivers are likely to decide that the coverage isn't worth the cost. Thus, the good drivers decline the insurance. Because of adverse selection, only the bad drivers have bought the insurance.

If this situation continues, the end result is no insurance. After good drivers decide not to buy insurance, the company finds that the average claim is higher than expected. The company had originally based its premium on insuring both good and bad drivers, but because good drivers decided not to buy the insurance, the actual claims reflect only bad drivers. Because the average claim is higher than originally estimated, the insurance company has to raise its premium. But once again, drivers with relatively good records decide the insurance isn't worth the cost, so they don't buy the policy. Claims again turn out to be higher than expected, and the cycle continues until finally, the insurance company gives up or goes bankrupt.

Dealing with Adverse Selection

One method for dealing with adverse selection is to force everyone to participate. For example, states commonly require drivers to have car insurance. Thus, it's possible for car insurance companies to charge a premium that reflects the average claim. However, participants who are unlikely to submit a claim may believe it's unfair for them to be forced to subsidize those likely to file a claim. I'm a good driver, so why should I subsidize somebody who's not?

An alternative method for dealing with adverse selection is to group individuals through indirect information, such as statistical discrimination. Insurance companies can't get individuals to admit whether they're good or bad drivers, so the companies develop statistical profiles of good and bad drivers. By determining who is most likely to be a bad driver, the insurance company can establish different premiums. Thus, young males are likely to pay more for insurance. Somebody living in Los Angeles pays more than someone in Hanover, Indiana. Drivers with speeding tickets and other traffic violations pay higher premiums. The list goes on and on because the better the characteristics, the more accurate the premiums, and competition among insurance companies helps develop better statistical profiles.

But neither of these alternatives — requiring participation or statistical discrimination — has the actual participants share information to overcome the asymmetry. Both direct and indirect methods lead to the revelation of information that resolves, or at least reduces, adverse selection. The direct method is to use an appraisal, while indirect methods include screening and signaling.

Appraising asymmetric information

Appraisal resolves asymmetric information by examining a characteristic that's objectively verifiable. In the case of a used car, if the buyer decides to take the car to his mechanic, the mechanic can provide a knowledgeable assessment of its condition. Or in the case of art, an appraiser can verify the painting as an original or a fake.

Appraisal directly resolves asymmetric information under two conditions:

- ✔ The characteristic associated with the asymmetric information must be objectively verifiable.
- ✔ The appraisal's benefit must exceed the seller's cost.

In the case of health insurance, a medical exam becomes an appraisal. The medical exam yields objective information about the individual's current health.

Signaling with warranties

While appraisal directly conveys information from one party to another, signaling is a method for indirectly conveying information. By using *signaling,* the individual with better information convincingly communicates that information to the individual who has less information.

To return to the example of the used car, going to your own mechanic provides you an appraisal of the car's value. Alternatively, the current owner of the car could signal to you that the car is well taken care of by offering a warranty — a guarantee to fix any repairs during a certain period of time or providing a CARFAX or similar report.

To be successful in resolving asymmetric information, signaling must induce self selection among the better-informed participants. Only participants offering well cared for used cars are willing to offer warranties or a CARFAX report. A warranty carries a real cost to the seller if the car breaks down. Thus, while a warranty may convince you, the buyer, that the car is well taken care of, a sign that simply states "Best Used Cars In Town" isn't likely to be convincing, because it doesn't cost much for those selling lemons to make the same sign.

Controlling through screening

Another indirect method for resolving information asymmetry is screening. In *screening,* the participant with less information controls a variable that leads to the participant with better information revealing that information. One screening method with insurance is the use of deductibles. An *insurance deductible* is an amount the insured must pay before the insurance company pays on a claim. High risk participants are likely to know they're high risk. Thus, high risk participants are likely to file a claim and want low deductibles — they don't want to have to pay very much before the insurance company starts paying. On the other hand, low risk participants know they're unlikely to file a claim — they're willing to have a higher deductible because they're less likely to have to pay it. The deductible provides a mechanism that leads the better-informed participant, the insured, to reveal information to the less well-informed participant, the insurance company.

The number of screening options must correspond to the number of choice characteristics. For example, individuals choosing low deductibles can do so because they're high risk or alternatively, because they're risk averse. Thus, deductibles are a good, but not perfect, screening device.

Working with Moral Hazard

Moral hazard is another asymmetric information problem. In the case of *moral hazard,* one party takes hidden actions or actions that are unknown to the other party after the transaction. Moral hazard encourages bad behavior like poorer driving with insurance.

Insurance provides an example of moral hazard. The probability that the insurance company has to pay a claim is based on the hidden actions of the policy owner. For example, if fire insurance covers 100 percent of the replacement cost of my house and contents, I have less incentive to reduce the chance of loss. I'm more likely to take a quick trip to the store while dinner cooks on the stove — a fire hazard. I'm less likely to incur the cost of installing a sprinkler system or buying a fire extinguisher to minimize fire damage. These efforts have costs, and the efforts' benefits are reduced given my fire insurance.

Health insurance is another example of moral hazard. If my health insurance covers 100 percent of the cost of medical care, I'm more likely to run to the doctor because the cost to me is so low — just the opportunity cost of my time. On the other hand, my trips have a very real cost to the health insurance company — it has to pay the doctor. The fact that I have insurance changes my behavior in a way that adversely affects the health insurance company.

One way to address moral hazard in health insurance is to have a high deductible. A high deductible shifts more of the cost of going to the doctor back on me. Of course, if something major is wrong, the deductible ends up being a very small part of the total cost. So, for potential big problems, I still go to the doctor. On the other hand, I'm more likely to ignore those small little problems, at least for awhile, to avoid paying the deductible. I don't go to the doctor as often, keeping healthcare costs down. And that's the point: For markets to work well, all participants must have the same information and incentives.

Chapter 18

Rules, Rules Everywhere: Government and Managerial Decision-Making

•••

In This Chapter

▶ Including externalities

▶ Getting something for nothing as a free rider

▶ Using government to provide goods

▶ Eliminating monopoly efficiency

▶ Regulating or preventing collusion

▶ Providing information equality

▶ Restricting foreign competition

•••

*T*he United States relies primarily upon a system of markets and prices for resource and commodity allocation. But remember, markets are a means, not an end. Ultimately, the goal is to produce as much stuff as possible with those resources. In some instances, markets don't work very well at producing and allocating stuff. In these instances, government can step in to improve the situation. The purpose of government intervention isn't to preserve competition, but rather to ensure an efficient allocation of resources or provide goods the market wouldn't necessarily provide on its own. Too often, however, the focus of regulation has been on competition, not efficiency.

Government intervention has always existed to varying degrees. In its early history, the United States regulated some areas of business by issuing licenses and, in the case of monopolies, fixing prices. For example, in his book *Notes on the State of Virginia,* Thomas Jefferson indicates that licensing and rate fixing were used with ferries.

During the last third of the 19th century, the rise of big business led to concerns regarding the power of business over consumers. Railroads represented the most extreme situation. Railroads often built lines parallel to one another to engage in rate wars and takeovers — for an example, see Chapter 14. At other times, railroads with monopolies in specific areas would charge extremely high rates. As a consequence, consumers, especially farmers, protested railroad rate setting. In *Munn v. Illinois,* the Supreme Court established that railroads were subject to government regulation. Ultimately, Court decisions led to the establishment of the Interstate Commerce Commission (ICC) in 1887. Within several years, government regulation of big business was extended through the Sherman Antitrust Act. So, government regulation has been around a long time and affects businesses in a lot of different ways.

In this chapter, I examine a few of the ways government intervention affects businesses. I give special attention to situations where markets don't work very well. I begin by examining what happens when non-participants in a private market exchange incur costs or receive benefits — what economists call externalities. In some cases, external benefits lead to government, instead of private businesses, providing what are called public goods. Governments do regulate monopolies, and I examine monopoly regulation's goal — just a hint, it's not to have more competition. A brief overview of antitrust legislation and asymmetric information is then followed by government intervention in international trade.

Examining the Nature of Regulation

Resources are limited; thus the quantity of goods and services that society produces is limited. The goal of any economy is to satisfy as many consumer wants and desires as possible given this scarcity. In a market economy, these wants and desires are satisfied by the goods and services that profit-maximizing businesses provide.

Nevertheless, at times markets don't work well — at times profit-maximizing behavior doesn't lead to maximum satisfaction. In these situations or market failures, government regulation and intervention can improve upon the market outcome.

Profiting from dinner

When Adam Smith published *The Wealth of Nations* in 1776, he concluded that markets are generally the best means for satisfying consumer wants and desires. (Smith believed government's role is limited to providing national defense, administering justice, and providing certain public goods, such as education.) Economists regard Adam Smith as the first economist, so what was he really? Nobody walked around in 1776 saying, "Hey, there's Smith. He's an economist." Adam Smith was a professor of moral philosophy. Indeed his other well-known book is *The Theory of Moral Sentiments*.

Smith is known for the idea of the invisible hand. In essence, individuals pursuing their own self-interest end up promoting what is best for everyone — even though that's not their goal. As an owner of a bakery, I don't produce high quality baked goods for a pat on the back. I produce those goods to earn a living by making profit. And in exchange, you get some great bread. Or as Smith said, "It is not from the benevolence of the butcher, the brewer, or the baker, that we expect our dinner, but from their regard to their own interest." Thus, Smith, the moral philosopher, concludes that self interest and pursuing profit isn't necessarily bad; indeed, self interest provides you your dinner.

Working through Market Failures

Price represents the last unit of a good's value to consumers, and marginal cost represents the cost of producing the last unit of a good. Markets are *allocatively efficient* when equilibrium results in the last unit's price or value to consumers equaling the actual marginal cost of producing that unit. A *market failure* exists when price doesn't equal marginal cost for the last unit produced. Market failures occur for a variety of reasons, including externalities (see the following section) and monopoly power (see Chapter 10 for details on monopoly).

Identifying Externalities

Externalities refer to beneficial or harmful effects realized by individuals or third parties who aren't directly involved in the market exchange. Thus, an externality is a cost (in the case of a negative externality) or benefit (in the case of a positive externality) that is not reflected in the good's price.

Producing too much with negative externalities: Pollution

Negative externalities result in social costs that are higher than the actual costs the firm pays. As a consequence, firms produce a larger quantity of output than is socially optimal. Government regulation attempts to internalize those costs for the firm, resulting in production decisions that represent true resource costs.

As Chapter 2 explains, commodity supply describes the relationship between the good's quantity supplied, and the price producers are willing to accept for that good. Therefore, because some costs are not paid by the producers when there are negative externalities, they are willing to accept a price that's lower than would be necessary if all costs were included.

An example of a negative externality is pollution. A fisherman who doesn't consume a firm's product experiences a negative externality if the firm's pollution adversely affects fishing. The fisherman incurs a cost, although he's not a consumer of that firm's product.

Figure 18-1 illustrates a perfectly competitive market. If there are no externalities, the equilibrium output level, Q_E, corresponding to the intersection of the demand and market supply curves, represents the socially optimal output level.

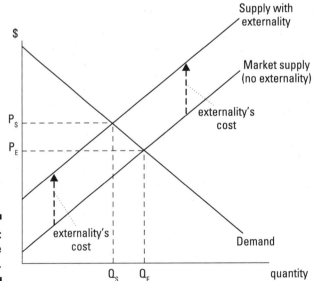

Figure 18-1:
Negative externality.

However, when pollution or another negative externality is present, the market supply curve in Figure 18-1 doesn't represent the good's true production cost. The true cost is now represented by the supply curve that includes the externality. In this situation, the good's social cost equals the firms' marginal cost curves represented by the market supply plus the marginal cost of the negative externality. As a consequence, marginal social cost results in the true supply curve with the externality being higher than the market supply.

Assuming the demand curve remains the same, the market's socially optimal output level is Q_S corresponding to the intersection of demand and the supply curve with externality. The corresponding price consumers pay to cover the full cost of production is P_S.

The purpose of government regulation is to reduce the market output from Q_E to the socially optimal level, Q_S. In order to accomplish this goal, government must internalize the cost of the negative externality for the firm. This is accomplished through various methods, such as fines, regulations requiring different production techniques, or taxes.

Producing too little with positive externalities: Honey

While negative externalities result in social costs that are greater than the actual costs paid by the firm, *positive externalities* exist when individuals receive uncompensated benefits through somebody else's consumption of the good. Positive externalities result in firms producing a smaller quantity of output than is socially optimal. Government regulation attempts to compensate firms for those benefits, resulting in production decisions that recognize the good's true value to society.

Commodity demand describes the relationship between the good's quantity demanded and the price consumers are willing and able to pay for the good. Therefore, price represents the value of an additional unit of the good to consumers. However, if other individuals receive benefits — even though they aren't part of the market transaction — those benefits aren't included in the demand curve the firm faces.

Honey is an example of a good with positive externalities. The market demand for honey is based upon the price individuals are willing to pay to consume the product. However, the bees that produce honey also pollinate flowers and other plants. The beekeeper doesn't receive any compensation for this benefit. If the beekeeper did receive compensation, the beekeeper may be inclined to have more bees, leading to greater plant pollination, as well as more honey.

Figure 18-2 illustrates a perfectly competitive market with a positive externality. If there are no externalities, the equilibrium output level, Q_E, and price, P_E, corresponding to the intersection of the market demand curve and supply curve represents the socially optimal output level.

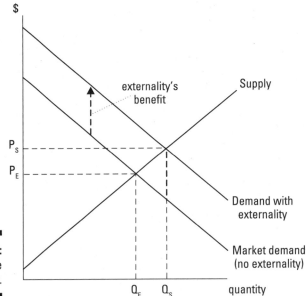

Figure 18-2:
Positive
externality.

The presence of a positive externality, however, means the market demand curve doesn't represent the good's true value to society. With a positive externality, the true demand is higher than the market demand. This higher demand incorporates the added benefit or value of the positive externality. The resulting socially optimal output level corresponds to the intersection of the new demand curve with the positive externality and the market supply curve resulting in the socially optimal quantity Q_S and price P_S.

Government intervention seeks to increase the market output to the socially optimal level. In order to accomplish this task, government may subsidize the producer to reflect the positive externality. In the case of honey, government may place a tax on plants and seeds and use the tax revenue to pay beekeepers a subsidy based on how many beehives they have. With the subsidy, beekeepers have an incentive to have more hives and bees.

Providing Public Goods: Free Riders

Public goods are goods that benefit individuals other than those involved in the market transaction. The consumption of public goods is nonrival and nonexclusionary. *Nonrival* means that the good's consumption by one person doesn't affect others consuming it. For example, when I listen to a radio broadcast, it doesn't affect your ability to listen to the same broadcast. *Nonexclusionary* means that after the good is provided, no one can be excluded from consuming it. For example, clean air is nonexclusionary. Because public goods are nonrival and nonexclusionary, private firms can't profitably provide them.

Given you're able to consume a public good after it's provided, you have little incentive to pay for it. A *free rider* is someone who enjoys the benefits of the good without paying for those benefits. If everyone acts as a free rider, private businesses can't profitably provide a good.

For example, ten neighbors live on a lake. Annual maintenance on the dam forming the lake necessitates that each neighbor pays $1,000 annually. One of the neighbors refuses. Because the dam is nonrival and nonexclusionary, that person gets to enjoy the benefits without having to pay any of the annual cost. The neighbor becomes a free rider, and as more and more people realize they can also free ride, they stop contributing to the dam's annual maintenance and the dam and lake ultimately disappear.

The free riding problem results in government providing these goods and financing them through taxes. Taxes compel everyone to pay for the benefits they receive. But because taxes are a lump sum and voters typically don't directly connect the cost of a specific item to its benefit, there is a tendency for public goods to be overproduced.

Regulating Monopoly

Chapter 10 examines profit-maximizing behavior for monopolies. As that chapter stresses, a monopolist's ability to set price is constrained by consumer demand. If the monopolist tries to raise price too high, you'll stop buying the product, or at the very least buy less of it.

In spite of this constraint, government still restricts the ability of many monopolies to set price. These restrictions are often described as "protecting" consumer interests, but more accurately, the restrictions lead to greater efficiency.

Losing through deadweight loss

Markets characterized by substantial economies of scale are typically better served by a monopoly rather than a large number of competitive firms. Figure 18-3 illustrates the production and pricing decisions for an unregulated monopolist with substantial economies of scale.

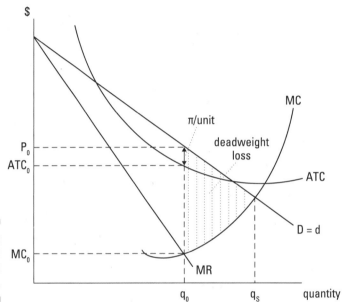

Figure 18-3: Unregulated natural monopoly.

Economies of scale exist when long-run average total cost or cost per unit decreases as the quantity of output produced increases. A monopoly that exists due to economies of scale is a *natural monopoly.*

The natural monopolist's profit-maximizing quantity, q_0, in Figure 18-3 corresponds to the intersection of marginal revenue and marginal cost. To determine price, the monopolist goes from q_0 up to the demand curve — hence the constraint of consumer demand — and across to P_0. Because price is greater than average total cost (ATC_0) at q_0, the monopolist earns positive economic profit per unit, π/unit.

This profit-maximizing solution results in a deadweight loss to society. The *deadweight loss* represents society's welfare loss because the price P_0 of the last unit, or the last unit's value to a consumer, is greater than the marginal cost MC_0, the cost of producing that unit. The deadweight loss corresponds to the shaded triangle in Figure 18-3.

Society's ideal quantity of output or socially optimal output corresponds to the intersection of the market demand and marginal cost curves — the output level q_S in Figure 18-3. At this output level, the last unit's value to a consumer as represented by price exactly equals the cost of producing that unit as represented by marginal cost.

Regulating for efficiency

Monopoly regulation's purpose is to induce the monopolist to produce the socially optimal output level. In Figure 18-4, this is accomplished by government establishing a price, p_R, that corresponds to the point where marginal cost intersects demand. Establishing a price through regulation results in the firm's marginal revenue corresponding to that price. Marginal revenue corresponds to price because the monopolist charges the same price established by the regulators for every unit of the good it sells. After P_R hits the demand curve, the monopolist must lower price to sell more units; therefore, marginal revenue develops a disjointed or vertical region at that output. The regulated monopoly's marginal revenue curve is MR_R.

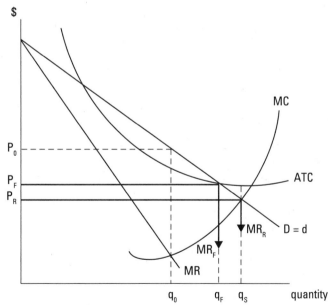

Figure 18-4:
Regulated
natural
monopoly.

The regulated monopolist maximizes profit by producing the output level associated with marginal revenue equals marginal cost. This output level is the socially optimal output level, q_S.

This regulation is self-defeating. At the regulation's profit-maximizing price P_R and quantity q_S, the monopoly is losing money or earning negative economic profit. This is apparent because at q_S, price is less than average total cost. As a result, you're better off in the long run closing down the monopoly and moving to your next best alternative. And, of course, after you close down, output goes to zero — this is not what regulators want.

Regulating for a fair return

In Figure 18-4, regulating for the socially optimal quantity of the good results in the monopoly shutting down in the long run. In order to avoid this situation, regulators often set price to guarantee that the monopolist receives a fair return. A *fair return* is zero economic profit or the firm's owners earning exactly as much as they could in their next best alternative. Accountants might call this a normal return.

In fair-return pricing, regulators establish a price that corresponds to the output level where demand intersects average total cost. In Figure 18-4, this is the price P_F. Once again, the monopoly must sell every unit it produces at the price regulators establish, so P_F is the monopoly's marginal revenue curve until it reaches the demand curve. After P_F hits the demand curve, the monopolist must lower price to sell more units; therefore, marginal revenue again develops a disjointed or vertical region.

The monopoly produces the profit-maximizing quantity of output associated with marginal revenue intersects marginal cost, or the output level q_F in Figure 18-4. Setting price at this level results in zero economic profit because price equals average total cost.

The monopoly stays in business with this price; however, it doesn't quite get the monopoly all the way to the socially optimal output q_S.

Restricting Interaction with Antitrust

With the rise of big business during the last third of the 19th century, laws were passed to encourage competition and prevent the concentration of economic power or monopoly. Continuing into the first half of the 20th century, additional legislation was passed to close loopholes or extend legislation into areas previously not covered. The legislations' intent is to prevent practices that reduce competition rather than lower costs through improved operating efficiency.

Prohibiting collusion

The first antitrust law passed was the Sherman Act in 1890. Its two major provisions state the following:

✔ "Every contract, combination in the form of trust or otherwise, or conspiracy, in restraint of trade or commerce among the several States, or with foreign nations, is hereby declared to be illegal. Every person who shall make any such contract or engage in any such combination or conspiracy, shall be deemed guilty of a felony."

✔ "Every person who shall monopolize, or attempt to monopolize, or combine or conspire with any other person or persons, to monopolize any part of the trade or commerce among several States, or with foreign nations, shall be deemed guilty of a felony."

The Sherman Act prevents executives representing rival firms from working together to reduce competition. For example, executives in the same industry can't discuss prices or agree to fix them.

Although it reduces anticompetitive practices, the Sherman Act doesn't cover all such practices. In addition, the Act is often regarded as too vague. These difficulties led to the passage of additional legislation.

In 1914, the federal government passed additional legislation supporting competition by addressing weaknesses in the Sherman Act. The Clayton Act prohibits price discrimination, tying contracts, and intercorporate stock holdings if they substantially reduce competitive practices. Section 2 of the Clayton Act prohibits price discrimination unless cost differentials in serving various customers justify the price differentials or the lower prices charged in certain markets are established to meet the competition in that area. Tying contracts require a firm purchasing one item to purchase other items. Section 3 of the Clayton Act prohibits tying contracts that reduce competition.

The Federal Trade Commission Act, also passed in 1914, prohibits unfair competitive practices and created the Federal Trade Commission to prosecute antitrust violations and to protect the public from false and misleading advertisements. Additional legislation directed at preserving competition includes the Robinson-Patman Act of 1936. This act prevents large-scale retailers from engaging in unfair price cutting in order to drive smaller retailers out of business.

The enforcement of antitrust legislation is the responsibility of the antitrust division of the Justice Department and the Federal Trade Commission.

Antitrust violations are resolved by dissolution and divestiture, injunction, and consent decree. In addition, fines and jail sentences can be imposed.

The Supreme Court usually enforces provisions of the Sherman Act that prevent the formation of cartels or informal collusion that results in price fixing, price leadership schemes, or market sharing. In addition, the Supreme Court prevents predatory pricing (selling a product below average variable cost in order to drive out rival firms) and other price behavior, such as price discrimination, that reduces competition.

Preventing mergers

Antitrust legislation is frequently applied to corporate mergers. The following are the three types of mergers:

- ✔ **A horizontal merger** occurs between firms that are direct competitors in the same product market. An example of a horizontal merger is two firms producing laundry detergent merging.

- ✔ **A vertical merger** occurs between a firm and its suppliers, or between different firms associated with different stages of the good's production process. An example is a merger between a coal and steel company.

- ✔ **A conglomerate merger** occurs between firms in completely unrelated lines of production. A merger between a firm providing financial services and a firm operating a chain of retail stores is an example of a conglomerate merger.

Section 7 of the Clayton Act prevents a firm from acquiring the stock of a rival firm if it reduces competition. The Celler-Kefauver Antimerger Act of 1950 extends the intent of Section 7 of the Clayton Act by making it illegal to acquire the assets of competing corporations if such an action results in a substantial reduction in competition or creates a monopoly. As a result, such mergers require government approval to determine whether or not there is a substantial reduction in competition.

Generally, the Supreme Court upholds antitrust prosecution of horizontal mergers between large, direct competitors. In the absence of a substantial increase in horizontal market power, vertical and conglomerate mergers typically don't result in antitrust violations.

Regulating Information Asymmetry: I Know Something You Don't Know

As Chapter 17 explains, information asymmetry refers to market situations where some participants have better information than other participants. Participants with better information are at a competitive advantage to those with less information. After rational individuals with less information recognize the situation, they will choose not to participate. As a result, there are fewer, perhaps no, market transactions when information asymmetry persists.

One of the most important areas of asymmetric information is in the buying and selling of stocks. Legislation restricting *insider trading* prevents company officials from acting on information that isn't publically known. For example, a company engaging in promising pharmaceutical research knows that the Food and Drug Administration has decided not to approve one of its previously promising drugs. An insider possessing this information before it's made public can sell the company's stock today at a high price before the price drops after the announcement. Purchasers end up losing money because they didn't possess the insider information. Over time, outsiders become very reluctant to trade the firm's stock because they fear others know something they don't.

By regulating insider trading through the Securities and Exchange Commission, the government supports an efficient market for stocks and bonds. Participants in the market, both buyers and sellers, know that the information behind the decisions to buy and sell stocks and bonds is accessible to everyone.

Government also regulates advertising to ensure claims are valid. Businesses have more information about the goods they produce than consumers. It's difficult for consumers to independently test the claims. The Lanham Act prohibits false and misleading advertising. Similarly, restaurant and public health inspections help insure health standards are maintained.

Yet another area of information asymmetry that government regulates is lending. The Truth in Lending Simplification Act requires creditors to make written declaration of important information including the annual interest rate, itemized finance charges, and the total purchase price.

As these areas illustrate, government attempts to reduce information asymmetry by requiring all parties to a transaction to fully disclose pertinent information. This asymmetry reduction facilitates market exchange by reducing the likelihood that individuals stop participating in the market because they have less information.

Determining Who's in Business by Licensing Providers

As a doctor, I'm ready to address any and all of your physical ailments. And just in case you hesitate, I do have a degree that says I'm a doctor — not a medical doctor but a doctorate in economics. Thus, if you have a sore back, you shouldn't see me, but if you have a sore bottom line, perhaps I can help.

This situation illustrates another important area of information asymmetry — how to assess professional expertise. I'm quite incapable of determining whether or not an individual possesses sufficient knowledge to care for my physical health. Thus, I require somebody with that expertise to make the judgment on my behalf.

Through licensure, the government relies on experts to evaluate a peer's credentials. Upon satisfactory completion of the evaluation, the individual receives a license certifying that expertise. Engineers, accountants, lawyers, and medical doctors are among the many occupations that require licenses.

Understanding Government's Role in International Trade

Consumers can purchase similar goods either produced domestically or internationally (imports). These imports are a major source of competition for domestic firms.

Charging tariffs

A *tariff* is a tax charged on imports. Government uses tariffs to protect domestic industries from foreign competition. As a result of a tariff, domestic firms typically are able to charge a higher price while also producing more output. In order to produce more output, it's not uncommon for tariffs to lead to higher employment in protected industries as compared to the employment level that would exist if the industry were unprotected.

Figure 18-5 illustrates a protective tariff's impact as compared to free trade. The underlying assumption for Figure 18-5 is that the United States government is imposing a tariff on imports in order to protect U.S. firms. The market illustrated in Figure 18-5 is the market for the good in the United States. Thus, the demand curve labeled D_{US} is the good's demand from customers in the United States. The supply curve S_{US} is the U.S. supply curve and illustrates the quantity of the good U.S. firms are willing to produce and sell at various possible prices. The supply curve S_{FT} is the world supply of the good to the U.S. market assuming free trade — no tariffs. The world's supply includes the quantity U.S. firms are willing to produce plus the quantity foreign firms are willing to produce to sell in the U.S. market.

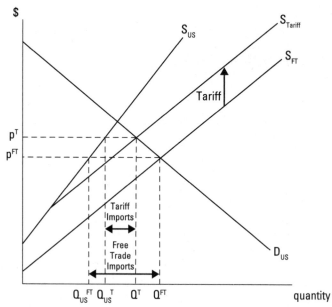

Figure 18-5:
International trade with tariffs.

If free trade exists and the market is in equilibrium, the good's equilibrium price is P^{FT}, which corresponds to the intersection of D_{US} and S_{FT}. The quantity of the good U.S. consumers purchase is Q^{FT}. The quantity of the good U.S. firms produce equals Q_{US}^{FT}. Given the good's free-trade price P^{FT}, this is the quantity U.S. firms are willing to provide based upon the U.S. supply curve S_{US}. The difference between the quantity purchased by U.S. consumers, Q^{FT}, and the quantity produced by U.S. firms, Q_{US}^{FT}, is made up with imports as labeled in Figure 18-5.

If U.S. firms are successful in lobbying the federal government for tariff protection, the world's supply of the good to the U.S. market shifts to S_{Tariff}. As illustrated on Figure 18-5, the vertical difference between the world supply curve with no tariffs, S_{FT}, and the world supply curve with tariffs, S_{Tariff}, represents the amount of the tariff as labeled. If the tariff is the same for each unit of the good imported, the vertical difference doesn't change.

With a tariff in place, the market adjusts to a new equilibrium. The good's equilibrium price increases to P^T, which corresponds to the intersection of D_{US} and S_{Tariff}. The quantity of the good U.S. consumers purchase is Q^T. The quantity of the good U.S. firms produce equals Q_{US}^T. Given the good's price with the tariff, P^T, this is the quantity U.S. firms are willing to provide given the U.S. supply curve S_{US}. The difference between the quantity purchased by U.S. consumers, Q^T, and the quantity produced by U.S. firms, Q_{US}^T, is made up with imports as labeled in Figure 18-5.

The tariff has the desired effect. It increases the price U.S. firms receive and, as a result, the firms increase their production from Q_{US}^{FT} to Q_{US}^T. Not surprisingly, imports also shrink because the foreign firms have to subtract the tariff from the price they receive.

Tariffs help protect domestic industries, but often at the expense of consumers. Tariff protection means that consumers of the good pay higher prices.

Restricting through quotas

Quotas restrict the quantity of imports from other countries. Quotas are another method government uses to protect domestic industries from foreign competition. Like a tariff, quotas lead to higher prices for domestic firms, which provides incentive to produce more output. Thus, quotas also lead to higher employment if an industry is protected for foreign competition.

Figure 18-6 illustrates an import quota's impact as compared to free trade. Similar to Figure 18-5, Figure 18-6 assumes the United States government is imposing an import quota to protect U.S. firms. Figure 18-6 illustrates the good's U.S. market. The demand curve labeled D_{US} is U.S. consumer demand for the good. The supply curve, S_{US}, is the U.S. supply curve and illustrates the quantity of the good U.S. firms are willing to produce and sell at various possible prices. The supply curve S_{FT} is the world supply of the good to the U.S. market assuming free trade — no quotas or tariffs.

The world supply includes both the quantity U.S. firms are willing to produce and the quantity foreign firms are willing to produce to sell in the U.S. market at various possible prices.

If free trade exists and the market is in equilibrium, the good's equilibrium price and quantity are P^{FT} and Q^{FT} as determined by the intersection of D_{US} and S_{FT}. U.S. consumers purchase the quantity Q^{FT}. Given free trade, U.S. firms produce Q_{US}^{FT} — this is the quantity U.S. firms are willing to provide given where the good's free trade price P^{FT} hits the U.S. supply curve S_{US}. The difference between the quantity purchased by U.S. consumers, Q^{FT}, and the quantity produced by U.S. firms, Q_{US}^{FT}, is made up with imports as labeled in Figure 18-6.

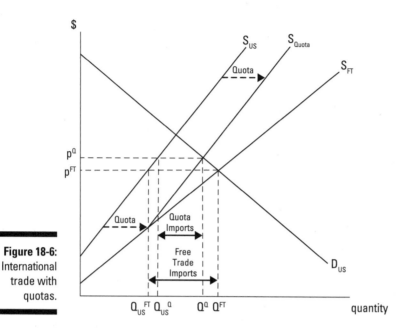

Figure 18-6:
International
trade with
quotas.

U.S. firms successfully lobby the federal government for an import quota. As
a result, the world's supply of the good to the U.S. market shifts to S_{Quota}. As
illustrated in Figure 18-6, the horizontal difference between the U.S. supply
curve, S_{US}, and the world supply with the quota, S_{Quota}, equals the quota. This
is the maximum permitted quantity of imports. The quota's impact on supply
is illustrated in Figure 18-6.

A quota leads to a new market equilibrium. The good's equilibrium price
increases to P^Q, which corresponds to the intersection of D_{US} and S_{Quota}. U.S.
consumers purchase Q^Q of the good. U.S. firms produce Q_{US}^Q — this is the
quantity U.S. firms are willing to provide given the market price P^Q and the
U.S. supply curve S_{US}. The difference between the quantity purchased by U.S.
consumers, Q^Q, and the quantity produced by U.S. firms, Q_{US}^Q, is made up
with imports as labeled in Figure 18-6. Thus, imports equal the amount of
the quota.

The quota accomplishes its intended goal by increasing the price U.S. firms
receive. As a result, U.S. firms produce more — moving to Q_{US}^Q from Q_{US}^{FT}.
This production increase may lead to higher employment in the protected
industry. At the same time, imports decrease to the amount of the quota.

Quotas, like tariffs, protect domestic industries. But that protection comes at
a price; more specifically, it comes at a higher price for consumers. In a real
sense, consumers are footing the bill for the domestic industry's protection.

Other types of trade restrictions include embargos that prevent trade with another country and negative lists that exclude items from free trade agreements.

Getting Ahead through Rent Seeking

Free markets permit individuals to pursue their own interests. Thus, consumers seek goods that allow them to maximize their satisfaction given the constraint imposed by their income. Given that constraint, consumers naturally want the lowest possible prices. Business owners want to maximize their profit because that profit becomes income as they purchase goods and services. Not surprisingly, business owners want prices to be very high, resulting in more profit.

Usually, these different and conflicting motives aren't a problem as Adam Smith recognized. Individuals are free to choose whether or not to buy and sell a good. Thus, given this freedom of choice, buyers and sellers engage in exchange only if it's mutually beneficial. Government intervention can change this. Such intervention is especially important when markets fail. Government intervention improves resource allocation by influencing business behavior when there's a market failure. But it's also possible for government to implement policies that benefit some parties at the expense of others. *Rent seeking* occurs when an individual's or group's efforts to get government intervention benefits them at another individual's or group's expense. These rent-seeking efforts can lead to inefficiency. Examples of rent-seeking include political lobbying for government subsidies or using government-issued licenses to prevent competitors from entering a market.

Given individuals are motivated by self interest and have limited information, markets don't always work and neither does government.

Part V
The Part of Tens

The 5th Wave   By Rich Tennant

"His only suggestion is to add more hotels."

In this part . . .

This part cuts to the chase by summarizing the things you have to remember as a business owner or decision-maker. In this part, you discover the ten concepts you have to remember and ten common mistakes you need to avoid.

Chapter 19

Ten Critical Concepts

A great line from the movie *Kung Fu Panda* is "there's no charge for awesomeness." In this chapter, I cover ten of the most awesome economic concepts — and there's no extra charge. Remembering these critical concepts when making economic decisions helps you avoid bad decisions. And what's really awesome is that you have just ten of them to remember!

Opportunity Cost

Every economic decision incurs a cost. Reading this sentence means you're giving up the opportunity to do something else — perhaps watch television. Decision-making is all about weighing alternatives, so it's critical that you recognize the opportunity cost associated with your decisions.

Opportunity cost is the cost of a decision measured by the next best alternative given up. An important condition in this definition is the best alternative. You don't have to evaluate every possible alternative; you simply need to think about the best alternative. As you make managerial decisions, you need to compare the decision you're making to its best alternative. For example, if you select the low bid contractor, you need to consider what you're missing or losing that the second-lowest bid would have offered. Obviously, the lowest bid is cheaper, but perhaps the second lowest bidder does better and more timely work. You must recognize the opportunities you miss if you decide to go with the lowest bid.

Opportunity cost affects how much you pay for inputs. During a recession, a lot of workers are unemployed, and college graduates have trouble finding jobs. Some graduates consider themselves fortunate to have one job offer.

When you offer a graduate a job, the graduate's opportunity cost of taking your job is very low (because they don't have any competing offers), so you don't have to pay as much. On the other hand, if unemployment is very low, each graduate may have numerous offers. Therefore, the opportunity cost of taking your job is much higher because the graduate is comparing your offer to other offers that may pay more. The applicant expects to be paid more.

One critical opportunity cost managers sometimes forget is the opportunity cost of money — interest. If you decide to hold cash, you give up the opportunity to earn interest. Similarly, if you invest cash to renovate a business, at the very least, you give up the opportunity to earn interest by saving.

Opportunity costs also include nonmonetary costs. Nonmonetary costs include things like the different levels of supervision in two alternatives, different levels of stress in the two alternatives, or employee morale. Quite frequently, these nonmonetary costs become monetary costs, such as when experienced employees quit due to low morale.

Supply and Demand

Supply and demand is a great example of the KISS principle: Keep It Simple Silly. In some ways, the silly here applies to economists who have developed lots of very complicated theories describing price determination. However, the basic idea of the price-quantity relationship is embodied in demand and supply. As price goes up, customers buy a smaller quantity — their quantity demanded decreases. This relationship is represented by the downward-sloping demand curve. On the other hand, as price goes up, producers provide a larger quantity — the quantity supplied increases. An upward-sloping supply curve represents this relationship.

Consumers and producers want exactly the opposite thing: Consumers want low prices, and producers want high prices. Demand and supply determine a compromise price — what economists call the *equilibrium price.* The equilibrium price corresponds to the point where the demand and supply curves intersect. At the equilibrium price, the quantity demanded determined off the demand curve is exactly the same as the quantity supplied determined off the supply curve. At the equilibrium price, the quantity consumers want to purchase exactly equals the quantity producers want to sell. Everyone's happy.

The most important aspect of the demand and supply relationship is what happens when the price is not at equilibrium — a situation where the price is too high or too low. If your price is too high, a surplus exists; you want to sell more of the product than customers want to purchase. Because you have a surplus, your inventories grow, and you should lower your price. It's time for a sale. As you lower price, consumers want to buy more, so your inventories start to go down. At the lower price, you'll also want to produce less because you can't sell the good for as much as you thought you could.

If your price is too low, customers want to buy more than you have to sell. This situation leads to a shortage, and you have very little product available to sell; it has already been bought. You should raise price in this situation. As a result, customers will want to buy less at the higher price (quantity demanded decreases), while you will want to provide more (quantity supplied increases). These changes in quantity demanded and quantity supplied eliminate the shortage.

Although customers want to purchase less of your product at the higher price, it really doesn't matter because you weren't producing enough to sell to all of them in the first place. Think of a restaurant with a very long line of waiting people — this represents the shortage. Some people may walk away because they have to wait too long. If you raise the price of a meal, your waiting line is going to be shorter, but that doesn't matter if all your tables are still full. You don't make money by people waiting.

The Price Elasticity of Demand

The law of demand states that consumers purchase less of a good at a higher price. This scenario is the general relationship. You also need to know how responsive quantity demanded is to a price change. When you raise price a little, does quantity go down a little or a lot? The price elasticity of demand measures how sensitive consumers are to price changes.

The price elasticity of demand, η, is simply a number that compares the percentage change in quantity demanded divided by the percentage change in price:

$$\eta = \frac{\%\Delta q}{\%\Delta p}$$

But be careful with this formula; it works only for very small percentage changes in price.

The larger the price elasticity of demand, the more responsive customers are to a price change. This situation is an *elastic demand.* When you raise price, you lose a lot of customers. Quantity demanded decreases a lot more than price increases, and, as a result, your sales revenue decreases.

Conversely, the smaller the price elasticity of demand, the less responsive customers are to a price change. This is an inelastic demand. As you raise price, quantity demanded decreases by a very small amount; you lose very few customers. Because the decrease in quantity demanded is a lot less than the increase in price, your sales revenue increases.

Three factors make demand more elastic — a large number of substitutable goods, goods that cost a large proportion of income, and a longer period of time for consumers to adjust to the price change. If these factors apply to your situation, be careful about raising price. An elastic demand doesn't mean you shouldn't raise price and sell a smaller quantity; it simply indicates that in order to increase profits, your cost savings associated with selling a smaller quantity would have to be greater than the revenue you lose.

Utility Maximization

Everybody wants to maximize satisfaction — what economists call *utility.* However, everybody is constrained by the amount of income they have and how much various goods cost. (Even Bill Gates has constraints, but I digress.)

In order to maximize satisfaction, you want the additional satisfaction, or *marginal utility,* you get from the last dollar's worth of a good to be equal for all goods. Therefore, utility maximization requires that the marginal utility per dollar spent be equal for all goods — goods a, b, c, and the rest of the goods' alphabet.

$$\frac{MU_a}{p_a} = \frac{MU_b}{p_b} = \frac{MU_c}{p_c} = \ldots = \frac{MU_{every\,good}}{P_{every\,good}}$$

The great thing about consumer behavior is you can influence it. Your advertising increases the marginal utility — I assume you have good advertising — and you obviously control the price you set. If you want customers to buy more, simply increase their marginal utility or lower the price.

Marginal Revenue Equals Marginal Cost

In order to maximize profits, the additional revenue you obtain from the last unit of the good sold, *marginal revenue,* must equal the additional cost of producing the last unit, *marginal cost.* The output level where marginal revenue equals marginal cost maximizes profit.

 To find the profit-maximizing output level, you simply need to find the point where the marginal revenue and marginal cost curves intersect or cross. That's it; it can't get much simpler. Awesome!

Mutual Interdependence

Your decisions affect others. That comment seems obvious enough, but too often, managers forget this simple rule. Think of a major highway intersection with two gas stations: yours and mine. I decide to lower the price of gasoline by 2 cents a gallon in order to steal your customers. Clever strategy — and it doesn't take much of a guess to think that you quickly respond by lowering your price 2 cents. So we both end up making 2 cents less a gallon for the gasoline we sell. I wish I'd thought of mutual interdependence.

 With mutual interdependence, incentives matter. If you're motive is to increase your happiness, you respond to expected cost and benefits. As Adam Smith said long ago, appealing to the baker's self-interest by buying bread is a lot more likely to get you bread than relying on the baker's charity. And because incentives matter, you and I respond to changing net advantages that our interactions generate. Thus, mutual interdependence leads to mutual adjustment as incentives change.

By recognizing mutual interdependence, you can avoid unintended consequences. Unintended consequences are outcomes you didn't anticipate. For example, asking your colleagues to put a "rush" on a project may get the project done, but it also can lead to them not wanting to work with you. That's an unintended consequence you don't want.

Risk

Everybody loves to take chances, and people often take chances without thinking about them.

As a manager or entrepreneur, you have to make decisions given an uncertain future. If you make well-informed decisions — that is, you correctly anticipate the future — you're rewarded with profit. On the other hand, bad decisions lead to losses.

Risk falls into two types:

- **Insurable:** With insurable risks, you can accurately estimate the frequency of occurrence. Fire, natural disasters, theft, and accidents are all examples of insurable risks. In the case of insurable risks, you can pay a fee — insurance premium — to avoid the potential losses. You don't have to take these chances if you buy the insurance.

- **Uninsurable:** Uninsurable risks are uncontrollable and unpredictable. These risks change your revenue and costs in ways that you can't anticipate. Because you can't anticipate these risks, insurance companies don't offer policies on them. They're insurance companies, not casinos (although, to be honest, casinos are a great example of "insurable" risks).

There are three sources of uninsurable risks. First, structural changes occur in the economy. Consider how the world has changed because of cellphones. As just one example, consider how Kodak's success depended on old technologies for taking pictures. Kodak has suffered tremendous loses because the new technology has made their products obsolete, or at the very least, less desirable.

A second source of uninsurable risks are changes in the general economic environment — think national or global recession. When the housing market collapsed, construction companies lost business with fewer new homes being built. Similarly, the resulting recession caused a significant decrease in new car purchases resulting in losses and layoffs in the automobile industry.

Finally, government policy changes. For example, a local government grants an exclusive contract to a private company for trash collection. Hopefully, it's your company and not a rival. Or, the federal government reduces a tariff on imports. Domestic firms producing the same good face greater competition.

If you successfully anticipate and prepare for these uninsurable risks, your firm earns greater profit.

Externalities and Rent-Seeking

Markets work well — awesome! Not perfectly — shucks! Externalities refer to situations where some of the benefits or costs spill over to nonparticipants in the market transaction.

Positive externalities exist when the nonparticipant receives a benefit. Honey is an example of a positive externality. The beekeeper takes care of bees in order to collect honey for sale that customers purchase. The beekeeper and customers engage in a market transaction. However, even though I don't buy honey or keep bees, I benefit from a positive externality as the bees pollinate the flowers in my garden. I receive a benefit without paying the beekeeper anything.

A negative externality exists when a cost is imposed on the nonparticipant. When the beekeeper's bee stings me while I work in my garden, that's a negative externality. A more important example of a negative externality is pollution. Frequently, government tries to reduce negative externalities through taxes or regulation.

Rent-seeking occurs when someone seeks to gain special benefits from government at taxpayers' or someone else's expense. Examples of rent-seeking include getting special tax incentives or tariff protection from cheaper foreign goods.

Present Value

Do not confuse a dollar today as being worth the same as a dollar one year from now. Time is money!

Time matters because you can use the money you have today to earn interest. A dollar today will be worth $1.05 one year from now if the interest rate is 5 percent. And you would much rather have the $1.05 than $1.00 next year. (Okay, the nickel may not matter much, but what happens if you're considering a $10 million investment that won't start generating revenue for three years?)

The time value of money and present value are especially important in investment decisions. But they are also important with accounts receivable — the money you're owed. In a big business, letting invoices go unpaid for several months can represent big losses in potential interest earnings.

The present value of money is determined by the formula

$$PV = \sum_{t=1}^{n} \frac{(R_t - C_t)}{(1+i)^t}$$

where PV represents the present value, $R_t - C_t$ represents the net revenue or cash flow in year t, i represents the interest rate, and t represents how many years in the future you'll receive the net revenue.

Calculus

I've saved the best for last — calculus. Okay, calculus may not be the best, and I've made my share of jokes about calculus in various sections of this book. Nevertheless, many situations are simply too complicated to analyze with two-dimensional graphs. Business decisions, even when simplified, can involve many variables. Equations enable you to specify more variables in the decision-making process.

After you have an equation with multiple variables, calculus is the tool that enables you to optimize the equation in order to maximize profit, minimize cost, maximize sales, and so on. And even better, calculus allows you to use a Lagrangian function (see Chapter 3) — and a Lagrangian is sure to impress any boss or significant other. (My wife still wonders what I do at work when I say I've been using Lagrangians all day.)

Chapter 20

Ten Managerial Mistakes and How to Avoid Them

. . . .

In This Chapter

▶ Recognizing common mistakes

▶ Identifying a better alternative

. . . .

*P*erhaps the Irish writer Oscar Wilde says it best, "Experience is the name everyone gives to their mistakes." Or as American humorist Franklin P. Jones notes, "Experience is that marvelous thing that enables you to recognize a mistake when you make it again." But despite these humorous, if not somewhat positive spins on mistakes, the bottom line is that if you make too many mistakes as a manager, you're going to get fired. Therefore, this chapter helps you avoid some common mistakes by showing a better alternative. As a result, you'll keep your job and hopefully use some of your income to buy other *For Dummies* books.

Minimizing Cost per Unit

Business's goal in a market economy is to maximize profit — the difference between revenue and cost. By its very definition, profit has two components — cost, which emphasizes what the firm must spend in order to acquire the resources necessary to produce the good, and revenue, what the firm receives when it sells the good.

Focusing solely on cost per unit ignores the revenue side of profit maximization. If minimum cost per unit occurs at 1,000 units of output, but the firm sells only 800 of them, the surplus or extra 200 units the firm produces don't help the bottom line. They don't add to profit. (In this example, I assume that the item can't be carried forward as inventory — perhaps it's perishable.)

Even if the firm sells all 1,000 units, minimizing cost per unit doesn't necessarily maximize the firm's profit. If cost per unit is minimized at $4.00 per unit when the firm produces 1,000 units, the total cost equals $4,000 — $4.00 × 1,000. If the firm sells those 1,000 units at a price of $6.00, total revenue equals $6,000 — $6.00 × 1,000. In this situation, the firm's total profit is $2,000 (the difference of the $6,000 revenue over the $4,000 costs).

Instead, you decide to produce 1,200 units. Your cost per unit increases to $4.20 and your total cost increases to $5,040 which equals $4.20×1,200. Remember cost per unit is minimized at 1,000 units. Assume you can still sell 1,200 units at a price of $6.00, so your total revenue equals $7,200. Now, your profit is $2,160 (the $7,200 revenue – $5,040 costs) — it's $160 higher than before. Indeed, it's $160 higher even though your cost per unit is now $0.20 higher at $4.20 as compared to $4.00.

This example simply illustrates that profit can be higher even when your cost per unit isn't minimized. In order to avoid this problem, you must focus on both revenue and cost. Does producing another unit of the good add more to your revenue than it adds to your cost? In other words, is your marginal revenue greater than your marginal cost (MR > MC)? If it is, your profit increases so you should produce that additional unit, even if it makes your cost per unit higher.

Maximizing Profit per Unit

Maximizing profit per unit is a corollary to minimizing cost per unit. On the surface, maximizing profit per unit appears to overcome the last mistake — the firm includes the revenue side. But the important distinction here is the difference between average and marginal.

Profit per unit equals price minus average total cost. So, if the firm sells 1,000 units at a price of $6.00 and the cost per unit — average total cost — is $4.00, the firm's profit per unit is $2.00 — price minus average total cost. Total profit simply equals profit per unit multiplied by the number of units sold; so, in this case, total profit equals $2,000 — $2.00 × 1,000.

As in the last section, once again assume you decide to produce 1,200 units, and your cost per unit increases to $4.20. But in order to sell 1,200 units, you now have to lower your price to $5.90. Your profit per unit now equals $1.70 — $5.90 – $4.20. Your total profit equals profit per unit multiplied by the number of units or $2,040 — $1.70 × 1,200. Your total profit is $40 higher even though your profit per unit is $0.30 lower. The reason, of course, is that you're getting $1.70 per unit profit on 1,200 instead of 1,000 units. You're getting less profit per unit but selling a lot more units.

Thus, total profit can be higher even when your profit per unit isn't maximized. In order to avoid this problem, you must focus on what each additional unit adds to your revenue — marginal revenue — and what each unit adds to your cost — marginal cost. If the marginal revenue of an additional unit is higher than its marginal cost (MR > MC), producing that unit adds to your profit. On the other hand, if marginal revenue is less than marginal cost (MR < MC), producing the extra unit reduces your profit because it's adding more to your cost than its adding to your revenue. So, total profit is always maximized when marginal revenue equals marginal cost (MR = MC), not necessarily where profit per unit is maximized.

Using Cost-Plus Pricing

Cost-plus pricing is a simple method of setting price that's convenient for business managers. Usually, cost-plus pricing is based upon some target, such as the desired profit per unit. But in this case, simple isn't necessarily good.

The problem with cost-plus pricing is that it completely ignores the good's demand. Managers may like its simplicity, but the price they set using this technique ignores what consumers are willing and able to pay for the good. If the price this method establishes is too high, consumers won't buy everything the firm produces. And if the price is too low, consumers will buy everything but the firm receives less revenue than it could have. In either situation, the firm doesn't maximize profit.

Cost-plus pricing can maximize profit. But in order to do so, your mark-up must be based on the price elasticity of demand. By basing your mark-up on the price elasticity of demand, you've incorporated the demand or revenue side of the market. In order to maximize profit with cost-plus pricing, the mark-up must equal the following:

$$\text{mark-up} = \frac{-1}{\eta + 1}$$

where η is the price elasticity of demand. This formula leads to a mark-up that's consistent with marginal revenue equals marginal cost. Thus, profit is maximized.

Pricing to Break Even

Pricing to break even is intended to reduce the risk of losses. In this strategy, price equals the cost per unit, so there are no losses, assuming consumers purchase everything that's produced.

Breakeven pricing is a very conservative strategy. Managers afraid of losing their job may adopt this strategy to reduce the risk of losses. Or a new firm that can't withstand losses because of its limited financial resources may adopt this strategy in order to reduce the risk of bankruptcy.

But as is the case with other simplistic pricing strategies, by failing to incorporate aspects of consumer demand, this strategy is unlikely to maximize profit. So, as a long-run strategy, breakeven pricing limits the firm's success and profit.

The only pricing strategy that always maximizes profit is setting marginal revenue equal to marginal cost. Satisfying this condition enables you to determine the profit-maximizing output level and then, by using the consumer demand, you can determine the price that maximizes your firm's profit.

Underestimating Rivals

No business owner or manager should forget the term coined by economist Joseph Schumpeter (1883–1950) — creative destructionism. (See Chapter 7 for details.) Schumpeter emphasizes capitalism's evolutionary nature — over time everything changes. By examining technological change and innovation, Schumpeter concludes that the inevitable tendency is for new businesses to destroy existing businesses. Thus, human ingenuity and creativity ensure capitalism's continual evolution and new businesses replacing existing businesses. Change is inevitable.

The lesson you can learn from Schumpeter is that there is no such thing as the status quo. Today, your business may be extremely successful, but recognize that others notice your success. Profit attracts competition. As other individuals pursue their self interest, they notice your profit and attempt to emulate if not actually improve upon your success. And the fact of the matter is that some will improve on your efforts and their success will diminish your own.

So, never assume rivals will continue with the same behavior. Never underestimate rivals or, in other words, never underestimate the attraction large profit provides. If you want to maintain profit, you have to continually make adjustments and changes in your business. Underestimating how others react to your success is the quickest way to ensure its end.

Falling into a Prisoner's Dilemma

Prisoner's dilemma is a situation where rational players pursue their own self interest. (I tell you more about it in Chapter 12.) However, by pursuing their own self interest, the players choose actions that lead to an outcome that's less than optimal. By acting out of self interest, players end up with a less than optimal outcome, but ignoring what their rival does is even worse.

Prisoner's dilemma typically exists in oligopolies, although it occurs in other situations as well. One key aspect of a prisoner's dilemma is a small number of participants. Thus, the ultimate outcome is based on the actions chosen by all players and every player recognizes this aspect. So, the existence of a prisoner's dilemma requires mutual interdependence among the players, and players take into account how rivals respond to their decisions.

Because collusion is illegal in the United States, a prisoner's dilemma can be very difficult for you to resolve. You know how rivals will respond to your decision, but you also know that those rivals pursue their own self interest. The only way to resolve a prisoner's dilemma is to try to change the nature of the game. This change can most easily be accomplished with games that never end. In a never-ending game, you may pursue trigger strategies such as tit-for-tat. When you use a tit-for-tat strategy, you initially assume all players will cooperate by choosing the best combined outcome. In any subsequent round, you do whatever your rival did in the previous round. Thus, if your rival pursued a less than optimal strategy in the last round, you pursue that strategy this round. If your rival cooperated in the last round, you cooperate this round. A tit-for-tat strategy tends to lead to cooperation because it punishes cheaters in the next round. In addition, it forgives cheaters if they subsequently decide to cooperate.

Ignoring the Future

Question: How many traditionalists does it take to change a light bulb?

Answer: What? Change!?!

It's very easy for companies to get into a rut — we do it this way because we've always done it this way. But the one thing that can be guaranteed is that circumstances change.

It's important to prepare for the future by investing in capital, research, and development, among other strategies. Profit attracts both imitators and innovators, so stagnation simply insures extinction.

Long-term business success requires evolution. You need to constantly evaluate current operations, while simultaneously anticipating what the future holds.

Being Insensitive to Risk

Risk and uncertainty exist when outcomes aren't known in advance. A situation is risky when objective probabilities can be assigned to the situation's possible outcomes — you possess information concerning the likelihood of each possible outcome. A situation is uncertain when objective probabilities can't be assigned to the possible outcomes. As a consequence, you have no objective information concerning the likelihood of a given outcome. In either situation, the consequences or payoffs resulting from a decision or action depend upon factors outside your control.

Given risk and uncertainty, it's essential to develop systematic methods to evaluate different actions. These methods can't guarantee you the highest payoff, because you don't control all factors, but the criteria must enable you to systematically evaluate alternative actions with variable and uncertain payoffs. The crucial issue with risk and uncertainty is to have objective criteria and information upon which you're basing a subjective decision. It's not necessary for everyone to agree a certain course of action is best, but it's critical that everyone understand the pros and cons of each alternative.

Forgetting Regulations

In general, the purpose of government intervention isn't to preserve competition, but rather to improve resource allocation. At times markets don't efficiently allocate scarce resources, and profit-maximizing behavior doesn't lead to maximum consumer satisfaction. Instances involving externalities like pollution, monopoly inefficiency, and collusion are a few examples. When markets don't work well, government regulation and intervention improve upon the market outcome.

Nevertheless, at times regulation focuses on competition, not efficiency. Thus, government intervention may be used to promote a specific goal, such as using trade restrictions to reduce foreign competition. Or government may require professional or business licenses. In some circumstance, government even fixes the good's price. (See Chapter 18 for more on government regulations.)

No matter what the circumstance, you must recognize the restrictions government establishes. Failure to recognize these restrictions can lead to negative consequences, including financial penalties or prison.

Disregarding Principal–Agent Issues

At first glance it seems that managers and owners always have the same goal — making the firm as profitable as possible. But what economists have long recognized is that incentives matter, and as individuals pursue their self interest, their actions reflect what gives them the most satisfaction. And given individuals have diverse interests, you have no guarantee they're all working toward the same goal.

In order for a business to be successful, employees must work together to achieve the owner's goal. But why should an employee make sacrifices in order for the owner to get more profit? The old adage, "What's in it for me?" immediately comes to mind. Given this circumstance, it's crucial for owners as principals to recognize that their agents — managers and employees — may pursue different goals. This is the principal–agent problem.

The principal–agent problem is most likely to occur when two conditions exist. First, the principal doesn't directly observe the agent's actions and, second, the agent's actions aren't the sole determinant of the ultimate outcome.

Successful businesses eliminate the principal–agent problem by aligning the goals of both principals and agents in order to get a coordinated, cooperative effort to maximize profit. There are many ways to do this, but generally the methods can be categorized as either involving reward or punishment. Reward recognizes good effort; thus employees have an incentive for continued hard work past the minimum effort necessary to keep their job. Profit-sharing is an example of a reward. But note that rewards are expensive. Punishment emphasizes supervision and negative consequences, such as an employee being fired. The advantage of punishment is it's inexpensive to implement. On the other hand, punishment motivates individuals only to a point. That point is the minimum effort necessary to avoid the punishment.

Regardless of the method used, the principal–agent problem needs to be recognized and addressed if your business is going to maximize its profit. (See Chapter 17 for details on avoiding this problem.)

Ignoring This Book

Yes, I can count, and I know this is the 11th managerial mistake for this chapter, and the section is supposed to be the Part of Tens. But because this is the 11th mistake, you can consider it a bonus mistake or as close to a free lunch as you're going to get.

As indicated in the heading, it's a mistake to ignore this book. Okay, I admit that sounds a little self-serving, so let me rephrase — it's a mistake to ignore economics. The economic theories presented in this book have stood the test of time. They form an excellent foundation for sound business decision-making, and that's your goal. So learn and apply these theories, and your success won't be an accident.

Index

● ●

Notes

Notes

Notes